T0384216

An Introduction to Cybernetic Synergy

An Introduction to Cybernetic Synergy

Improving Decision-Making and Cost Efficiency in Business and Commercial Environments

Mark Rowbotham

A PRODUCTIVITY PRESS BOOK

First published 2021
by Routledge
600 Broken Sound Parkway #300, Boca Raton FL, 33487
and by Routledge

2 Park Square, Milton Park, Abingdon, Oxon, OX14 4RN

Routledge is an imprint of the Taylor & Francis Group, an informa business

ISBN: 9780367761356 (hbk)
ISBN: 9780367761387 (pbk)
ISBN: 9781003165682 (ebk)

Typeset in Minion Pro
by codeMantra

Contents

Preface

The subject of cybernetic synergy, although emanating from a socio-economic experiment of economic control by cybernetic means in Chile in the early 1970s, has never been approached as an applied subject in its own right. Indeed, the subject of applied business cybernetics has never been addressed as a separate issue, although it has been shown that the overall subject of cybernetics applies to a wide range of disciplines, from biology to business via mathematics and engineering, and indeed a variety of articles have been published from time to time on the generic subject.

There are already several books available on the subject of cybernetics, but they are mostly concerned with mathematical approaches along with very heavy technical and formulaic texts, most of which are completely alien to the layman or the simple practitioner. Furthermore, other than references to business or economic practice in some books, particularly those written by the eminent cybernetician Stafford Beer, former Professor of Business Management at Manchester University and author of several books, there has never, according to the view of the author, been a book published purely about the subject of applied cybernetics relating to business practices.

Business cybernetics is a discipline per se. It deals with business practice, efficiency, and quality control in business. It encompasses much of today's business practice in terms of lean management, continuous improvement, Six Sigma, ISO, and much much more. Contrary to the views of many, it has nothing to do with Artificial Intelligence (AI), cyberspace, cybersecurity, and other subjects which have deviated wildly from the original concepts. Cybernetics as a discipline concerns the art (or science) of finding one's way through a morass of information and concepts, by employing the services of some form of helmsman, or, as in the Greek, *Kubernetes*, from which the word "cybernetics" is derived. Helmsmen use simple forms of navigation to steer a ship. I should know this, as I come from a nautical family, where working with the sea as part of the merchant navy was a tradition handed down from one generation to another, apart from one relation, a cousin of my mother, who joined the Royal Navy (having been born in as much the UK interior as possible, namely the West Riding of Yorkshire!). Indeed, I was expected to go to sea in accordance with my North-Eastern forbears, but I rebelled, instead becoming an Officer of HM Customs & Excise (HMC&E), and latterly, a Customs & Excise Consultant. However, that did not sever my connections with the sea. I was assigned to port Customs controls, and boarded and examined several ships as part of my job in HMC&E as an Import and Export Controls Officer, ultimately becoming a specialist in maritime cargo controls. Cybernetics was originally an external interest, fuelled by a cousin of my mother who practised cybernetics as part of his job with a major US management consultancy firm, until it became part of my job as a Customs Consultant by pure chance, auditing companies to determine their compliance with established Customs regulations and practices as well as international supply chain analysis.

I soon discovered that there was some isolated literature on the subject of cybernetics for business purposes but that it was extremely fragmented and had little or no cohesion and was either located in specific articles on the internet or incorporated in books written by specialists such as Oskar Lange and Stafford Beer, both of whom addressed economic cybernetics from a more socialist viewpoint. It was Stafford Beer who established the original concept of cybernetic synergy when he devised the project to introduce cybernetic planning into the Chilean economy at the invitation of the Chilean Economic Minister, supported by the then Chilean President, Salvador Allende. Admittedly, the principle of the project was to adhere to the socialist policy of a planned economy but controlled by cybernetic means. This would appear to fly in the face of free market economics, but in a world of increasing competitiveness and cost efficiency, cybernetics can enjoy a renaissance, in its application to the corporate entity in terms of monitoring and control of corporate activities for efficiency and cost-effectiveness purposes. In this respect, it applies not so much at a national or supranational level, but principally at a corporate level. Planned economies have a propensity to failure, whereas corporate policy tends towards competitiveness based on efficiency and profitability.

This was the time, therefore, to redress the balance and write a book on commercial cybernetics and its applications, around the concept of cybernetic synergy within and between predominantly commercial organisations, be they productive or service-based. This is not so much for my own purposes, although my idea has been to use my own commercial experiences, but also for the benefit of those control freaks or savvy business managers out there who want to be able to control business practices either for self-gratification or to genuinely strive for commercial and corporate efficiency in an uncertain economic and commercial world. As time progresses, there is an increasing need for competitiveness based on efficiency and cost-effectiveness, and in my view, cybernetics is the definitive way to achieve this. I have tried to steer (kybernetika) clear of mathematical wizardry and complex formulae as found in several textbooks, as well as a mountain of technical jargon to be found in most books of the subject of cybernetics. Instead, I have concentrated on simple language and practicalities that (hopefully) can be easily understood by most people. I have used certain diagrams and the occasional formula, but I have aimed to keep it as simple as possible to facilitate an easy understanding and application of the subject, and to cybernetically steer through the swamp that is the discipline of the subject.

The primary cybernetic concepts analysed include the following:

- The Viable Systems Model
- Feedback
- Requisite Variety
- Dynamic Systems
- The Neural Network

These concepts are then applied to a series of business concepts and practices, and finally, conclusions are drawn.

It is all too easy to become emotional and passionate about the subject, particularly in its application to present global crises, but in the cold light of day, when it comes to objective thinking, the principle of cybernetics can easily be applied to present circumstances as a means of providing answers to complex and controversial subjects. It is easy to have hindsight, but if cybernetics were to be viewed as a pertinent discipline in today's world of business and government, as it was in the past, it could have far-reaching and radical consequences and outcomes for what appear to be almost surmountable challenges presently faced by the world as a whole. It is, thankfully, never too late to redress the balance.

May this book be a blessing and inspiration to all who read it.

Mark Rowbotham

Abstract

"Cybernetics" comes from the Greek word *Kybernetike*, meaning "the art of steering".

Cybernetics is about having a goal and taking action to achieve that goal. Knowing whether you have reached your goal (or at least are getting closer to it) requires "feedback", a concept that was made rigorous by cybernetics.

From the Greek, "cybernetics" evolved into Latin as "governor", and it has, as a result, come to mean a form of government and hence control, in an all-embracing way. It has therefore come to mean not only an understanding of the applied environment, in terms of the mechanisms used to find one's way through the complexities of that environment, but also the means of controlling that environment using the facilities of a central control facility, hence the concept of government as a form of central control.

Cybernetics as a process operating in nature has been around for a long time; indeed, it has existed for as long as nature has been around, and as a concept in society, it has been in existence at least since the Greek philosopher Plato used it to refer to government in general. Its function as a link between nature, the machine, and administration was largely developed by Norbert Wiener in the late 1940s, based on the function of the brain as a means of control and synergy.

Cybernetic synergy is the study of relationships and controls of and between corporate entities, on an external basis, and departments within corporate entities, on an internal basis. It concerns the decision-making process, and how decisions can be made on the basis of feedback from any part of the organisation being managed. It therefore concerns the issue of input of raw material or information, the output of the transformed information and materials, and the rectification of any issue based on negative feedback related to the productive process. It investigates not only the basic theory of the subject but also its applications in the commercial and business environment, as well as touching on government and administrative issues where shortcomings have emerged owing to a lack of synergy and communication.

Author

Mark Rowbotham is an International Consultant, Trainer, and writer in Customs and VAT Compliance and Risk issues, as well as other areas including International Trade, Excise, Export Controls, Oil & Gas Offshore, and Marine issues. He has spent a considerable length of time working in both the Government, Commercial, and Academic sectors. He deals primarily with Compliance, Control, and Procedural issues in Customs, Excise, VAT, and Logistics, and is a trainer in these issues as well as International Trade, the Supply Chain, Finance, and Risk Management courses.

He was originally an Officer in HM Customs & Excise, dealing with Import and Export Controls on maritime freight traffic into and out of UK Ports, and became an independent consultant and trainer in 2000, dealing primarily with Customs compliances, procedures, and documentation. He advises on these issues, and undertakes training, advisory, and consultancy work in these areas.

He gained a Masters' Degree in International Relations and Political Economy in 1995 and is a Chartered Fellow of the Chartered Institute of Logistics and Transport (UK), as well as a member of the Institute of Export in the UK.

He has written extensively on the subjects of Customs, International Supply Chain, and Marine Compliance issues for a wide variety of International Trade and Logistics publications and journals and has had a book published in 2008, entitled *Introduction to Marine Cargo Management*, Second Edition published in 2015. He also advises several Chambers of Commerce in the UK on Customs, VAT, and International Trade issues, frequently delivering advice, training courses, and seminars on these subjects. He is an accredited trainer for the British Chambers of Commerce, and has also been an adviser to UK Trade & Investment (now DIT) on Customs Procedures pertaining to trade with the Americas.

1

Introduction to Cybernetics

"Cybernetics" comes from the Greek word *Kybernetike*, meaning "the art of steering".

Cybernetics is about having a goal and taking action to achieve that goal. It is therefore about knowing whether you have reached your goal (or at least are getting closer to it) and requires "feedback", a concept that was made rigorous by cybernetics, in order to measure the degree or extent to which you are achieving or arriving at that goal. If we use the example of a boat crossing from one side of a wide and fast-flowing river to the other, the steering principle comes into its own. The boat starts out from its mooring and moves into the river. However, the flow of the river causes the boat to deviate from its original course in the direction of the flow of the river. The task of the steersman is to move the boat back onto its original course, all the time making adjustments to the boat's direction against the flow of the river, until the boat arrives safely at its destination on the other side of the river. The steersman uses "feedback" based on the effect of the river flow on the boat's course to apply corrective action.

From the Greek, "cybernetics" evolved into Latin as "governor". From this, one can draw one's own conclusions, as this can lead to "control".

Cybernetics as a process operating in nature has been around for a long time; actually, for as long as nature has been around, and as a concept in society, cybernetics has been around at least since the Greek philosopher Plato used it to refer to government in general.

Cybernetic synergy, the subject of this book, is the study of the monitoring and control of relationships between corporate entities, on an external basis, and departments within corporate entities, on an internal basis.

The word **cybernetics** comes from the Greek κυβερνητική (*kybernētikḗ*), meaning "governance", i.e. all that are pertinent to κυβερνάω (*kybernáō*), the latter meaning "to steer, navigate, or govern"; hence κυβέρνησις (*kybérnēsis*), meaning "government", is the government, while κυβερνήτης (*kybernḗtēs*) is the governor or "helmperson" of the "ship". During the second half of the 20th-century cybernetics evolved in ways that distinguish first-order cybernetics (about observed systems) from second-order cybernetics (about observing systems). More recently there is talk about a third-order cybernetics (doing in ways that embrace first- and second-order cybernetics).

In modern times, the term became widespread because the American mathematician Norbert Wiener wrote a book called "Cybernetics" in 1948. His sub-title was "control and communication in the animal and machine". This was important because it connects control (actions taken in *hope* of achieving goals) with communication (connection and information flow between the actor and the environment). So, Wiener is pointing out that effective action requires communication. Later, Gordon Pask proposed conversation as the core interaction of systems that have goals.

Wiener's sub-title also states that both animals (biological systems) and machines (non-biological or "artificial" systems) can operate according to cybernetic principles. This was an explicit recognition that both living and non-living systems can have *purpose*. This was a somewhat scary idea back in 1948.

The term itself began its rise to popularity in 1947 when Norbert Wiener used it to name a discipline apart from, but touching upon, such established disciplines as electrical engineering, mathematics, biology, neurophysiology, anthropology, and psychology. Wiener, Arturo Rosenblueth, and Julian Bigelow needed a name for their new discipline, and they adapted a Greek word meaning "the art of steering" to evoke the rich interaction of goals, predictions, actions, feedback, and response in systems of all kinds (the term "governor" derives from the same root; Wiener, 1948). Early applications in the control of physical systems (aiming artillery, designing electrical circuits, and manoeuvring simple robots) clarified the fundamental roles of these concepts in engineering, but the relevance to social systems and the softer sciences was also clear from the start. Many researchers from the 1940s to the 1960s worked solidly within the tradition of cybernetics without necessarily using the term, such as R. Buckminster Fuller, who referred to cybernetic principles as part of his work, but many less obviously, namely Gregory Bateson and Margaret Mead, who used the principle of cybernetics in their own analytical work.

In working to derive functional models common to all systems, early cybernetic researchers quickly realised that their "science of observed systems", i.e. the first order, cannot be divorced from "a science of observing systems", i.e. the second and higher order, because it is we who observe, as stated by Heinz von Foerster in 1974. The cybernetic approach is centrally concerned with this unavoidable limitation of what we can know, i.e. our own subjectivity. In the words of the German mathematician David Hilbert, "We must know; we will know". In this way cybernetics is aptly called "applied epistemology". At minimum, its utility is the production of useful descriptions, and, specifically, descriptions that include the observer in the description. The shift of interest in cybernetics from "observed systems"—physical systems such as thermostats or complex auto-pilots—to "observing systems" – language-oriented systems such as science or social systems—explicitly incorporates the observer into the description, while maintaining a foundation in feedback, goals, and information. It applies the cybernetic frame to the process of cybernetics itself. This shift is often characterised as a transition from "first-order cybernetics" to "second-order cybernetics". Cybernetic descriptions of psychology, language, arts, performance, or intelligence (to name a few) may be quite different from more conventional, hard "scientific" views – although cybernetics can be rigorous too. Implementation may then follow in software and/or hardware, or in the design of social, managerial, and other classes of interpersonal systems.

Artificial Intelligence (AI), which has been linked with cybernetics and which has given rise to words concerning the completely separate field of information technology, such as "cyberspace", is predicated on the presumption that knowledge is a commodity that can be stored inside of a machine and that the application of such stored knowledge to the real world constitutes intelligence, whether by electronic or written means. Only within such a "realist" view of the world can, for example, semantic networks and rule-based expert systems appear to be a route to intelligent machines. Cybernetics in contrast has evolved from a "constructivist" view of the world, where objectivity derives from shared agreement about meaning and where information (or intelligence for that matter) is an attribute of an interaction rather than a commodity stored in a computer, as stated by Winograd and Flores in 1986. These differences are not merely semantic in character, but rather determine fundamentally the source and direction of research performed from a cybernetic, versus an AI, stance.

The term "cybernetics" has been widely misunderstood, perhaps for two broad reasons. First, its identity and boundary are difficult to grasp. The nature of its concepts and the breadth of its applications, as described above, make it difficult for non-practitioners to form a clear concept of cybernetics. This holds even for professionals of all sorts, as cybernetics never became a popular discipline in its own right; rather, its concepts and viewpoints seeped into many other disciplines, from sociology and psychology to design methods and postmodern thought. Second, the advent of the prefix "cyb" or "cyber" as a referent to either robots ("cyborgs") or the Internet ("cyberspace") further diluted its meaning, to the point of serious confusion to everyone except the small number of cybernetic experts. The media talks of "Cyberattacks". These are not attacks by robots but refer to unauthorised computer hacking. This has nothing whatsoever to do with cybernetics. Indeed, cybernetics could be used to avoid this sort of unwanted and unjustified invasion or incursion and ensure that control systems prevent this kind of occurrence.

However, the concepts and origins of cybernetics have become of greater interest recently, especially since around the year 2000. Lack of success by AI to create intelligent machines has increased curiosity toward alternative views of what a brain does, as proposed by the cybernetician W. Ross Ashby in 1960, and alternative views of the biology of cognition, according to the Chilean philosopher Humberto Maturana in 1970. There is growing recognition of the value of a "science of subjectivity" that encompasses both objective and subjective interactions, including conversation. Designers are rediscovering the influence of cybernetics on the tradition of 20th-century design methods and the need for rigorous models of goals, interaction, and system limitations for the successful development of complex products and services, such as those delivered via today's software networks. And, as in any social cycle, students of history reach back with minds more open than was possible at the inception of cybernetics, to reinterpret the meaning and contribution of a previous era.

Cybernetics is a transdisciplinary approach for exploring regulatory systems, i.e. their structures, constraints, and possibilities. Norbert Wiener defined cybernetics in 1948 as "the scientific study of control and communication in the animal and the machine". In other words, it is the scientific study of how humans, animals, and machines control and communicate with each other.

Cybernetics is applicable when a system being analysed incorporates a closed signalling loop, originally referred to as a "circular causal" relationship, that is, where action by the system generates some change in its environment and that change is reflected in the system in some manner, known as "feedback" that triggers a system change. Cybernetics is relevant to, for example, mechanical, physical, biological, cognitive, and social systems. The essential goal of the broad field of cybernetics is to understand and define the functions and processes of systems that have goals and that participate in circular, causal chains, i.e. actions that cause effects that move from action to sensing to comparison with desired goal, and again to action. Its focus is how anything digital, mechanical or biological, processes information, reacts to information, and changes or can be changed to better accomplish the first two tasks. Cybernetics includes the study of feedback, black boxes, and derived concepts such as communication and control in living organisms, machines, and organisations including self-organisation.

In cybernetics, theories tend to rest on four basic pillars, namely variety, circularity, process, and observation. **Variety** is fundamental to its information, communication, and control theories and emphasises multiplicity, alternatives, differences, choices, networks, and intelligence rather than force and singular necessity. **Circularity** occurs in its earliest theories of circular causation or feedback, leading to rectification, later in theories of recursion and of iteration in computing and now involving self-reference in cognitive organisation and in autonomous systems of production. Traditional sciences have shied away from if not exorcised the use of circular explanations. It is this circular form which enables cybernetics to explain systems from within, making no recourse to higher principles or a priori purposes, expressing no preferences for hierarchy. Nearly all cybernetic theories involve process and change, from its notion of information, as the difference between two states of uncertainty, to theories of adaptation, evolution, and growth processes. A special feature of cybernetics is that it explains such processes in terms of the organisation of the system manifesting it, e.g. the circular causality of feedback loops is taken to account for processes of regulation and a system's effort to maintain an equilibrium or to reach a goal. Negative feedback tells the control system that something is wrong, leading the control system to rectify the issue before it causes further, and greater, problems. Finally, observation including decision-making is the process underlying cybernetic theories of information processing and computing. By extending theories of self-reference to processes of observation including cognition and other manifestations of intelligence, cybernetics has been applied to itself and is developing an epistemology of systems, i.e. *how* an observer knows, as opposed to *what* he knows, involving their observers qualitatively unlike the earlier interest in the ontology of systems, i.e. what actually exists as opposed to what appears to exist but in reality does not, which are observed from the outside.

Studies in cybernetics provide a means for examining the design and function of any system, including social systems such as business management and organisational learning, including for the purpose of making them more efficient and effective. Fields of study which have influenced or been influenced by cybernetics include game theory, as proposed by the American economist John Nash, system theory, which is a mathematical counterpart to cybernetics, perceptual control theory, sociology, psychology, philosophy, architecture, and organisational theory.

Cybernetics has been defined in a variety of ways, by a variety of people, and from a variety of disciplines. Cybernetician Stuart Umpleby reports some notable definitions:

- "Science concerned with the study of systems of any nature which are capable of receiving, storing and processing information so as to use it for control" – A.N. Kolmogorov
- "'The art of steersmanship': deals with all forms of behaviour in so far as they are regular, or determinate, or reproducible: stands to the real machine – electronic, mechanical, neural, or economic – much as geometry stands to real object in our terrestrial space; offers a method for the scientific treatment of the system in which complexity is outstanding and too important to be ignored" – W. Ross Ashby
- "A branch of mathematics dealing with problems of control, recursiveness, and information, focuses on forms and the patterns that connect" – Gregory Bateson
- "The art of securing efficient operation [lit.: the art of effective action]" – Louis Couffignal
- "The art of effective organization" – Stafford Beer
- "The art and science of manipulating defensible metaphors" (with relevance to constructivist epistemology. The author later extended

the definition to include information flows "in all media", from stars to brains.) – Gordon Pask

- "The art of creating equilibrium in a world of constraints and possibilities" – Ernst von Glasersfeld
- "The science and art of understanding" – Humberto Maturana
- "The ability to cure all temporary truth of eternal triteness" – Herbert Brun

Other notable definitions include the following:

- "The science and art of the understanding of understanding" – Rodney E. Donaldson, the first president of the American Society for Cybernetics
- "A way of thinking about ways of thinking of which it is one" – Larry Richards
- "The art of interaction in dynamic networks" – Roy Ascott
- "The study of systems and processes that interact with themselves and produce themselves from themselves" – Louis Kaffman, President of the American Society for Cybernetics

Cybernetics as a discipline was firmly established by Norbert Wiener, Arturo Rosenblueth, and others, such as W. Ross Ashby, mathematician Alan Turing, and W. Grey Walter, who was one of the first to build autonomous robots (known as Cybernetic Organisms) as an aid to the study of animal behaviour. In the spring of 1947, Wiener was invited to a congress on harmonic analysis, held in Nancy, France. France was at the time an important centre of cybernetics research along with the United Kingdom and United States. During this stay in France, Wiener received the offer to write a manuscript on the unifying character of this part of applied mathematics, which is found in the study of telecommunication engineering. The following summer, back in the United States, Wiener decided to introduce the neologism *cybernetics*, coined to denote the study of "teleological mechanisms", into his scientific theory, and it was popularised through his book *Cybernetics: or Control and Communication in the Animal and the Machine*, published by MIT Press/John Wiley and Sons, New York, 1948. In the United Kingdom, this became the focus for the Ratio Club, a dining club where scientists met to discuss prevalent issues in cybernetics.

In 1950, Wiener popularised the social implications of cybernetics, drawing analogies between automatic systems (such as a regulated steam engine), and human institutions in his best-selling book *The Human Use of Human Beings: Cybernetics and Society* (Houghton-Mifflin).

The design of self-regulating control systems for a real-time planned economy was explored by economist Oskar Lange, cyberneticist Viktor Glushkov, and other Soviet cyberneticians during the 1960s. By the time information technology was developed enough to enable feasible economic planning based on computers, such as in the Chilean Cybersyn project of 1971–1973, the Soviet Union and eastern bloc countries began moving away from planning and eventually collapsed.

More recent proposals for socialism involve "New Socialism", outlined by the computer scientists Paul Cockshott and Allin Cottrell, where computers determine and manage the flows and allocation of resources among socially owned enterprises.

On the other hand, the Austrian-British economist Friedrich Hayek, who championed classical liberalism as part of free-market economics, also mentions cybernetics as a discipline that could help economists understand the "self-organizing or self-generating systems" called markets. Being a "complex phenomena", the best way to examine the market functioning is by using the feedback mechanism, explained by cybernetic theorists. That way, economists could make "pattern predictions". From this, the market as seen by Hayek is a "communication system", i.e. an "efficient mechanism for digesting dispersed information". The economist and a cyberneticist are like gardeners who "provide the appropriate environment". However, Hayek's definition of information is idiosyncratic and precedes the information theory used in cybernetics and the natural sciences.

Finally, Hayek also considers the 18th-century economist Adam Smith's idea of the "invisible hand", i.e. prevailing forces, as an anticipation of the operation of the feedback mechanism in cybernetics. In the same book, *Law, Legislation and Liberty*, Hayek mentions, along with cybernetics, that economists should rely on the scientific findings of the general systems theory of Ludwig von Bertalanffy, along with information, communication theory, and semiotics.

The **viable system theory** concerns cybernetic processes in relation to the development/evolution of dynamical systems. They are considered to be living systems in the sense that they are complex and adaptive, can learn, and are capable of maintaining an autonomous existence, at least within the confines of their constraints. These attributes involve the maintenance of internal stability through adaptation to changing environments. One can distinguish between two strands of this theory, namely **formal systems** and principally **non-formal systems**. Formal viable system theory is normally referred to as viability theory and provides a mathematical approach to explore the dynamics of complex systems set within the context of control theory. In contrast, principally non-formal viable system theory is concerned with descriptive approaches to the study of viability through the processes of control and communication, though these theories may have mathematical descriptions associated with them.

The concept of viability arose with the British cybernetician Stafford Beer in the 1950s through his paradigm of management systems. Its formal relative, viability theory began its life in 1976 with the mathematical interpretation of a book by Jacques Monod published in 1971 and entitled *Chance and Necessity*, and which concerned processes of evolution. Viability theory is concerned with dynamic adaptation of uncertain evolutionary systems to environments defined by constraints, the values of which determine the viability of the system. Both formal and non-formal approaches ultimately concern the structure and evolutionary dynamics of viability in complex systems.

The viable system theory of Beer is well known through his viable systems model (VSM) and is concerned with viable organisations capable of evolving. Through both internal and external analysis, it is possible to identify the relationships and modes of behaviour that constitute viability. The model is underpinned by the realisation that organisations are complex, and recognising the existence of complexity is inherent to processes of analysis. Beer's management systems paradigm is underpinned by a set of propositions, sometimes referred to as cybernetic laws. Siting within this is his VSM, and one of its laws is a principle of recursion, so that just as the model can be applied to divisions in a department, it can also be applied to the departments themselves. This is permitted through Beer's viability law which states that *every viable system contains and is contained in a viable system*. The cybernetic laws are applied to all types of human activity systems such as organisations and institutions.

Now, paradigms are concerned with not only theory but also modes of behaviour within inquiry. One significant part of Beer's paradigm is the development of his VSM that addresses problem situations in terms of control and communication processes, seeking to ensure system viability within the object of attention. Another is Beer's Syntegrity protocol which centres on the means by which effective communications in complex situations can occur. VSM has been used successfully to diagnose organisational pathologies, i.e. conditions of social ill health. The model involves not only an operative system that has both structures (e.g. divisions in an organisation or departments in a division) from which behaviour emanates that is directed towards an environment but also a meta-system, i.e. an overall supervisory system, which some have called the observer of the system and which applies to Ashby's Law of Requisite Variety (RV), which states that a control system must be as large as or greater than the system which it is designed to control. The system and meta-system are essentially different, so that, for instance, where in a production company the system is concerned with production processes and their immediate management, the meta-system is more concerned with the management of the production system as a whole. The connection between the system and meta-system is explained through Beer's Cybernetic map. Beer considered that viable social systems should be seen as living systems.

Stafford Beer coined the term *viable systems* in the 1950s and developed it within his management cybernetics theories. He designed his VSM as a diagnostic tool for organisational pathologies, i.e. conditions of social and organisational ill health, i.e. lack of well-being and overall good management. This model involves a system concerned with operations and their direct management and a meta-system that "observes" the system and controls it.

HIGHER ORDERS OF AUTONOMOUS AGENCY

Stafford Beer's (1979) VSM is a well-known diagnostic model that emanates from his management cybernetics paradigm. Related to this is the idea of first-order (observing the system) and second-order (observing the observer) cybernetics. Cybernetics is concerned with feed-forward and feedback processes.

Feed forward refers to the practice of giving a control impact in a downlink to a subordinate to a person or an organisation from which you are expecting an output. A feed forward is not just a pre-feedback, as a feedback is always based on measuring an output and sending respective feedback. A pre-feedback given without measurement of output may be understood as a confirmation or just an acknowledgment of control command.

However, a feed forward is generally imposed before any wilful change in output may occur. All other changes of output determined with feedback may, for example, result from distortion, noise, or attenuation. It usually involves giving a document for review and giving an ex post information on that document which you have not already given.

However, social feedback is the response of the supreme hierarch to the subordinate as an acknowledgement of a subordinate's report on output, hence the subordinate's feedback to the supreme.

First-order cybernetics is concerned with this relationship between the system and its environment. Second-order cybernetics is concerned with the relationship between the system and its internal meta-system (that some refer to as "the observer" of the system).

Management cybernetics is the application of cybernetics to management and organisations. "Management cybernetics" was first introduced by Stafford Beer in the late 1950s. Beer developed the theory through a combination of practical applications and a series of influential books. The practical applications involved steel production, publishing, and operations research in a large variety of different industries.

As practised by Beer, research into operations involved multidisciplinary teams seeking practical assistance for difficult managerial issues. It often involved the development of models borrowed from basic sciences and put into isomorphic relationships with an organisational situation. Beer initially called this "Operations Research" (OR) but, along with Russell Ackoff, became increasingly disenchanted with that term as the field transitioned into one in which a predefined set of mathematical tools was applied to well-formulated problems. Beer's critique of traditional OR, in part, was that it became a matter of experts in mathematics looking for situations that could be conformed to their methods, rather than solutions derived by looking at business or other methods. Indeed, OR became increasingly related to the use of statistical analysis and theoretical solutions, rather than practical solutions derived from the problem itself. Beer maintained that what was needed for effective research into operations was to first understand the key dynamics within the situation, and only then to select the theory or methods that would allow one to understand that situation in detail. Beer's book *Decision and Control*, especially Chapter 6, discusses the methodology in some detail.

Viable means capable of independent existence and implies both maintaining internal stability and adaptation to a changing environment. "Internal stability" and "adaptation" can be in conflict, particularly if the relevant environment is changing rapidly, so the VSM, which will be explained in a later chapter, is about maintaining a balance between the two such that the system is able to survive.

The VSM is a model of the structures and functions that are both necessary and sufficient for the long-term survival of a system in a changing environment. Allenna Leonard, Beer's longtime partner, suggested that the most useful way to think about the VSM is as a language. The VSM is a language of viability. The VSM is a language for diagnosing organisations and managerial teams in terms of their viability or lack thereof. The VSM is also a language for designing organisations and managerial teams that will be viable.

One of the great difficulties in managing the modern large organisation is that many of the issues are far too complex for even small groups. The critical knowledge is often dispersed among a substantial number of people. Organisations are often faced with choosing between (1) very costly and time-consuming meetings of large groups or (2) making bad decisions based on an inadequate grasp of the relevant factors, partly owing to lack of knowledge or understanding of the issues concerned. Syntegration is a group method designed to solve this conundrum.

Syntegration, or integration of synergies, melds a number of cybernetic principles with the principle of **tensegrity**, or tensional integrity, based on a system of isolated components under compression inside a network of continuous tension. These components cannot escape the network but instead display continuous activity within it, in much the same way that atomic molecules function within a substance such as gas, air included. In scientific terms, particularly the discipline of physics, when a gas (or, for that matter, a liquid) is cool, molecules are slow to react. When the gas or liquid is heated, these molecules react with significant force, creating turbulence, or, in the case of liquid such as water, evaporating. As any aircraft pilot knows, air turbulence can be a major problem, especially over hotter countries close to the equator. These molecules are displaying, therefore, a form of aggravated syntegrity in that they are moving around in close proximity to each other, although the medium in which they are operating is more global and extensive than a limited finite network function as defined by the corporate entity. The initial "team syntegrity" format involved 30 people divided into 12 overlapping teams to deal with some broad and initially ill-defined issue. The teams and roles within the teams are arranged to achieve the mathematically optimum degree of resonance of information throughout the entire group. In practice, syntegration achieves a remarkable degree of shared understanding of the initial issue based on the overlap of knowledge, inherent or acquired. In syntegrations intended to develop a plan of action, the implementation phase is usually very quick and effective, probably because of the shared understanding developed among the participants.

Organisational cybernetics (OC) is distinguished from management cybernetics. Both concepts use many of the same terms but interpret them according to another philosophy of systems thinking. The full flowering and development of management cybernetics is represented in Beer's books, in particular *The Brain of the Firm* and *Decision and Control*, including his own observation and experiences in the use of the concept. OC is more scientific and theoretical and studies organisational design and the regulation and self-regulation of organisations from a systems theory perspective that also takes into consideration the social dimension. To this extent, it deals more with theoretical and hypothetical issues, whereas management cybernetics addresses more practical and applicable issues. Extending the principles of autonomous agency theory (AAT), cultural agency theory (CAT) has been formulated for the generation of higher cybernetic orders. Researchers in economics, public administration, and political science focus on the changes in institutions, organisation, and mechanisms of social steering at various levels, namely regional, sub-national, national, European, and international, and in different sectors, including the commercial (private, semiprivate) and public sectors, including government itself.

Overall therefore, the concept of cybernetics as a generic subject revolves significantly around control and communication in a variety of areas. The purpose of this book is to examine cybernetics and its applications in the context of business and management and to suggest where the concept can apply to present-day challenges and crises in the commercial, and more loosely, government and administrative sectors.

2

A Brief History of Cybernetics

Cybernetics is essentially the discipline that studies communication and control in living beings and the machines invented, created, and built by man. A more philosophical definition, suggested by Louis Couffignal in 1958, considers cybernetics as "the art of assuring efficiency of action". The word *cybernetics* was reinvented by Norbert Wiener in 1948 from the Greek *kubernetes*, pilot, or rudder. The word was first used by Plato in the sense of "the art of steering" or "the art of government". Ampère used the word cybernetics to denote "the study of ways of governing". One of the very first cybernetics mechanisms to control the speed of the steam engine, invented by James Watt and Matthew Boulton in 1788, was called a *governor*, or a ball regulator. Cybernetics has in fact the same root as government: the art of managing and directing highly complex systems. Governors do not just refer to people controlling an administration, but they can also refer to mechanical objects designed to regulate flows, such as speed governors in an engine.

The most important initiator of cybernetics was the American Norbert Wiener (1894–1964) with his book *Cybernetics or Control and Communication in the Animal and the Machine*. He compared artificial neural networks, especially the control of machines, with the brain and its control function over the human and animal body, and was, in effect, the pioneer of the discipline of cybernetics as we know it today. The contribution of Warren S. McCulloch (1898–1969) may be compared to that of Wiener. Warren McCulloch was an American neurophysiologist and cybernetician, known for his work on the foundation for certain brain theories and his contribution to the cybernetics movement. In 1943, together with Walter Pitts, McCulloch created computational models based on mathematical algorithms called "threshold logic" which used two distinct approaches, of which one was focussed upon biological processes in the brain and the other focussed on the application of neural networks to artificial intelligence.

Cybernetics has also had precursors such as A. M. Ampère, who introduced the word *cybernétique* to the French language, as well as B. Trentowski who did the same in Polish. H. Schmidt, S. Odobleja in the 1930s, and P. Postelnicu in the early 1940s recognised the general importance of the idea of negative feedback as a means of influencing decisions.

Wiener was part of a group of very intellectual people with various specialisms (psychology, mathematics, sociology, philosophy, knowledge management), including Stefan Odobleja, Arturo Rosenblueth, Julian Bigelow, Warren McCulloch, and Walter Pitts, who seem to have been at the centre of developing the theories surrounding cybernetics around 1940, much of which was based in France, where Wiener's work was first published. Other reference sources cite earlier origins and use of the word cybernetics (or translated equivalent) dating back to Plato, 428–348 BC, in which he used the term in his work *Republic* to describe systems of government and how these systems constituted a form of control. More recently, others used the cybernetics term prior and closer to Wiener's ideas, notably André-Marie Ampère, 1775–1836, well-known for his studies into electromagnetism, and later Louis Couffignal, 1902–1966, also deemed to be a French "cybernetics pioneer". In short, the study of control and response to complex systems has been concentrating great minds for thousands of years, and Wiener is generally regarded as the chief modern architect and pioneer of the modern concept of the discipline.

Particularly, Wiener appears to have combined the main contributory cybernetics perspectives which have been developed by many and various people over the past 2000 years, i.e. the principles of regulating and responding to

- mechanical and electrical systems,
- social and governmental systems,
- human and animal nervous systems, and
- human and animal social systems.

His work has influenced many others in the field, and even some 80 years later, he is still accepted as the father of cybernetics. From Wiener's work, cybernetics is central to our understanding of life, organisations, and the way we relate to our world, however we define it.

D. J. Stewart of the UK Cybernetics Society explained the formal establishment of the cybernetics term as follows:

> By the summer of 1947, the science of control and communication had developed to such an extent that it was beginning to be inconvenient not to have a name for it, and so the term 'cybernetics' was coined...

(and Stewart then quotes Weiner from 1948)

> Thus as far back as four years ago, the group of scientists about Dr Rosenblueth and myself had already become aware of the essential unity of the set of problems centering about communication, control, and statistical mechanics, whether in the machine or in living tissue. On the other hand, we were seriously hampered by the lack of unity of the literature concerning these problems, and by the absence of any common terminology, or even of a single name for the field. After much consideration, we have come to the conclusion that all the existing terminology has too heavy a bias to one side or another to serve the future development of the field as well as it should; and as happens so often to scientists, we have been forced to coin at least one artificial neo-Greek expression to fill the gap. We have decided to call the entire field of control and communication theory, whether in the machine or in the animal, by the same 'Cybernetics', which we form from the Greek kubernetes or 'steersman'.

(Stewart concludes):

> Further justification for the new term is that *kubernetes* is the root of the Latin verb *gubernare*, 'to govern', and that one of the earliest forms of automatic control mechanism was the speed governor of the steam engine. Incidentally, the word *cybernétique* had been used, in something approaching the present sense, when Ampère used it as a name for his science of civil government.

(Ampère, 1834)

This in itself is a natural progression of the studies of cybernetics in its earliest known form by the Greek philosopher Plato, who himself referred it to the science of government.

The basic concepts of cybernetics are negative feedback and information. A famous example of negative feedback is given by Watt's governor, the purpose of which is to maintain the speed of the wheel of a steam engine, at a given value, despite perturbations. The theory of information, mainly due to Claude E. Shannon, gives a measure of the unexpectedness of a message carried by a signal.

Other traits of cybernetics must be noted, such as the "principle of requisite variety" introduced by W. Ross Ashby. It tells that to efficiently resist a given level of variety of aggressions or challenges it is necessary to dispose of or use a comparable level of variety of opposite actions, which could loosely be described as a mindset change. "First Order cybernetics" deals with systems operation, in the form of control, negative feedback, and adaptation. "Second Order cybernetics", as proposed by Heinz von Foerster, emphasises the role of observation played by a cybernetic device which has to perceive in order to adjust its behaviour to its aims.

Cybernetics began properly with the publication in 1948 of a book by Norbert Wiener entitled *Cybernetics or Control and Communication in the Animal and the Machine*. The word cybernetics had been chosen by Wiener, in agreement with other colleagues, from the Ancient Greek *kubernetike*, or the art of steering. Another initiator, almost as important as Wiener, is Warren S. McCulloch who published, in 1943, in collaboration with N. Pitts, an article on logics and the nervous system. The directions of approach of Wiener and McCulloch were different, in that Wiener saw Leibniz as the historical patron of cybernetics, whereas McCulloch was inspired by Descartes. Wiener's preference was due to Leibniz's interest in the construction of a calculating machine and his attempt to build up a general calculus of logics (calculus ratiocinator). Contrastingly, McCulloch observed that Descartes, in his treatise on man, had introduced negative feedback in his description of how an individual escapes the inconvenience of a fire close to his foot. He feels the pain generated by the heat of the fire on the skin of his foot and therefore retreats to safety in a rapid manner.

Other initiators to be covered in more detail below are Claude E. Shannon and William Ross Ashby. The importance of Shannon, for his essential contribution to communication theory, was recognised by Wiener himself. The eminent role of Ashby had more to do with control seen from the point of view of "requisite variety". Other contemporary initiators were P. Vendryès, with his early theory of autonomy, S. Odobleja, and P. Postelnicu who understood the general role of retroaction. H. Schmidt also deserves special mention for his introduction of a "general science of regulation loops", as does J. Lafitte who recognised the interest of what he called "reflex machines".

The importance of older influences must not be overestimated, but Plato, A. M. Ampère, S. Trentowski, and C. Bernard should definitely be mentioned. Plato, in "The Republic" and "Gorgias", used the metaphor of steering (*kubernetike*) to present the art of government. A. M. Ampère, in the second volume of his essay on the philosophy of science, introduced the word *cybernétique* with the same purpose as Plato. S. Trentowski, in a book on a management, proposed *kibernetiki* as a new Polish word. C. Bernard, in his introduction to experimental medicine, emphasised the role of regulations in the equilibrium of the body, an idea which W. B. Cannon made famous with the concept of homeostasis, also used by P. Vendryès. More precisely, Bernard emphasised the importance of the constancy of the "milieu intérieur" defined by parameters such as blood pressure, temperature, concentration of glucose in blood, and so on, achieved by physiological processes.

The word "cybernetics" was coined in the year 1948 by Wiener:

> I first looked for a Greek word signifying 'messenger', but the only one I knew was angelos. This has in English the specific meaning 'angel', a messenger for God. The word was thus pre-empted and would not give me the right context. Then I looked for an appropriate word from the field of control. The only word I could think of was the Greek word for steersman, kubernetes. (…) What recommended the term cybernetics to me was that it was the best word I could find to express the art and science of control over the whole range of fields in which this notion is applicable.
>
> *(Wiener, 1964)*

At this time controlling devices had been in use for at least 200 years and some important contributions to the theory of information were already 20 years old. Therefore, cybernetics was not an invention but rather a new way of looking at and solving problems. The question then arises as to why was cybernetics not born until the year 1948, why not 50 or 100 years earlier?

At about the same time Wiener was developing his ideas, another scientist, working independently, came to the same conclusion. His name was Hermann Schmidt, and he was professor at the Technische Hochschule in Berlin (now the technical university). He published his ideas in several papers. Although his interests tended more towards a type of anthropological philosophy, his basic results concerning the theory of control in the animal and the machine were exactly the same as Wiener's, and even though Schmidt published his basic ideas a few years earlier than Wiener, he never achieved his popularity. He was not even well known in Berlin, where he died in 1968. Keeping this in mind, one should not be surprised to find other scientists at a time as far back as the 19th century who developed ideas similar to the basic concepts of cybernetics. The problem of communication was less relevant to 19th-century science than control.

At that time, the inventor of the governor could only be traced to a drunken wandering millwright who either invented it or at least popularised it in England. Before that time, i.e. about 1750, machines with feedback control had already been used by some mechanics, including the mechanical engineers James Watt and Matthew Boulton, for more than 2000 years. But these mechanical devices were not used in large numbers and were not generally known. Since the skill required to build mechanisms was handed down from craftsman to craftsman, the principle itself was obviously not elaborated on or explored. A detailed history of the early development of feedback mechanisms is given by Mayr (1969). At the beginning of the 19th century, steam engines were widely distributed and, along with them, the governor. Although the governor was continuously being improved on, the problem of how to construct regulators had not yet been solved in theory. All regulators for new machines had to be tested first, and quite often they had to be modified.

The Scottish engineer James Clerk Maxwell (1867/1868) was the first to formulate the problem of the creation of regulators, and the German mathematician Adolf Hurwitz (1895) who gave a suitable mathematical solution to the problem, along with the British mathematician E.J. Routh, by way of the Routh-Hurwitz Stability Criterion, which provided much of the basis for what is now known as control engineering. In Maxwell's paper "On governors" (**1868**) he mathematically described the behaviour of governors, devices that control the speed of steam engines, thereby establishing the theoretical basis of control **engineering**, which was made more definitive by the Routh-Hurwitz solution.

Besides the governor, other regulators were developed during the 19th century, such as thermostats and regulators for fluid levels. The technical side of control was not as easy to solve, although the problem was clear, namely that the engineer had to develop a theory for a regulating mechanism, construct it, and then see whether or not it would work. The problem was far less clear when dealing with organisms. That control mechanisms are essential for life was evident to most people who had dealt with the problem, since the time of Alcmaion of Croton. But the question remained of how one could grasp the problem at a time when it had not yet been solved in theory or expressed in a clear and logical manner. In fact, most scientists were content with the statement that there is some kind of regulation in living organisms without being able to define parameters or state how the mechanisms work.

The problems for biologists are quite different from the problems engineers might have: engineers have to construct a control device, so they are familiar with every detail concerning the operation of the machine. On the other hand, biologists see the complex reactions of organisms. They have to explore whether some parameters can be found that are held constant or demonstrate patterns of change. An analysis would reveal whether

- the parameters are controlled with feedback;
- they are controlled without feedback; or
- their constancy is the result of a steady state mechanism.

Without having theoretical and mathematical tools one could not expect biologists of the 19th century to give detailed analyses of biological control mechanisms. Yet one can investigate whether they found the behaviour of control mechanisms to exhibit certain characteristics and whether they recognised them as something particularly worthy of further research. Indeed, Darwin's study of the human species revealed much about human development and behaviour as a result of comparisons with the animal kingdom, although his assertions that humans evolved from the ape still give rise to controversy and doubt as to the evidence of his observations.

However, it was Wiener who brought far more cohesion to the concept of cybernetics, when he related biological control mechanisms to artificial and mechanical control mechanisms, by comparing the animal or human brain with the control mechanism of a machine. In effect, this was a study of the brain and hence neural mechanisms, an area which is discussed and explained later in this book. Wiener did not so much invent cybernetics; rather, he brought a greater level of understanding, definition, and cohesion to the concept. In turn, Wiener's concepts were further developed by other famous cyberneticians such as Oskar Lange, Viktor Glushkov, Stafford Beer, and W. Ross Ashby. These people were to more greatly influence the course and application of the concept of cybernetics to the level which we understand today.

PROJECT CYBERSYN

Project Cybersyn was a Chilean project from 1971 to 1973 during the presidency of Salvador Allende aimed at constructing a distributed decision support system (DSS) within the production environment to aid in the management of the national economy. The project consisted of four modules: an economic simulator, customised software to check factory performance, an operations room, and a national network of telex machines that were linked to one mainframe computer. It was largely designed and implemented by Stafford Beer, albeit with significant support from Chilean technicians (Figure 2.1).

Project Cybersyn was based on the viable systems model (VSM) theory and a neural network approach to organisational design, and featured innovative technology for its time: it included a network of telex machines (*Cybernet*) in state-run enterprises that would transmit and

FIGURE 2.1
The operations room (or Opsroom): A physical location where economic information was to be received, stored, and made available for speedy decision-making. It was designed in accordance with Gestalt principles in order to give users a platform that would enable them to absorb information in a simple but comprehensive way.

receive information with the government in Santiago. Information from the field would be fed into statistical modelling software (*Cyberstride*) that would monitor production indicators, such as raw material supplies or high rates of worker absenteeism, in "almost" real time, alerting the workers in the first case and, in abnormal situations, if those parameters fell outside acceptable ranges by a very large degree, also the central government. The information would also be input into economic simulation software (*CHECO*, for CHilean ECOnomic simulator) that the government could use to forecast the possible outcome of economic decisions. Finally, a sophisticated operations room (*Opsroom*) would provide a space where managers could see relevant economic data, formulate feasible responses to emergencies, and transmit advice and directives to enterprises and factories in alarm situations by using the telex network.

The principal architect of the system was British operations research scientist Stafford Beer, and the system embodied his notions of organisational cybernetics in industrial management. One of its main objectives was to devolve decision-making power within industrial enterprises to their workforce in order to develop self-regulation of factories.

The project's name in English (Cybersyn) is a portmanteau of the words "cybernetics" and "synergy", hence the title of this book, partly as a tribute to the CyberSyn project. Since the name is not euphonic in Spanish, in that language the project was called *SINCO*, both an initialism for the Spanish *Sistema de INformación y COntrol*, "system of information and control", and a pun on the Spanish *cinco*, the number 5, alluding to the five levels of Beer's VSM. It also gave rise to the principle of cybernetic networks (Cybernet), where all factories throughout Chile that were involved in the structure were linked to the central control function by way of computerised network links. In itself, this same architecture could be used in today's world of transnational and multinational corporations.

Stafford Beer (formerly Anthony Stafford Beer) was a British consultant in management cybernetics as well as Professor at Manchester Business School. He also sympathised with the stated ideals of Chilean socialism of maintaining Chile's democratic system and the autonomy of workers instead of imposing a Soviet-style system of top-down command and control. He had originally been in the British Armed Forces and had used his advanced education in devising control systems for army operations. Once out of the Armed Forces, he set his knowledge to management techniques in the steel industry in the 1950s.

In July 1971, Fernando Flores (Carlos Fernando Flores Labra), a Finance Minister in the government of the Chilean President Salvador Allende, and a high-level employee of the Chilean Production Development Corporation (CORFO), contacted Beer for advice on incorporating Beer's theories into the management of the newly nationalised sector of Chile's economy. Beer saw this as a unique opportunity to implement his ideas on a national scale. More than offering advice, he left most of his other consulting business and devoted much time to what became Project Cybersyn. He travelled to Chile often to collaborate with local implementers and used his personal contacts to secure help from British technical experts. The implementation schedule was very aggressive, and the system had reached an advanced prototype stage at the start of 1973.

As Beer stated: *the Cybersyn project aimed to acquire the benefits of cybernetic synergy for the whole industry, while developing power for the workers at the same time* (How Many Grapes, 1994, p. 322). Allende sought a form of Communist control where the workers were themselves involved in the decision-making process at local level, rather than the Soviet policy of totally centralised decision-making and government.

The entire story of the Chilean project has been told on several occasions, but some accounts miss the essential nature of this, and indeed all VSM applications. The principal key is to enhance and encourage autonomy at all levels (as the only way of dealing with environmental variety) but also to ensure that the autonomous parts work together in a harmonious, coherent fashion and thus enjoy the synergy which comes when parts join together to create a whole system. Beer calls this the "explosion of potential", which happens in teams, and also pervades collaborative projects of all kinds.

The empowerment of the working people of Chile was at the heart of Allende's vision. Even when the country was under severe political and ideological attack by the United States, the issue of industrial democracy remained firmly established, with the workers having a substantial degree of influence in the functioning of Chilean industry. In August 1973, a month before the brutal coup that ousted the president, Beer asked Allende to what extent he expected worker control of the social economy. Allende replied "El maximo" (the maximum). For this to work, the usual approach of command and control, as promoted by the Soviet system, must be replaced by a pattern of relationships which are based on continuous flows of information, and thus a crucial element of Cybersyn was to run the entire national economy in real time, thus giving Chile potentially the most advanced system of governance on the planet.

The project started in the middle of an economic crisis, when inflation was rising dangerously and there was massive international opposition to Allende's government. Recently, declassified documents reveal that US President Richard Nixon ordered the CIA to "make the economy scream". The economic blockade by most of the developed world provided the context for the entire project.

There were 500 unused telex machines bought by the previous government. Each was put into one factory and linked to a central computer system in the control centre in the Chilean capital Santiago, the so-called operations room. In the control centre in Santiago, data coming from each factory each day (several numbers, such as raw material input, production output, and number of absentees) were entered into a computer, which made short-term predictions and necessary adjustments. There were four levels of control (firm, branch, sector, total), with algedonic (negative or positive) feedback. If one level of control did not remedy a problem in a certain interval, the higher level was notified. The results were discussed in the operations room, and a top-level plan was made. Where the feedback was negative, remedial action would be taken. Where the feedback was positive, the strategy behind it was enhanced and used as standard practice.

The software for Cybersyn was called *Cyberstride*, which used Bayesian filtering and Bayesian (intelligent) control, which embraces neural network control, machine learning control, and reinforced learning. It was written by Chilean engineers in consultation with a team of 12 British programmers. Cyberstride was a system to collect performance indicators from production plants, examine the flow of data for algedonics, and send the information directly back to its source to encourage self-regulation. The system would support decision-making to provide the required resources and support to alleviate any crises. It included the computers and software to process performance indicators from each factory and sector of the economy. The software, known as *Cyberfilter* (Cybernetic Filtration), provided statistical filtration, based on time series analysis that could forecast incipient instability and generate algedonics, i.e. early alarm signals. It was a joint pioneering effort between Chilean and British engineers and scientists. Despite its relatively primitive nature when compared with present-day technology, it was very advanced for its time, and proved extremely useful in providing solutions to several Chilean economic problems. Had it been allowed to work beyond Allende's presidency, it could have proven the basis for several other similar initiatives globally.

Cybernet was a sub-project that created a communication network between factories, state enterprises, sector committees, and the state government, using an existing telex network previously used to track satellites. They expanded the existing network to include every firm in the nationalised industries; it was intended to serve as a real-time economic control tool and transmitted data once every day. Raul Espejo, at the time the main facilitator of the Cybersyn project, later revealed that at the beginning of the project, someone discovered a warehouse full of unused telex machines and these provided the hardware on which Cybernet was based.

The futuristic operations room for the Cybersyn project was designed by a team led by the interface designer Gui Bonsiepe. It was furnished with seven swivel chairs (Tulip chairs, considered the best for creativity) with buttons, which were designed to control several large screens that could project the data, and other panels with status information, although these were of limited functionality as they could only show pre-prepared graphs. These graphs consisted of slides. Based on the information available, the operations directors could make decisions concerning rectification of the issues as they arose. Given the lack of state-of-the-art equipment and technology in Chile at the time, the system was still way ahead of its time, and, even given its short life, enabled the decision-makers to reach major decisions in real time concerning rectification of the problems that emerged.

The vision had been to facilitate the distribution of control and involvement of workers in business planning, via the workers' committees in each plant contributing to the system. The design looked more like bureaucratic centralisation of control via bottom-up reporting and top-down direction. Workers were expected to perform processes and use resources in the ways that had been modelled and planned. Any significant deviation from this was to be reported upwards, and corrective directives were to be cascaded downwards. However, the difference was that decision-making was not of itself the driving force. The bottom-up reporting drove the system based on a system of decentralisation, and decisions were made from the top down based on the reports issued from each element of the network, i.e. the feedback.

The system was most useful in October 1972, when the Gremio strike took place. About 40,000 striking truck drivers blocked the access streets that converged towards Santiago. According to Gustavo Silva (executive secretary of energy in CORFO, the Chilean Economic and Production Development Agencyi), the system's telex machines helped organise the transport of resources into the city with only about 200 trucks driven by strike-breakers, lessening the potential damage caused by the 40,000 striking truck drivers.

Gremios were trade associations that controlled the majority of the transportation network in Chile. They were generally of middle-class origins and were not supportive of Allende's initiatives to redistribute wealth to the poorest people in Chile. In 1973, the CIA persuaded the Gremios to strike and thus bring to a standstill the vast majority of the transportation system in Chile. After a few hours, algedonic signals began to flood into the capital, and the Cybernet systems were immediately taken over by the government. A temporary control centre (the operations room had not been completed) was established next to the communications room and began to receive demands for transportation. Supplies were needed in manufacturing plants. Food had to be delivered to shops. Patients needed to get to hospital. Due to the real-time design of the system, they knew exactly what needed to be moved, and the location and availability of the few remaining trucks (from the army, ambulances, etc.) that were under the control of the government. After 24 hours, everything important had been delivered, and the strike was abandoned. Beer estimated that this was achieved with between 10% and 30% of the normal transport capacity of Chile. If one applies the same logic to the present Covid-19 pandemic in 2020, much of the chaos brought on by the spread of the pandemic could have been avoided. However, it is, unfortunately, easy to be wise after the event, when the clichés of shutting the stable door after the horse has galloped off, and learning about geology the morning after the earthquake, apply.

The response to the Gremios strike and the ability to break the strike demonstrate the power of the Cybersyn experiment. One Chilean senior minister stated that the government would have collapsed without the cybernetic tools. Despite the unfinished network, the use of Telex machines, and the lack of a finished operations room, the real-time data that was derived enabled the government to quickly respond to the crisis and overcome the problem. In the present day, salutary lessons could be learned from this.

The project is described in some detail in the second edition of Stafford Beer's books *Brain of the Firm* and *Platform for Change*. The latter book includes proposals for social innovations such as having representatives of diverse "stakeholder" groups in the control centre, although in hindsight this would have required extensive training in the system for all concerned.

Computer scientist Paul Cockshott and economist Allin Cottrell referenced Project Cybersyn in their 1993 book *Towards a New Socialism*, citing it as an inspiration for their own proposed model of computer-managed socialist planned economies. The project was, after all, a pioneer in the use of cybernetics in a socialist environment, although it must be pointed out that cybernetics spans all forms of politics and is as useful and applicable in a free-market economy as it is in a socialist economy.

After the CIA-backed military coup on 11 September 1973 which ousted President Allende and removed his whole administration, the Cybersyn project was abandoned and the operations room was destroyed. In its short life, it had already revolutionised the whole use of cybernetics in national economic planning and control. Had it been allowed to continue, and had more modern computer technology been implemented, it could have had a far greater impact on such management techniques and could have been applied globally, especially where the national economy was based on a command structure, rather than a free-market structure, particularly in socialist countries, or at least where state control prevailed over many of the national authorities and institutions.

In many ways, Project Cybersyn should still inspire and inform present-day thinking. It offers an alternative to the two paradigms which diametrically oppose each other and have dominated political thinking for the last 100 years, namely free markets and centralised state socialism. It is, of course, impossible to know what would have happened if the coup had not taken place, or if, as Beer hoped, the existing institutions would have withered away as the more effective cybernetic institutions began to establish themselves. However, Raul Espejo, who was given the task of facilitating the project and making Cybersyn work, still remains optimistic. His perspective is as follows:

> With the benefit of hindsight I think that had the 1973 coup failed, and had the people and its socialist government supported the 3rd way offered by Beer's vision, Chile would have emerged, after several years of painful learning and development, as a more cohesive and fair society with a large social capital of engaged citizens.

Project Cybersyn may not be completely dead. It was very successful in providing a solution for national emergencies such as national strikes by the Chilean truck drivers, namely the movement of vital materials to where they were most needed, and in this respect provides a solution for present-day emergencies, such as emergency planning in war zones, and, more prevalently and critically, the Coronavirus (Covid-19) pandemic. The onslaught of the pandemic occurred so quickly that nobody outside its origin, considered to be China, was prepared for it. Whatever the circumstances behind its inexorable spread, cybernetic synergy could have provided (and still could provide) a means of providing vital resources to the health and retail sectors. In many countries, panic buying quickly emptied supermarket shelves, and in the health service, there is a woeful breakdown in the supply of essential preventive materials, such as masks and medical equipment, to hospitals and other medical centres. It has been established that there is a chronic short supply of face masks and other basic medical material. Using a cybernetic synergy strategy, this could have been avoided. A simulated plan had been implemented in the United States against such a scenario a few years ago but was never sanctioned for actual use. The secret, if that is what it can be called, is to implement an emergency contingency plan based on cybernetic synergy and the Chilean model that activates an immediate form of action to locate vital supplies of materials and move them by the quickest possible means to the locations that require them. This is based on previously input information into a central computer control system that shows which locations are stocking materials and the means of moving them from their existing location to the locations of need and emergency. In this way, the deficiencies and evident shortcomings of the health service would be overcome and reorganised based on the ability for the system to act swiftly and organise a logistics strategy that would address the need at its absolute point. Materials could be moved at high speed from one location to another, thus enabling the locations under pressure to use the material to relieve that pressure and address the need at its critical point. This strategy worked for Chile, even considering its Socialist/Marxist regime, and therefore can work for present-day regimes, assuming that they are in a state of preparedness and readiness for such an emergency.

The essence of the project is explained in detail in the book *Brain of the Firm* by Stafford Beer, now in its second edition, and recounts his experiences in creating and implementing the project, even though it was in its advanced prototype stage at the time of the coup d'état which ousted the President and his regime. If it worked then, then it can work today in an even better and more advanced and efficient way, given the advances in technology and the use of Enterprise Resource Planning (ERP) that exist today. It must be remembered that in the early 1970s, when the Cybersyn project was conceived and implemented, information technology was far more basic and by no means as advanced and complex as it is today. Today's level of technology makes the task of emergency planning far less cumbersome and far more efficient and simple to create and implement. What took 3 years to create and implement in the 1970s should only take a matter of weeks to accomplish in today's world. It takes will and consensus ad idem to create such a system, along with a little originality and initiative, but the end result will be a solution that would save many lives, as well as preparing for a far less certain future. There is still time to create such a project, but it would need to be carefully considered, planned, created, and implemented. An electronic database that show the types, quantities, and location of materials can be easily created and used, based on instructions to move those materials to the locations required on an instant basis, based on the analysis of the location and extent of the problem or emergency. Once the level of the emergency has been assessed, which amounts to negative feedback in terms of the cybernetic process, instructions are issued through the computer system to allocate resources to their point of need and to identify those resources and locations, and then move those resources to the location of need, thus combatting the emergency and relieving the acute situation. The solution is not that complex, but it requires careful planning and organisation.

Today, cybernetics has become diluted in other concepts which use either limited elements of the original discipline or deviate from it completely. Control theory refers to engineering concepts and controls of production than it does neural networks or commercial applications which it does not touch. Artificial Intelligence now refers to electronic processes and applications, and indeed the word or prefix "cyber" has more to do with robotic controls and electronic security than it does the neural network or the VSM. Indeed, the VSM of Stafford Beer is largely unknown, although its basic principle is used in indirect ways to determine company practice and performance without recognising its true value to commercial practice and efficiency. The time has come to re-establish the importance of cybernetics as an applicable and powerful discipline, and use it accordingly.

3

The Viable Systems Model

The English cybernetician Stafford Beer devised, applied, and refined the viable systems model (VSM) over a period of 30 years. It is aimed at the diagnosis and design of organisations as autonomous systems capable of self-organisation and adaptation to changing contexts. The VSM, rooted in a cybernetics (regulation theory) approach, offers a framework for gaining vital information on a system's functioning and ensuring its viability through requisite variety. It promotes the appropriateness and the repertoire of the system's responses to challenges by striving to make the responses as nuanced as the problems themselves.

Beer described the VSM as an *insight machine* rather than a *technocratic solution to problems*. Others have described the VSM as a *paradigm shifter* because of its indisputable validity and practical utility. Although his theory and the implementation of it are complex, the VSM nevertheless provides a framework according to which non-mathematicians can understand systems functioning.

This chapter provides a brief summary of Beer's work and main ideas but does not cover the theoretical subtleties and nuances in detail, as these are of no importance to the notion of applied cybernetics, especially within a business context. To gain a more complete understanding of the VSM, it is best to read some of Beer's own publications, such as his books, *The Brain of the Firm* and *The Heart of Enterprise*.

THE THEORETICAL UNDERPINNINGS OF THE VSM

The VSM stems from a transdisciplinary cybernetics perspective which can be described as the science of effective organisation through communication and control, or the regulation of systems to ensure their sustainability.

The epistemology of Beer's approach is informed by Relativity Theory and Hegel's Axiom of Internal Relations. According to Beer, all organising and management activities are aimed at dealing with **complexity**. He describes the measure of complexity as that of **variety** or *the number of possible states of a system*. The variety of a system also depends on the context in which it is embedded. Variety grows rapidly and exponentially with increased systems complexity. Real-world systems thus show variety that is mathematically infinite. Appropriate responses to the complexity involved depend on the attenuation of the variety, or how it is filtered or amplified. Here, Beer incorporates the principles of Ashby's Law of Requisite Variety according to which the capacity to control depends on the equilibration of the varieties of the controller with that of the system being controlled.

As suggested by the naming of his book, *The Brain of the Firm* (1972), Beer created the VSM to mimic the structure of the human brain. The brain, with its estimated 10 billion neurons, each of which has thousands of interconnections, shows astounding variety. The information picked up through our senses is also tremendously complex and varied. However, due to human system limits and social conditioning, the variety from the environment is, however, filtered or screened out (attenuated) by perceptual processes. Without such filtering the brain will be overwhelmed. The VSM also leverages measures of *variety* to align systems components and to match people, machines, and money to jobs.

Beer refers to ignorance as the most lethal attenuator. Systems, such as companies, which filter out important information (variety) about their environments, are also bound to fail due to their ignorance of new trends, new technologies, and new competitors. To ensure the purposeful adaptation of a system, variety needs to be attenuated, but it is the way in which this is done through filtering and/or amplification which is important. Design initiatives are therefore required to optimise attenuation processes.

Various systems overlap and dynamically interact with one another. This embeddedness of systems, Beer refers to as the principle or theorem of **recursion**. Viable systems have a recursive structure in that all viable systems contain, and are contained by, other viable systems. Continuous adaptation of these systems is required, and the term **autopoiesis** refers to the capacity of a system to recreate itself but maintain its identity and purpose.

The interaction between systems needs to be regulated or coordinated from a meta-level to prevent conflict. Just as pain and pleasure guide responses in the brain, **algedonic alerts**, or alarms and rewards, regulate **purposive** (which means "done with purpose") systems recursion.

Regulation aimed at effective interaction between systems requires maximum flexibility and freedom. Beer points out that rigid systems offer reductionist solutions to complex contextual challenges. Company organograms, for example, represent inflexible structures which largely fail to accommodate the dynamics of systems functioning.

The VSM offers the concept of **self-organisation** to overcome the challenges of rigid or inappropriate organisation. In nature, systems are characterised by self-organisation. In social systems, optimal self-organisation occurs when the freedom of participants is maximised within the restrictions necessary for the system to fulfil its purpose. According to Hilder (1995), self-organising systems have a hierarchy of purposes. A lack of purpose signifies the collapse of a system.

Design aimed at the maintenance and adaptation of systems focuses on the relationships between the components within a system as opposed to the components themselves. In other words, how information flows between system components is much more important than the individual components.

COMPONENTS OF VIABLE SYSTEMS

The VSM, which reflects a cybernetics theory of management, capitalises on the ideas of recursion, self-organisation, purpose, and that of fuzzy borders. Self-organising systems contain **three main elements**, namely

- environments (with fuzzy borders), where certain
- processes (operations) are implemented, as guided by
- management (meta-systems)

The first two elements are systems within themselves, i.e. they operate on an independent basis, not necessarily connected with other processes. The third element, i.e. management, is concerned with the control of all the previous two elements, as the management of the overall organisation must control each individual element of that organisation. In that respect, management is a meta-system, not a system or subsystem.

The environment refers to the domain of action of the system, which contextualises the interactions of the organisation. The reference to fuzzy borders illustrates the fact that environments can overlap, thus inferring that they are not mutually exclusive and isolated from all other environments. For example, production refers to the manufacturing environment, but it impinges on the procurement environment in that it requires the input of materials to function, and these materials must be procured from elsewhere. It impinges upon the inventory environment, as the materials that are procured will be kept in storage on the company's premises until they are required for production. It also impinges upon the logistics environment, as materials need to be moved into the company and products despatched elsewhere following production, in order to fulfil the whole throughput environment (Figure 3.1).

Whereas natural systems are self-organising, social systems need to be designed to ensure their viability. Beer's VSM, as graphically depicted below, is aimed at providing a blueprint for such a design:

According to Beer, viable systems consist of five interacting subsystems, levels, or components:

- The **first three levels or subsystems** are focused on internal operational functions in the shorter term (here-and-now). Included are primary activities, communication channels, and control structures.
  - **System 1** refers to the fundamental operations and management of the implementation process. The environments of operations may overlap and interfere with one another and must be coordinated to reduce oscillations and disruptions.
  - **System 2** involves the (often informal) coordination of System 1 elements (through timetables, schedules, or production plans). System 2 management of System 1 normally dictates operations because senior management does not have the requisite variety to do so. In other words, senior management is too far removed from the daily problems to be able to fully understand and help solve them.
  - **System 3** involves the control of the internal and immediate activities of System 1 as well as the supervision of System 2.

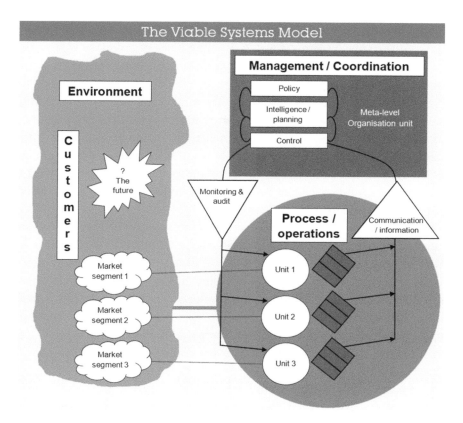

FIGURE 3.1
The viable systems model (www.cognadev.com).

- **The fourth level or subsystem** is responsible for integrating internal and external factors aimed at balancing the current situation with the demands of the broader context in the future (there-and-then).
  - **System 4** is referred to as the intelligence function aimed at ensuring adaptation to changing external circumstances. It requires channels to the environment and rich interaction with System 3. The intelligence of System 4 does not operate in a vacuum, though it stems from the ethos, nature, and character of System 5.
- **The fifth level or subsystem** balances the short-term internal functioning (here-and-now) with the long-term internal and external contexts (there-and-then). It includes decisions to direct the entire organisation to ensure its sustainability.

- **System 5** defines the ethos or the identity of the organisation and manages Systems 3 and 4. It is the basis of policy as well as the organisation's unwritten constitution.

The functioning described above applies to all viable systems, including those that are natural as well as man-made as both these systems rely on adaptation to changing environments for their survival over time. Compared to the architecture of the brain and nervous system, Systems 3, 2, and 1 of the VSM reflect the autonomic nervous system. System 4 represents reasoning and communication, whereas System 5 replicates introspection and decision-making.

In more simple terms, a viable system is composed of five interacting subsystems which may be mapped onto aspects of organisational structure. In broad terms Systems 1–3 are concerned with the "here and now" of the organisation's operations, and System 4 is concerned with the "there and then" – strategical responses to the effects of external, environmental, and future demands on the organisation. System 5 is concerned with balancing the "here and now" and the "there and then" to give policy directives which maintain the organisation as a viable entity.

- *System 1* in a viable system contains several primary activities. Each System 1 primary activity is itself a viable system due to the recursive nature of systems as described above. These are concerned with performing a function that implements at least part of the key transformation of the organisation (individual departmental functions).
- *System 2* represents the information channels and bodies that allow the primary activities in System 1 to communicate between each other and that allow System 3 to monitor and coordinate the activities within System 1. It represents the scheduling function of shared resources to be used by System 1 (internal electronic database systems, e-mails, etc.).
- *System 3* represents the structures and controls that are put into place to establish the rules, resources, rights, and responsibilities of System 1 and to provide an interface with Systems 4/5. It represents the big picture view of the processes inside of System 1 (enterprise resource planning, e.g. SAP, Oracle).
- *System 4* is made up of bodies that are responsible for looking outwards to the environment to monitor how the organisation needs to adapt to remain viable (ISO, AEO, etc.).

- *System 5* is responsible for policy decisions within the organisation as a whole to balance demands from different parts of the organisation and steer the organisation as a whole (overall management, use of ERP, etc.).

In addition to the subsystems that make up the first level of recursion, the environment is represented in the model. The presence of the environment in the model is necessary as the domain of action of the system, and without it, there is no way in the model to contextualise or ground the internal interactions of the organisation.

Algedonic alerts (from the Greek αλγος, pain and ηδος, pleasure) are alarms and rewards that escalate through the levels of recursion when actual performance fails or exceeds capability, typically after a timeout. Where the algedonic alert is positive, this notifies the operator that the system is working well and can thus be enhanced or developed further. Where the alert is negative, this notifies the operator that a problem exists which requires immediate rectification.

The model is derived from the architecture of the brain and nervous system. Systems 3-2-1 are identified with the ancient brain or automatic nervous system. System 4 embodies cognition and conversation. System 5, the higher brain functions, includes introspection and decision-making.

THE FOUR PRINCIPLES OF ORGANISATION

Beer's Four Principles of organisation specify the *primary sources of certain outcomes.*

In describing the functioning of these systems, Beer capitalises on Ashby's Law of Requisite Variety which specifies that control is only possible if the variety of the controller is equal to, or greater than, the variety of what is being controlled. This notion forms the basis of Beer's **First Principle of Organisation**, namely that environmental, operational, and management varieties should be designed to equate with each other, but with minimal costs and damage to people.

Organisations should therefore naturally search for the most efficient way to institute variety, without making major or radical wholesale changes to any areas of the organisation and still preserving individual freedom. Although radical reviews are essential from time to time, these should be carried out in such a way as to avoid instability or inconvenience. Change can only be implemented with the tacit or manifest agreement of all concerned and should never be imposed on any part of the organisation without consultation or consent.

In other words, different varieties characterise the environment, the process and the management of the process. The variety of the management system is, however, less than that of the process system and requires amplification to match the requirements of the processes or operations. This can, for example, be achieved through performance contracts and policies. The variety characterising the process system also needs amplification to match that of the environment – through advertisement, for instance. The potentially infinite variety posed by the environment, however, needs to be filtered or attenuated through market research, for example, to optimise operations in the environment, in the same way that process variety has to be filtered for management purposes through progress reports and accountability measures.

The variety of the various interacting subsystems thus needs to be designed and controlled to match one another to ensure the homeostasis and equilibrium of the broader systems. The communication channels involved in these processes also need requisite variety for the effective transmission of messages. Should the systems not be able to accommodate one another's variety, the systems will become unstable and collapse.

Beer's **Second Principle of Organisation** states that the four channels carrying information between the three systems should have a higher capacity to transmit information at the time of messaging than the originating system which generates the message. The *time factor* is thus important as the stability of a dynamic system depends on timing. Where there are delays in timing, the message is no longer timely and thus ceases to be effective. Information that is delayed is out of date, and thus ineffective, as it has been superseded by newer, more applicable information.

This is the first instance in which time is included in the scenario. Communication along any channels must be fast enough to maintain pace with the rate at which variety is generated; otherwise, there is a risk of instability. It is important to note that the stability of the system is dynamic and constantly changing, rather than remaining static.

The **Third Principle of Organisation** refers to the crossing of the boundaries between a channel and a system at which point transduction, or translation of the message, or energy conversion from one form to another, takes place. Here the variety of the transducer must be at least equivalent to the variety of the channel. The effectiveness by which messages are transduced or translated is a critical factor in systems functioning.

Every entity and part of the organisation operates with its own unique "language" or means of communication. It is therefore possible to envisage how the language used differs between the staff operating on the production line and those occupying executive and senior management positions. In many cases, these languages are mutually incomprehensible and, in equally many cases, can lead to a breakdown in communication between departments and functions. The same is true of international organisations which are part of the same multinational organisation or supply chain. Comprehensive communication in such environments is essential. Unless the communicator is fluent in other languages, it will be impossible for a person speaking only English to understand a Brazilian, whose language is Portuguese, or a Chilean, whose language is Spanish, or a Canadian Québecois, whose language is French, albeit with a Joual accent. In the author's case, this is not an issue, as the author is fluent in French, Portuguese, and Spanish, as well as his own language, English! Similarly, a computer programmed in one language is incompatible and hence cannot communicate with a computer programmed in another language.

Subsequently, language crossing a boundary between entities needs to be translated or transduced. These facilities should be present at all boundaries and are crucial for clear communication between different levels of an organisation.

The **Fourth Principle of Organisation** stipulates that the first three principles are to be cyclically maintained without time lags or delays. In other words, the speed of communication and responses are to keep up with changes that affect the system. Other systems theories of organisational design also emphasise the critical impact of time delays.

Although organisations often refer to activities using discrete time periods, such as a month or a week, real-world activity does not operate in the same way, in that timing in the real world is not discrete but continues constantly and continuously throughout any given time period. Managerial processes need to occur continuously for organisations to cope with changes in variety which are dictated and governed by the environment. Therefore, communication and response to any changes must be fast enough to keep up and maintain pace with any fluctuations and changes in the environment, especially the external environment; hence, the issue of externalities dealt with in System 4 of the VSM.

FUNCTIONS OF VIABLE SYSTEMS

Beer identifies **six functions** that are necessary for systems to acquire viability, and which are present at every level of recursion, namely:

- operation
- coordination
- audit
- direction
- planning
- identity

Operation

Operation is the definition of the activities performed in an organisation and how they function. An operation is in general a process, i.e. production, transport and logistics, mechanical, supply chain, etc., even down to a basic physical function, i.e. the movement of arms and legs in a human or animal body. This also implies organisation or cooperative work between individuals. On this basis, most viable systems contain subsystems as a means of handling the complexity of their various environments. These subsystems are capable of and responsible for carrying out the value-adding tasks of each system.

Coordination

Coordination is the control over operations and the communication required to exercise that control. In a human body, this is governed and controlled by the brain; in an organisation, the controlling element is the management structure, and, most likely, a computerised function. This also implies that primary sub-units operating within the framework of the same "parent" or supervisory/controlling unit need to operate synergistically, i.e. in total synergy with each other. In this respect, they cannot operate completely independently from each other but must be able to work within the same overall function as part of an overall unit, albeit with a degree of semi-autonomy, in that they may operate within their own scope or remit.

Audit

An audit, in its accepted sense, is a control mechanism, carried out internally and externally, which monitors and checks performance, feedback and results, especially for financial and fiscal purposes. An audit or monitoring process therefore reflects the accuracy of the status of primary activities within the organisation. An audit identifies weaknesses in a system and seeks to provide the means to rectify them. Audits in an organisation are an independent means of checking whether a system works or not. The Sarbanes-Oxley audit system was implemented in the wake of the Enron collapse and was designed to ensure financial transparency in an organisation, especially in the United States, although the Sarbanes-Oxley audit system now extends globally.

Direction

Direction is the very essence of cybernetics. It determines where an organisation is heading. Direction, like a compass bearing, refers to the manner in which an entity is steered, whether a means of transport or an organisation itself. Direction is the controlled way in which such an entity moves from one position to another by way of a controlled means. The Hebrew word *Derekh* means "way", and this is the very description of how to move from one place to another, by a defined route adhered to by the steersman or driver. The driver, manager, steersman, or pilot directs the movement of the entity, in order to ensure that it reaches its objective or destination in a timely and efficient manner.

Planning

A goal or objective cannot be reached without planning. A strategy for development requires planning at every stage, or else it will go wrong. A modeller of any form of model, be it aircraft, ship, car, etc. will always state that he/she will require a set of instructions to build the model, in the same way that an engineer requires plans to build a full-scale item. Boeing engineers require plans and blueprints to invest in tooling, production processes and tests before the aircraft has even left the drawing board. This might suggest that the expensive delays on the Boeing 737 Max were the result of insufficient planning and advance testing of the Manoeuvring

Characteristics Augmentation System (MCAS) software prior to its installation on the 737 Max aircraft. This may be a question that will never be fully answered, but planning is always a requirement prior to execution and implementation of any project.

Identity

Identity is equally crucial in any organisation. An organisation, as with any project, must be identified, and all the elements of that organisation or project must be equally identified and identifiable. In this way, any issues arising can be defined and associated with a specific identifiable function or operation, and addressed and rectified accordingly. Humans and animals, like organisations and products, must be identifiable for many reasons. Human beings all have names, according to their first name (i.e. the name by which they are called) and the family name. Similarly, materials and products are defined by name and description, even right down to their identification by Commodity Code for the purposes of tariff classification in terms of Customs control in international trade movements, for import and export purposes.

These six functions allow viable systems such as living organisms and organisations, to control the flow of materials, energy, and information that comes from the environment. Every line of communication between a system and its regulator represents a homeostatic circuit or exchange system. The attenuation processes of amplification and filtering are required to navigate recursively upwards and downwards within any viable system regardless of its size.

There also two other functions which may be included, namely Intelligence and Policy. These work alongside each other, as Policy is often dependent upon Intelligence.

INTELLIGENCE

The Intelligence function is the two-way link between the primary activity, i.e. the viable system, and its external environment. Intelligence provides the primary function with continuous feedback, i.e. vital information, on marketplace conditions, changes in technology, and all external factors which are likely to be relevant to it in the future. In this respect, it relates significantly to System 4 in the VSM.

POLICY

Policy is often seen as the overall determination of the mission or objective of the organisation in question and is extremely dependent on the information it receives from the rest of the organisation, and therefore be selective with that information and its uses. The main roles of Policy are to provide clarity about the overall direction, values, and purpose of the organisation and to design at the highest level the conditions for organisational effectiveness.

MEASUREMENT OF SYSTEMS VIABILITY

To calculate the viability or requisite variety of a system, Beer (1979) applies

- two regulatory aphorisms which state that while it is necessary to *enter the black box* of a system to understand the nature of its functions, entering the black box is not necessary for calculating its potential variety;
- the four principles of organisation as discussed above, which are aimed at optimally equating managerial, process and environmental varieties;
- the recursive systems theorem indicating that all viable systems are contained by, or nested within, viable systems;
- the three Axioms of Management reflecting Ashby's Law of Requisite Variety, or statements regarding the variety disposed by interacting systems which should be equal and in proper balance; and
- the Law of Cohesion for multiple recursions of viable systems refers to the balancing or equating of System 1 variety which is accessible to System 3 of recursion, with the variety disposed by the sum of the meta-systems of recursion for every recursive pair.

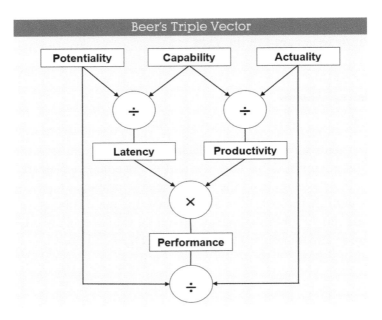

FIGURE 3.2
The triple vector.

In his book, *Brain of the Firm* (1972, p. 163), Beer proposes a triple vector to measure the performance of a system. He refers to the concepts of **actuality** (what we are doing now), **capability** (what we could do), and **potentiality** (what is required, i.e. target or objective). These three concepts can be used to calculate the system's **productivity** (ratio of actuality to capability); **latency** (ratio of capability to potentiality) and **performance** (ratio of actuality to potentiality as well as productivity to latency) can be estimated. These aspects are graphically represented in Figure 3.2.

If we address the **potentiality** of a system, we can attain a specified target, e.g. levels of efficient and cost-effective production. However, at present we are nowhere near that target and instead occupy a position of **actuality** (i.e. where we are now), which is always less than the potentiality. Our **capability** tells us what we are capable of doing to attain that target, in terms of performance and the use of resources.

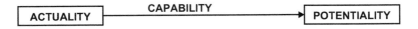

Our potentiality is 100%. If our actuality is only 60%, then we need to establish a capability of an extra 40% to reach our potentiality.

The VSM concept of variety is also used to match people, machines, and money to jobs that produce products or services. Jobs can be performed by one or many people. One person can also perform many jobs. A specific job may require of a person to shift focus between internal and external Systems 1–5. The type of decisions made and the effort (and cost) involved determine the resources, hence the variety, of a job.

Applications in Work Environments

The VSM model offers a framework for gaining vital information on systems functioning, aimed at ensuring the requisite variety, or viability, of systems. It uses variety measures to enable the system's repertoire of responses to challenges, to be as nuanced as the problems themselves.

Regardless of its valuable contribution, Beer's VSM is not widely known. The VSM is, however, applied to analyse and understand organisational structures and structural relationships, to diagnose organisational problems and to guide business process engineering. It is applied in the military, government administration, virtual communities, higher educational institutions, as well as in the fields of engineering, web technologies, collaborative and service networks, supply chains, health and safety systems, etc.

The VSM in Brief

Stafford Beer, the inventor of the VSM, described it as a "holistic model involving the intricate interactions of five identifiable but not separate subsystems". The model was developed during the 1950s while Beer was a manager in the steel industry in Sheffield (United Kingdom), as a practical tool capable of dealing with issues of organisational structure.

The VSM is firmly based on systems theory and is inspired by the way the brain coordinates the muscles and organs, as per the original concept of the American cybernetician Norbert Wiener. Its theoretical basis is the work carried out by W. Ross Ashby, particularly the Law of Requisite Variety. Other work was based on Wiener's development of cybernetics, the mathematics of recursive systems, and McCulloch's theories of neural networks.

What can be derived from all of this is a body of knowledge which describes the way in which all viable systems work. As part of his own work, Beer identified the **invariances** which apply universally, regardless of the size or nature of the viable system, and it is this concept which has been applied at all scales from small work-groups to nation states.

Beer's first models were mathematical, but these proved impossible for most people to understand, given the nature of complex mathematical formulae. He then designed the graphical model which illustrates the five subsystems, i.e. the building blocks of the VSM, and the "intricate interactions" which connect them. The diagram also shows the interactions between the viable system and its environment – the niche within which it operates.

A simple VSM diagram looks like this representation as Figure 3.3.

The diagram shows the three main elements: the operation (O), the management (M), and the environment (E).

As can be seen, the operational ellipse is composed of three operational units (labelled 1a–1c), and the management diamond is composed of four subsystems (labelled 2–5). These are the five systems: the operation is System 1 – in this case composed of three operational elements – and the management is composed of Systems 2–5. The various arrows represent

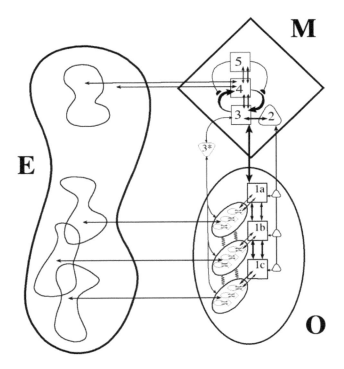

FIGURE 3.3
The simple VSM diagram.

the many and often highly complex interactions between the five systems and the environment, represented by a more nebulous entity.

An understanding of the theory begins with the observation that operational units must be as autonomous as possible, and thus Beer's model of sees any organisation as a cluster of autonomous operational parts which bind together in a cohesive manner in mutually supportive interactions to create a new, larger, whole system, similar in a way to the human and animal physical system. Thus, the function of overall management is to provide the "glue", i.e. the manner of cohesion, which enables this to happen. Beer named this function the meta-system, which is defined by him as **"A collection of sub-systems which looks after the operational elements so that they cohere in that totality called the Viable System".**

Systems 2–5, between themselves, make up the meta-system. Their roles are as follows:

System 2 deals with the inevitable problems which emerge as a number of autonomous, self-organising operational parts interact. However, there will be conflicts of interest which must be resolved. System 2 exists to harmonise the interactions, to keep the peace, to deal with the problems and to resolve any potential or actual conflicts. Without System 2, the system would shake itself to the point of disintegration.

System 3 is concerned with synergy, i.e. reciprocal communication to the point of consensus ad idem. It looks at the entire interacting cluster of operational units from its meta-systemic perspective and considers ways to maximise its effectiveness through collaboration. System 3 ensures that the whole system works better than the operational parts working in isolation. Beer postulates an "explosion of potential" which emerges from collaboration and symbiotic relationships. Without a System 3 this could not happen.

System 4 ensures that the whole system can adapt to a rapidly changing and sometimes hostile and challenging environment. It scans the outside world in which it operates, looks for threats and opportunities, undertakes research and simulations, and proposes plans to guide the system through the various possible pathways it could follow, using the definition of cybernetics to this effect, i.e. guiding the organisation through what could be seen as a morass or jungle. Without a System 4, the system would be unable to cope with the complexity of the external environment in which it operates.

System 5 provides closure and ultimate resolution to the whole system. It defines and develops the vision and values of the system through policies.

System 5 creates the identity, the ethos, and the ground rules under which everyone operates. It aligns the tasks of everyone in the organisation. In Beer's words, **Rules come from System 5: not so much by stating them firmly, as by creating a corporate ethos – an atmosphere.**

Without a System 5, fragmentation would be inevitable. In other words, System 5 holds the whole organisation together, as it represents the overall corporate policy.

The interactions between these five subsystems and the way they respond to and affect the external environment define the VSM. The essence of these interactions is as follows:

1. The operational units are given as much autonomy as possible so they can respond quickly and effectively. This is limited only by the requirements of system cohesion.

2. Systems 1–3 between them make up the internal environment of the viable system – the Inside and Now. The autonomous parts function in a harmonising internal environment which maximises its effectiveness through creating mutually supportive relationships.

3. System 4 is concerned with the Outside and Then. It formulates plans in the context of both the outside world and its intense interaction with System 3 which ensures all plans are grounded in the knowledge of the capabilities of the organisation.

4. System 5 monitors the interaction between S3 and S4 to ensure all plans are within policy guidelines. If not, it steps in and applies its ultimate authority.

5. All parts of the system work together holistically. Information is designed to flow throughout the structure in real-time, binding together the various subsystems.

Applications involve rethinking the workings of any organisation in these terms.

Take any enterprise and identify the operational parts: this is System 1.

Conflicts of interest are resolved by way of System 2.

As the process continues, a diagram something like Figure 3.3 will develop. Once this is complete, the diagnosis can begin, with questions such as: are the identified systems properly connected? Are they fit for purpose? And so on.

After 50 years, nobody has been able to find a case study in which the VSM has failed: in all its many and varied applications, it has provided to be an insightful diagnosis and has directed organisational restructuring to create effective organisations, based on individual autonomy and creativity.

A QUICK GUIDE TO THE VSM

For those less technical in their outlook, the following is a quick guide to how the VSM works in practice.

The Model

The VSM looks at an organisation interacting with its environment.

The organisation is viewed as two parts: **the operation** which does all the basic work (production, distribution, earning the money) and the bits which provide a service to the operation by ensuring the whole organisations work together in an integrated way (scheduling, accounts, strategic planning…) These bits are called **the meta-system**.

The following diagram illustrates the basic VSM (Figure 3.4).

The operation will consist of a number of operational units. These could be production units or teams of people doing various jobs.

The meta-system can be divided into three main functions:

- **The internal eye** looks at the entire collection of operational units and deals with ways of getting them to work together in mutually beneficial ways, and with the resolution of conflicts. This is "Inside and Now".
- **The external eye** looks at the external environment, assesses the threats and opportunities, and makes plans to ensure the organisation can adapt to a changing environment. This is "Outside and Then".
- **Policy systems** establish the ground rules which set the tone for the whole organisation. Policy rounds off the system. The policy systems must have ultimate control.

This is the basic model: The VSM sees any viable system as a collection of operational elements which are held together by a meta-system.

Both operation and meta-system must be in contact with, and interacting with, their environment.

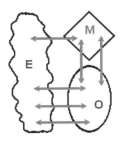

FIGURE 3.4
Basic VSM.

E represents the environment.
O represents the operation.
M represents the meta-system.
The arrows indicate the many and various ways that the three parts interact. Each arrow may have several aspects – it may be information, or trucks, a phone call, or a delivery of steel ingots.

The operational units themselves must be viable and thus can be looked at as smaller viable systems embedded in the larger system (Figure 3.5).

The Model – Slightly Elaborated

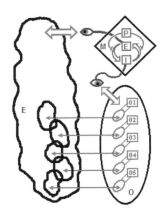

FIGURE 3.5
The managerial hierarchy.

Note: The three main parts – operation, environment, and meta-system. Note the meta-system is shown with its internal and external eyes; the operation is shown with five operational units, all of which are smaller embedded viable systems.

Preliminary Diagnosis

In the Preliminary Diagnosis it is necessary to look at one's own organisation and examine the units which compose it. That is, it is necessary to list the elements that do things, the coordination functions, the accounting and scheduling functions, and so on.

It is then possible to draw a large VSM which will look something like the pictures on the previous pages to identify

- the operational parts;
- the parts which have inputs from the internal eye and which deal with stability and optimisation of the operational units;
- the parts which have inputs from the external eye and which make long-term plans in the light of environmental information; and
- the policy systems.

At the end of this process, there will be a large picture which gives a representation of the organisation in its totality.

This is the basic model from which the rest of the diagnosis will follow.

In some cases the Preliminary Diagnosis will be the most useful aspect. You may find that your organisation has no way to carry out some of the functions which are vital for viability. Thus, you may decide to create new jobs to ensure these functions get performed. You may also find that some jobs do not seem to have anything to do with the viable systems. You may decide they are not necessary.

Designing Autonomy

It is essential to create the right conditions for all the operational units to function with as much autonomy as possible.

Thus they will need

- individual mission statements;
- budgets for the resources they need to carry out this mission; and
- an agreement that they can decide on their own internal development as long as they are working to the agreed mission.

There will also have to be safeguards to ensure that the units cannot threaten the overall viability of the organisation of which they are a part.

Thus:

- They must be accountable and able to demonstrate they are working to the agreed plan.
- There must be pre-agreed intervention rules, which means that autonomy is forfeit under certain conditions. The worst-case scenario must be considered in advance.

Balancing the Internal Environment

By this stage you will have looked at the various parts of your organisation and decided how they map onto the VSM. You will also have considered the autonomy of the operational units.

The internal environment consists of all the operational units and those jobs which are dedicated to looking at them (the internal eye) and to ensuring that conflicts are resolved and that their performance is optimised.

Internal balance is concerned with these (meta-systemic) jobs and with ensuring that they have the capabilities to function properly. So for example, a committee which meets once every three months would be an absurd idea – most of these jobs need to be done on a continuous basis.

The approach to internal balance is as follows:

- Maximise autonomy so that the vast majority of problems are dealt with within the operational units.
- Examine the exchange of goods and services between the operational units, and see if improvements may be made.
- Examine the bits of the external environment peculiar to each operational unit, and see if changes can be made (perhaps they all use the same suppliers and thus benefit from joint buying).
- Optimise the allocation of resources to the operational units. It may be possible to cut back in one unit and reinvest in another, thus creating synergy in the whole system.
- Examine the scheduling and coordination functions.
- Ensure that the information systems which inform the meta-system of the goings on at the operational level are well designed. How complete is the information? How up-to-date is it?
- And lastly, after all the above have been exhausted, it may be necessary to "beef up" the capabilities of the meta-system in order to

ensure it can discharge its functions of overseeing the operational units. This is the usual way that traditional businesses operate and in terms of both efficiency and human working conditions should be seen as the very last alternative.

The essence of the internal balance is to view the Inside of your enterprise as a system of autonomous operational elements, which need to be overseen (the internal eye) to look for ways of generating synergy.

The imposition of dictates from *above* should only be used when the viability of the whole enterprise is at risk and not, as in traditional businesses, as the usual way of dealing with most problems.

Information Systems

The VSM requires thorough and up-to-date information systems.

The perfect information system would measure everything it needs to know continuously, so that a real-time model of the goings on within any part of the enterprise may be maintained.

The compromise between this and the usual management information, which is weeks or months out of date, is the use of daily performance indicators.

These measure whatever is seen as important within each operational unit (productivity, morale, wastage, sales, breakages…) at the end of each day. The figures are then plotted onto a time series so that the trends may be assessed.

The essence of the VSM approach to information is that we only need to know if something changes, usually in a negative fashion. If everything is operating as normal, we can leave it alone. Hence, the maxim "If it ain't broke, don't fix it". In other words, do not throw valuable resources at something which is working perfectly well. However, as soon as something changes (e.g. dramatic fall in productivity, leading to negative feedback) it is essential that we are notified immediately, as something needs fixing, and fixing fast, lest it leads to greater damage and inconvenience.

Therefore:

- Huge printouts of standard information which say *nothing much has changed* are useless and completely unnecessary.

- Immediate alerting signals which say *something dramatic or major has happened* are essential, as they act as alarm bells.

These signals, which are called **algedonics**, are the basis of information handling in the VSM. They can be designed to provide operational units with the information they need to learn and adapt to environmental changes, to define clear limits to autonomy, to guarantee that each operational unit is working as an integrated part of the whole system and so on.

The design of these information systems is crucial to the effective operation of the enterprise and can be used as an alternative to authority.

Balance with the Environment

The external eye maintains contact with the relevant parts of the external environment and enables the future planning systems to develop strategies for adapting to change in the market, or to new technology, or whatever.

Again, the various parts must be balanced:

- The future planning system must have the capabilities to examine and find the relevant information.
- It must be capable of planning and simulating various options.
- It must be aware of the capabilities of the operational units and develop any strategies within this context.
- It must be able to agree and implement its plans through the connections to the operational units.
- It must function within policy guidelines.

Policy Systems

The policy systems oversee the entire organisation. They constitute the ultimate authority. Clearly, they must be designed with great care.

For a cooperative, it is crucial that everyone is involved in policy decisions, and this usually involves a meeting of all members.

However, the practicalities of this need to be addressed. How often can the entire membership meet? How effective are big meetings? The answer to the question of how you involve all members in policy decisions and how you ensure that everyone has to work within these ground rules is perhaps one of the biggest questions for any social economy enterprise and will determine the extent to which it may describe itself as democratic.

Basic Vocabulary

This guide deals with how the VSM looks at organisations and how it ensures that the various parts of the organisation are balanced, while introducing the following main points:

- Autonomous operational units
- Meta-system – concerned with ensuring the operational units hang together or cohere into a single integrated organisation
- Synergy – the added efficiency which comes from working together in a cooperative fashion
- Daily performance indicators – which measure the goings on within each operational unit
- Algedonics – signals which are generated to say "Look out... something unusual has occurred"

It also uses the five systems to describe the various functions within the organisation.

System 1	The entire collection of interacting operational units.
System 2	The system responsible for stability/resolving conflict between operational units.
System 3	The systems responsible for optimisation/generating synergy between operational units.
System 4	Future plans and strategies. Adaptation to a changing environment. Externalities.
System 5	Overall policy.

Of all the systems, System 5 is perhaps the most dynamic and overseeing function of all. It represents the policy-making and decision function of the organisation and relies on all the other systems to make and direct policy. In this respect, it is the thinking, or *brain* part of the organisation, and is therefore represented by the senior management. Its organisation is represented by the following diagram.

The diagram depicts the highest managerial echelon of the organisation as it might be seen on a typical organisation chart. MM represents the

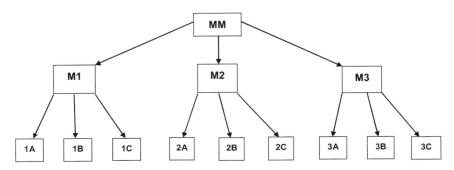

FIGURE 3.6
Sub-systems of the viable systems model.

manager of the whole organisation, i.e. the Chief Executive/President, and in this case, he has three main subordinates, namely M1, M2, and M3, who are Directors or Vice-Presidents. Each of these also has three subordinates (Divisional Heads), so in this case there are 13 people considered in the illustration (Figure 3.6).

MM calls M1, M2, and M3 and explains to them the specific situation. He tells them that each should come and see him independently, so that they can convey their views to him individually. This also means that their individual views will count for far more, as if they conferred together, they could reach a consensus ad idem and come back with an agreed solution. If they did, the Chief Executive could hardly contradict their combined view and would therefore not be in a controlling situation. However, each individual out of M1, M2, and M3 could present an entirely separate view and leave the Chief Executive with a choice of options. In reality, m1, m2, and M3 will go away and consult with their divisional managers, i.e. 1A-C, 2A-C, and 3A-C. For the same reasons, each Director/Vice-President asks their divisional heads not to conspire against them but talks to them individually, in order to hear their independent views. Therefore, the protocol is continued throughout. In so many ways, this would seem to be the orderly and disciplined way to deal with such matters, which would avoid petty squabbles and differences of opinion so evident in many boardroom meetings.

In reality, however, everyone is different, and each of us is entitled to their own opinions. As Oliver Cromwell said, "I may not like what you have to say, sir, but I uphold your right to say it". The main issue is that the divisional heads only know their side of the business and are not able to take into account all other aspects of the business. Indeed, there may be a different level of intelligence and intellect amongst the divisional managers, thus determining their level of awareness or even competence. After all, most people in any organisation are not expected to have PhDs in rocket science, let alone Masters' Degrees. Many, however, are dedicated professionals and know their professional disciplines with all the sharpness of a finely machined razorblade. Above all this, each individual may display a natural fallibility which prevents them from being master of everything, and so this continues from top to bottom in any organisation. Even the Chief Executive is specialist in his own field and still requires the advice of his subordinates in order to make balanced decisions. On this basis, what is the value of the advice of 1A, when he gives it to M1, or even m1, when he gives his advice to MM? This must be based on the collective knowledge of all associated subordinates based on a combination of knowledge, understanding, and perception of a specific situation. The same will be true of the advice given to M2 and m3, and their subsequent advice to MM. To this extent, the probability of error or misjudgement at each of the subordinate stages means that the probability of error at the top level may be higher. Indeed, if vital information is withheld or even not known at the subordinate level, then the risk of misjudgement at the top level is significantly higher. Hence the principle that the Chief Executive is only as good as those advising him and therefore cannot be expected to make decisions based on his own intuition.

However, the overreaching premise is that management is only as good as its subordinates. If the essential structure and operating system of the company do not work properly, whatever the policy adopted by the management will fail. This is true of any major organisation, from government to small-to-medium enterprise. The scenario detailed above will still fail on the grounds that regardless of any face-to-face meeting between the Chief Executive and his subordinates, if vital information relating to negative feedback is withheld, the Chief Executive will not be able to reach a balanced decision, whether personally or at boardroom level. The collapse of the US energy giant Enron was in reality a series of systematic failures, in that vital information concerning the true state of the organisation's financial affairs was withheld from the auditor, Arthur Andersen, and, even when Andersen knew of the dire state of affairs, it did nothing to either rectify the situation or report it. By the time the damage was done and Enron collapsed, the dire situation could not have been rectified, and

Andersen itself was ultimately called to account. In cybernetic terms, Enron was definitely not viable and had not been for some time. Effectively, all the systems of the VSM had totally failed. If Systems 1–4 fail, including the auditing and monitoring process at the level of System 3*, so will System 5. The management of the organisation was little or no better than its internal structure, which, as it is now known, was a disaster waiting to happen. Indeed, the management actively sought to cover up the dire financial situation, partly by shifting debts from one part of the organisation to others to make it appear as though the company was still solvent, when, in reality, it was not. Thankfully, the Sarbanes-Oxley legislation of 2002 sought to close the gap and ensure that such a scandal could never happen again, but it could not stop the fact that the stable door had been secured well after the horse had galloped off. In reality, the Sarbanes-Oxley legislation mandates the strict auditing and monitoring of financial affairs and reporting in order to ensure that any anomalies and discovered and reported in time to rectify a potentially damaging financial adversity, thus fulfilling the cybernetic principle of input and output of information coupled with positive and negative feedback.

System 5 shows that management must be in control as the brain of the organisation if true viability is to prevail. The management not only must know about all aspects of the organisation but also must be able to control it fully, hence the application of W. Ross Ashby's Law of Requisite Variety. If we review the law itself, we determine that:

> The controlling element of the organisation must be at least as large as, if not larger than, all the elements of the organisation which it is to control.

By nature of this statement, if management cannot control the organisation as a whole, the organisation cannot be viable and therefore cannot function properly. Management policy exists to exercise total control over the organisation, right down to the last nut and bolt used to secure an internal heating or air-conditioning duct. The automotive and aviation sectors have experienced such issues to their cost. The scandal that emerged from the crashes of two new Boeing 737 MAX aircraft showed that the intended MCAS software system installed in the aircraft malfunctioned in a big way, largely because it had not been properly tried and tested beforehand, and severe short-cuts had been taken in ensuring its safety and certification, along with the aircraft in which it was installed. In this respect, System 3* had failed as far as the VSM was concerned, and indeed, both Systems 2 (interdepartmental communication) and 5 (management control) had equally failed. Eventually, the Boeing scandal resulted in the removal of Boeing's CEO Dennis Muilenburg. As per the famous phrase of former US President Harry S. Truman, "The Buck stops here".

Another notable scandal was that of the Volkswagen catalyst installations. In the United States, VW was tasked with ensuring that the diesel-powered VW cars met the strict US carbon emission standards but failed to do so. VW was issued with a notice of violation of the US Clean Air Act by the US Environmental Protection Agency (EPA) in September 2015.

The agency had found that Volkswagen had intentionally programmed turbocharged direct injection (TDI) diesel engines to activate their emissions controls only during laboratory emissions testing, which caused the vehicles' NOx (nitrogen oxide) output to meet US standards during regulatory testing, but emit up to 40 times more NOx in real-world driving. Volkswagen deployed this software in about 11 million cars worldwide, including 500,000 in the United States, in model construction years 2009 through to 2015.

Regulators in several countries began to investigate Volkswagen, resulting in a sharp fall in the value of its stock price by a third in the days immediately following the news. Volkswagen Group CEO Martin Winterkorn resigned, as well as the head of brand development Heinz-Jakob Neusser, Audi research and development head Ulrich Hackenberg, and Porsche research and development head Wolfgang Hatz were suspended. Volkswagen announced plans in April 2016 to spend €16.2 billion (US$18.32 billion at April 2016 exchange rates) on rectifying the emissions issues and planned to refit the affected vehicles as part of a recall campaign. In January 2017, Volkswagen pleaded guilty to criminal charges and signed an agreed statement of facts, which drew on the results of an investigation Volkswagen had itself commissioned from US lawyers Jones Day. The statement set out how engineers had developed the defeat devices, because diesel models could not pass US emissions tests without them, and deliberately sought to conceal their use. In April 2017, a US federal judge ordered Volkswagen to pay a $2.8 billion criminal fine for "rigging diesel-powered vehicles to cheat on government emissions tests". The "unprecedented" plea deal formalised the punishment which Volkswagen had agreed to. Winterkorn was charged in the United States with fraud and conspiracy on 3 May 2018. As of 1 June 2020, the scandal had cost VW $33.3 billion in fines, penalties, financial settlements, and buyback costs. Various government and civil actions are currently undergoing in the United States, as well as the European Union, where most of the affected vehicles are located; while they remain legal to drive there, consumers' groups and governments seek to make sure Volkswagen has compensated these owners appropriately as they had to do in the United States.

Yet again, this was a clear case of a dramatic failure in the systems structure of the VSM. In particular, Systems 3, 3*, and 5 failed because of what amounted to a wilful cover-up conspiracy, rather than a breakdown in communication. System 3* (monitoring and auditing) particularly failed, because of deliberately fraudulent statements concerning the vehicles' emissions threshold based on false monitoring and reporting practices. The management may have known about these false reports, or, because of a question of honour, decided to resign. Whatever the element of blame, the overall VSM system failed because of deliberate actions to falsify the system and possible to avoid costly negative feedback. In the event, the overall feedback was negative, and it costs the organisation dear.

Such examples may be prominent, but they are not isolated cases. There are many instances where corporate scandals have rocked the industry as a whole. Indeed, the rationale behind the initiative of Stafford Beer to create the VSM lay in his experiences as a manager at British Steel, where he observed enough deficiencies to warrant creating a model which was designed to revolutionise the whole of the corporate and organisational management system. It is difficult to state whether a full cybernetic control over the affairs of both Boeing and VW would have prevented the scandals that emerged, but it would certainly have alerted the independent auditors of both organisational structures and practices much earlier in the process and could perhaps have avoided the scandals which ultimately emerged.

Subsystems

For each system within the VSM, there are five subsystems, and these are arranged as follows:

Subsystem 1 – external sensory
Subsystem 2 – internal sensory
Subsystem 3 – internal motor (or driver)
Subsystem 4 – external motor (or driver)
Subsystem 5 – link and coordination between subsystems 1–4

Two of the subsystems are sensory, in that they receive feedback, and two are motor, i.e. driving or activity-generating factors linked to the sensory subsystems. This implies that the motor-based subsystems rely on the sensory subsystems. Furthermore, two of the subsystems are internal, and two are external. All four subsystems function in accordance with each other, with the overall control and coordination function exercised by subsystem 5. Therefore, each system of the VSM has this five-subsystem structure as part of its overall function, as all five systems must work together to ensure that the overall organisation remains viable at all times. Should any one of the subsystems fail, the whole system fails, and consequently so too does the organisation as a whole.

Summary of the Viable Systems Model

- The model is **recursive**, i.e. there is a possibility of multiple different iterations of the systems and occurrences, creating multitudes of activity combinations.
- Each of the systems is nested within each other, creating a smaller VSM at each level.
- Each level could be considered top operated as System 1, should there be a higher level of recursion above it.
- There are often numerous departments within organisations, and organisations operate in multi-institution environments, each of which operates as a VSM in its own right.
- The functions described in the VSM do not necessarily have to correspond to a single role description, team, or department – multiple functions can be operated by a single individual/group, and simultaneously, functions can be shared between many other individuals or groups.
- For example, senior individuals often carry out the functions of Systems 3–5, which may cause confusion (i.e. those concerned with System 5 functions may intrude into System 3). Any transmissions coming from above should be concerned with regulation, not control, unless absolutely necessary.
- Every single level of the organisation must hold requisite variety – being able to amplify their own variety when necessary, and attenuate any input – whilst channels for communicating variety must hold higher capacity than their transmissions in order to account for errors.

The VSM considers an organisation as a number of operational units, and the systems needed to ensure they cohere, or work together, as an integrated, harmonious whole.

The three basic elements are the operation, the meta-system, and the environment.

All three are in continuous interaction.

The **operation** is called **System 1** and carries out the organisation's **primary activities**.

The **meta-system** is composed of Systems 2–5.

System 2	**Conflict resolution, stability**
System 3	**Internal regulation, optimisation, synergy**
System 4	**Adaptation, dealing with a changing environment (externalities), forward planning**
System 5	**Ultimate authority, policy, ground rules, identity**

The model is recursive, namely that the same principles of organisation *recur* at all organisational levels, regardless of scale. This means that any viable system is composed of smaller viable systems and is embedded in a larger viable system.

The Recursive System Theorem

An extension to the VSM as proposed by Stafford Beer applies to subsystems within the organisation. The theorem, as stated by Beer, is that:

> If a viable system contains a viable system, then the organisational structure must be recursive.

The implication of this is that as a complete system is recursive, i.e. it contains processes that recur on a regular basis, then any subsystem within that overall system must also be recursive. This therefore implies that all subsystems within an overall system are also recursive. If the viable company is organised in this way, so is its viable sub-unit, e.g. the individual department, factory, subsidiary, or branch. If that sub-unit is also organised in the same way, so too is the viable division within that sub-unit, and so it goes on. The organisation of the entire company and its subsidiary elements is based on the same principle, i.e. the VSM. What applies at top corporate level permeates throughout the organisation, and thus applies at all levels and within all elements. That which recurs at one level recurs at all levels, albeit in a different manner depending upon the operation concerned within the organisation as a whole. If this structure and pattern did not exist, the company would be completely dysfunctional and would thus collapse because of an inherent lack of internal control, especially if any externalities were to prevail. There must be an inherent coordination of all activities, and this means that all such activities must be subject to the same level of control at all levels, regardless of the subsidiary, its functions, and its relationship with the central controlling function. We can therefore expect that an organisation of viable systems and its integration into some large viable whole will be organisationally recursive, in other words, self-perpetuating in its entirety. Furthermore, any attempt to integrate other external functions, e.g. new practices, regulations, and procedures, as well as takeovers of other organisations, must also obey the same characteristics as the existing viable entity if the system is to function properly.

4

Input, Output and Decision Support

Another way of looking at the cybernetics principle is to compare two processing machines in a process. These machines are M1 and M2. Each has an input (I) and an output (O). The input for machine M1 is I(1), and its output is O(1). Correspondingly, the input for machine M2 is I(2) and its output is O(2). The function that converts input to output is F; therefore, the function for machine M1 is F(1), while the function for machine M2 is F(2).

A simplified diagram of this concept is as shown in Figure 4.1.

These machines are both used in the same overall organisation, but for different productive functions. One machine function controls the production of one type of material, while the other controls the production of another material.

Assuming that input is of the same level for both machines, where both machines operate equally efficiently, output for each machine will be relatively the same.

It has been decided to adopt new technology to upgrade each of the computers. This is duly implemented, but as a result, one computer operates more efficiently than the other, and as a result, the output from one machine is greater than that from the other machine. The feedback from one computer is negative, while the other is positive.

It should be noted at this point that the output variety, or number of elements, has to be at least equal to, if not greater than, the input variety. This means that everything that enters the machines is processed and reappears from the machines as a tangible output, either as a direct process or as a result of rectification. This corresponds to Ashby's Law of Requisite Variety, proposed by W. Ross Ashby, that states that the control of a function can only be obtained if the variety of the controller, i.e. the number and type

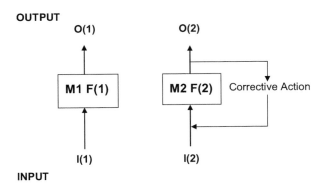

FIGURE 4.1
First order cybernetic control system.

of functions which it performs, including all the parts of the controller, is at least as great as the variety, i.e. number of elements and functions, of the situation to be controlled. That means that any controlling system must be able to control all elements of the system which it is designed to control. For example, in a production company, a control system is designed to control all aspects of the function of the plant, right down to administration and site security, let alone the internal functions such as procurement, sales, accounts, stores and inventory, costs, logistics, and so on.

The use of cybernetics and the viable systems model (VSM) determine the issues at stake, for example, older technology being unable to accept new technology, or even a situation such as a greater workload being placed on either machine owing to greater demand for production. This can, in turn, lead to a loss of efficiency and productivity, and this will be reflected in operational data being derived from the machines and entered into the organisation's computer system. Using electronic technology, it may be possible to use the computer system controlling the more efficient machine to operate the less efficient machine, or it may be necessary, as a last resort, to replace the less efficient machine with a new one. In the case of the first solution, the more efficient machine dominates the less efficient machine, thus reducing the risk of lower productivity. Thus, where $F(1) = F(2)$, a balance prevails. However, where $F(1) > F(2)$ or $F(1) < F(2)$, overall productivity is compromised, the VSM itself is compromised, and a remedial solution is required to redress the balance. This is mainly resolved by decision support systems (DSS).

The Chilean CyberSyn project was designed to carry out this same procedure in order to avoid expensive compromises to the national economy, and it is argued that had the military coup of 1973 not occurred, the cybernetics project could have resulted in a significant advantage to the national economy, notwithstanding the command nature of the economy. However, in a national economy based on free market economics, thus generating a more competitive environment, such a system would not have worked owing to a fragmented approach to corporate functioning based on free market economics as opposed to the socialist principle of national government control over the economy as a whole, where all organisations are controlled by the government system, i.e. a command economy. Another prevalent issue was that the project relied on an economic simulator based on a command economy structure, where the solutions were based on ideologies, not practicalities. Where real-time operations occur, ideologies do not prevail, and the system is based on real time fact, not supposition or assumption.

However, cybernetics can be and is used in a competitive and free-market economy, in that it is used to maximise the efficiency of an organisational structure by addressing the issues within that structure and thus make the organisation more efficient and consequently more competitive, by concentrating on the organisation as a whole, as well as all the parts within it.

DECISION SUPPORT SYSTEMS

A **DSS** is a computer-based information system that supports business or organisational decision-making activities. It is used to support determinations, judgments, and courses of action in an organisation or business. A DSS sifts through and analyses massive amounts data, compiling comprehensive information which can be used to solve problems as well as determine the decision-making process. To a degree, it stemmed from the cybernetic analysis used by Stafford Beer in the Chilean Cybersyn project, although the use of electronics in this project was nowhere as sophisticated as today's electronic systems. DSS serve the management, operations, and planning levels of an organization (usually mid and higher management) and help people make decisions about problems that may be rapidly changing and not easily specified in advance, i.e. unstructured and semi-structured decision problems. DSS can be either fully computerised or human-powered, or a combination of both.

Typical information used by a DSS includes target or projected revenue, sales figures or past information from different time periods, and other inventory- or operations-related data. A DSS gathers and analyses data, synthesising it to produce comprehensive information reports. In this way, as an informational application, a DSS differs from an ordinary operations application, whose function is just to collect data.

The DSS can be either completely computerised or powered by humans. In some cases, it may combine both. The ideal DSS analyse information and actually make decisions for the user based on a combination of their programs and the data input into the system. At the very least, they allow human users to make more informed decisions at a quicker pace.

The DSS can be employed by operations management and other planning departments in an organization to compile information and data and to synthesise it into actionable intelligence. In fact, these systems are primarily used by mid- to upper-level management.

For example, a DSS may be used to project a company's revenue over the upcoming 6 months based on new assumptions about product sales. Due to a large number of factors that surround projected revenue figures, this is not a straightforward calculation that can be done manually. However, a DSS can integrate all the multiple variables and generate an outcome and alternate outcomes, all based on the company's past product sales data and current variables. However, it should be noted that the system is only as good as the information fed into it. If the information is full of assumptions, the accuracy and reliability of the resulting output decisions must be brought into question. Only when balanced information based on pure fact is fed into the system, can it provide more reliable and accurate predictions and hence decisions. For example, extrapolation based on forecasting and regression analysis is totally valid, as long as it takes in any residuals, outliers, or data, which may exceed the norm. Extrapolation can be based on sudden or even seasonal demand and may only reflect a short period of time. It can also be based on the exception, rather than the rule, and this is why feedback based on a constant stream of data, rather than a specific event, is vital to the exercise, lest it should distort the whole decision-making process.

It is also important to note that a DSS can be tailored for any industry, profession, or domain including the medical field, government agencies, agricultural concerns, and corporate operations, hence the important relationship it has with the cybernetic process. It is a communications application given the nature of data inputs and outputs, and the inner process carried out by the computer being the analytical process, very similar to the neural network that constitutes the theory of cybernetics.

The primary purpose of using a DSS is to present information to the customer in an easy-to-understand way. A DSS system is beneficial because it can be programmed to generate many types of reports, all based on user specifications. For example, the DSS can generate information and output its information graphically, as in a bar chart that represents projected revenue or as a written report.

With the steady advance in technology, data analysis is no longer limited to large, bulky mainframe computers and indeed relies much more on computer networks that can be linked by desktop or laptop appliances. Since a DSS is essentially an application, it can be loaded on most computer systems, whether on desktops or laptops. Certain DSS applications are also available through mobile devices. The flexibility of the DSS is extremely beneficial for users who travel frequently. This gives them the opportunity to be well informed at all times, providing the ability to make the best decisions for their company and customers on the go or even on the spot. It also means that one of the main criteria of the VSM, the issue of communication and synergy, is therefore complied with as a matter of course.

While academics have perceived DSS as a tool to support decision-making processes, DSS users see DSS as a tool to facilitate organisational processes and thus simplify and enhance the decision-making process. Some authors have extended the definition of DSS to include any system that might support decision-making, and some DSS include a decision-making software component; Sprague (1980) defines a properly termed DSS as follows:

1. DSS tends to be aimed at the less well-structured, underspecified problem that upper-level managers typically face.
2. DSS attempts to combine the use of models or analytic techniques with traditional data access and retrieval functions.
3. DSS specifically focuses on features which make them easy to use by non-computer-proficient people in an interactive mode.

4. DSS emphasizes flexibility and adaptability to accommodate changes in the environment and the decision-making approach of the user.

DSS include knowledge-based systems. A properly designed DSS is an interactive software-based system intended to help decision-makers compile useful information from a combination of raw data, documents, and personal knowledge, or business models to identify and solve problems and make decisions.

Typical information that a decision-support application might gather and present includes

- inventories of information assets (including legacy and relational data sources, data warehouses, and data marts),
- comparative sales figures between one period and the next, and
- projected revenue figures based on product sales assumptions (although pure assumptions do not necessarily provide accurate projections).

A **data mart** is a structure/access pattern specific to data warehouse environments, used to retrieve client-facing data. The data mart is a subset of the data warehouse and is usually oriented to a specific business line or team. Whereas data warehouses have an enterprise-wide depth, the information in data marts pertains to a single department. In some deployments, each department or business unit is considered the *owner* of its data mart including all the *hardware, software* and *data*. This enables each department to isolate the use, manipulation, and development of their data. In other deployments where conformed dimensions are used, this business unit ownership will not hold true for shared dimensions such as customer, product, and so on.

Typical information used by a DSS includes target or projected revenue, sales figures or past ones from different time periods, and other inventory- or operations-related data. A DSS gathers and analyses data, synthesizing it to produce comprehensive information reports. In this way, as an informational application, a DSS differs from an ordinary operations application, whose function is just to collect data.

The DSS can be either completely computerised or powered by humans. In some cases, it may combine both. The ideal systems analyse information and actually make decisions for the user. At the very least, they allow human users to make more informed decisions at a quicker pace. The DSS can be employed by operations management and other planning departments in an organisation to compile information and data and to synthesize it into actionable intelligence. In fact, these systems are primarily used by mid- to upper-level management.

For example, a DSS may be used to project a company's revenue over the upcoming 6 months based on new assumptions about product sales. Due to a large number of factors that surround projected revenue figures, this is not a straightforward calculation that can be done manually. However, a DSS can integrate all the multiple variables and generate an outcome and alternate outcomes, all based on the company's past product sales data and current variables. However, the weakness is that assumptions can be very different from reality, and to this extent, an additional provision for variance analysis based on actual figures versus projected figures can prove very useful, especially concerning lengthy timescales of 1 year or more. Short timescales such as monthly periods are unlikely to yield huge differences between actuals and projected data, but annual estimates can show much larger variances. Demand amplification is one area where assumed figures that are projected based on previous data can result in a significant amount of variance which overestimates demand for a particular product, whereas in reality the actual demand for that product may be nowhere near the projected figures. This is where the principle of feedback enters the equation, and which would notify the control system that the projected figures were completely out of line, thus giving the system the chance to rectify itself and revert to a more controllable solution.

The primary purpose of using a DSS is to present information to the customer in an easy-to-understand way. A DSS system is beneficial because it can be programmed to generate many types of reports, all based on user specifications. For example, the DSS can generate information and output its information graphically, as in a bar chart that represents projected revenue or as a written report.

As technology continues to advance, data analysis is no longer limited to large, bulky mainframe computers. Since a DSS is essentially an application, it can be loaded on most computer systems, whether on desktops or laptops. Certain DSS applications are also available through mobile devices and can therefore be used remotely from a mainframe system.

The flexibility of the DSS is extremely beneficial for users who travel frequently. It gives them the opportunity to be well informed at all times, providing the ability to make the best decisions for their company and customers on the move or even on the spot in one location.

DSS include knowledge-based systems. A properly designed DSS is an interactive software-based system intended to help decision-makers compile useful information from a combination of raw data, documents, and personal knowledge, or business models to identify and solve problems and make decisions.

Typical information that a decision support application might gather and present includes

- inventories of information assets (including legacy and relational data sources, cubes, data warehouses, and data marts),
- comparative sales figures between one period and the next, and
- projected revenue figures based on product sales assumptions.

Using the relationship with the user as the criterion, Haettenschwiler differentiates *passive, active,* and *cooperative DSS*. A *passive DSS* is a system that aids the process of decision-making, but that cannot bring out explicit decision suggestions or solutions. An *active DSS* can bring out such decision suggestions or solutions. A *cooperative DSS* allows for an iterative process between human and system towards the achievement of a consolidated solution: the decision-maker (or its advisor) can modify, complete, or refine the decision suggestions provided by the system, before sending them back to the system for validation, and likewise the system again improves, completes, and refines the suggestions of the decision-maker and sends them back to them for validation.

Another taxonomy for DSS, according to the mode of assistance, has been created by Daniel Power. He differentiates *communication-driven DSS, data-driven DSS, document-driven DSS, knowledge-driven DSS,* and *model-driven DSS*.

- A **communication-driven DSS** enables cooperation, supporting more than one person working on a shared task; examples include integrated tools such as Google Docs or Microsoft SharePoint Workspace.
- A **data-driven DSS** (or data-oriented DSS) emphasizes access to and manipulation of a time series of internal company data and, sometimes, external data.

- A **document-driven DSS** manages, retrieves, and manipulates unstructured information in a variety of electronic formats.
- A **knowledge-driven DSS** provides specialized problem-solving expertise stored as facts, rules, procedures or in similar structures such as DeciZone interactive decision trees and flowcharts.
- A **model-driven DSS** emphasizes access to and manipulation of a statistical, financial, optimization, or simulation model. Model-driven DSS use data and parameters provided by users to assist decision-makers in analysing a situation; they are not necessarily data intensive. Dicodess is an example of an open-source model-driven DSS generator.

Using scope as the criterion, power differentiates *enterprise-wide DSS* and *desktop DSS*. An *enterprise-wide DSS* is linked to large data warehouses and serves many managers in the company. A *desktop, single-user DSS* is a small system that runs on an individual manager's PC.

Three fundamental components of DSS architecture are

1. the database (or knowledge base),
2. the model (i.e. the decision context and user criteria), and
3. the user interface.

The users themselves are also important components of the architecture.

Similarly to other systems, DSS require a structured approach. Such a framework includes people, technology, and the development approach.

The Early Framework of Decision Support System consists of four phases:

- **Intelligence**: Searching for conditions that call for decision
- **Design**: Developing and analysing possible alternative actions of solution
- **Choice**: Selecting a course of action among those
- **Implementation**: Adopting the selected course of action in a decision situation

DSS technology levels (of hardware and software) may include the following:

1. The actual application that will be used by the user. This is the part of the application that allows the decision-maker to make decisions in a particular problem area. The user can act upon that particular problem.
2. Generator contains hardware/software environment that allows people to easily develop specific DSS applications. This level makes use of case tools or systems such as Crystal, Analytica, and iThink.
3. Tools include lower level hardware/software. DSS generators including special languages, function libraries, and linking modules.

An iterative developmental approach allows for the DSS to be changed and redesigned at various intervals. Once the system is designed, it will need to be tested and revised where necessary for the desired outcome.

There are several ways to classify DSS applications. Not every DSS fits neatly into one of the categories but may be a mix of two or more architectures.

Holsapple and Whinston classify DSS into the following six frameworks: text-oriented DSS, database-oriented DSS, spreadsheet-oriented DSS, solver-oriented DSS, rule-oriented DSS, and compound DSS. A compound DSS is the most popular classification for a DSS; it is a hybrid system that includes two or more of the five basic structures.

The support given by DSS can be separated into three distinct, interrelated categories: personal support, group support, and organizational support.

DSS components may be classified as follows:

1. **Inputs:** Factors, numbers, and characteristics to analyse
2. **User knowledge and expertise:** Inputs requiring manual analysis by the user
3. **Outputs:** Transformed data from which DSS "decisions" are generated
4. **Decisions:** Results generated by the DSS based on user criteria

DSS which perform selected cognitive decision-making functions and are based on artificial intelligence or intelligent agents technologies are called intelligent decision support systems (IDSS).

The nascent field of decision engineering treats the decision itself as an engineered object and applies engineering principles such as design and quality assurance to an explicit representation of the elements that make up a decision.

DSS can theoretically be built in any knowledge domain. One example is the clinical decision support system (CDSS) for medical diagnosis. There are four stages in the evolution of CDSS: the primitive version is standalone and does not support integration; the second generation supports integration with other medical systems; the third is standard-based, and the fourth is service model-based.

DSS is extensively used in business and management. Executive dashboard and other business performance software allow faster decision-making, identification of negative trends, and better allocation of business resources. Due to DSS all the information from any organization is represented in the form of charts and graphs, i.e. in a summarized way, which helps the management to take strategic decision. For example, one of the DSS applications is the management and development of complex antiterrorism systems. Other examples include a bank loan officer verifying the credit of a loan applicant or an engineering firm that has bids on several projects and wants to know if they can be competitive with their costs.

A growing area of DSS application, concepts, principles, and techniques is in agricultural production and marketing for sustainable development. For example, the DSSAT4 package, developed through financial support of USAID during the 1980s and 1990s, has allowed rapid assessment of several agricultural production systems around the world to facilitate decision-making at the farm and policy levels. Precision agriculture seeks to tailor decisions to particular portions of farm fields. There are, however, many constraints to the successful adoption on DSS in agriculture. In some parts of the world, this policy has been severely hampered, as with the EU's Common Agricultural Policy (CAP), where certain elements of farming in some part so the EU have been reduced or eliminated altogether, in order to transfer the production of certain crops elsewhere in the EU, or to transfer it overseas altogether. This has, unfortunately, created severe shortfalls in the production of certain crops and has left some regions in the EU, especially on the Iberian Peninsula, in a much worse off position than they originally were.

DSS are also prevalent in forest management where the long planning horizon and the spatial dimension of planning problems demand specific requirements. All aspects of forest management, from log transportation and harvest scheduling to sustainability and ecosystem protection have been addressed by modern DSS. In this context, the consideration of single or multiple management objectives related to the provision of goods and services that traded or non-traded and often subject to resource constraints and decision problems. The Community of Practice of Forest Management Decision Support Systems provides a large repository on knowledge about the construction and use of forest DSS.

A specific example concerns the Canadian National Railway System, which tests its equipment on a regular basis using a DSS. A problem faced by any railroad is worn-out or defective rails, which can result in hundreds of derailments per year. Under a DSS, the Canadian National Railway system managed to decrease the incidence of derailments at the same time that other companies were experiencing an increase. It was effectively using a cybernetic system that incorporated feedback concerning the incidence of accidents or derailments and used this to reduce the likelihood of such adverse events based on anticipated incidence, therefore providing a rectification strategy to avoid such problems.

The application of DSS to cybernetic control can be clearly seen in various industrial and commercial scenarios. The retail and automotive sectors use a Japanese system called Kanban, which is used to ensure that supplies are received by a specific plant or outlet as required. The system operates in such a way that, once stocks in the plant or outlet reach a specific minimum, generally 10% of what is normally stocked, a message is automatically generated from the plant to the distribution centre, calling off another delivery of stocks. The automotive industry requires this as a matter of course, as in most cases, any automotive plant only stocks 4 hours' worth of material at any time. It relies on continuous supplies of materials throughout the day to maintain continuous production. Similarly, retail outlets such as the main supermarkets rely on continuous deliveries to maintain fully stocked shelves. The problem arises if there is panic-buying, as in the Coronavirus outbreak, where supplies disappeared off supermarket shelves within hours. There was no provision to trigger automatic emergency supplies, and as a result, the shelves were left empty for days. The cybernetic VSM would have immediately triggered an emergency procurement from whichever distribution centre held the stocks; the problem was that even the distribution centres may not have had the capacity available of products required to fulfil the sudden demand. The purpose of the exercise, in this case, is to have contingency stocks available, as long as the products are not perishable, so that in the event of unforeseen emergencies or sudden demand, stocks are available at the distribution centres for immediate dispatch to the locations where these stocks are required the most.

In the automotive business, it is general practice that supplies reach the automotive plant on a regular basis based on constant supply, using an automatic procurement procedure based on DSS and cybernetic control management. Should the chain of supply be compromised by delays or short shipments, the system allows for the use of alternative suppliers should the need arise, based on a short-term strategy to use these suppliers until the supply problem has been resolved. However, such systems do not always work, and the following account explains how and why.

The author had his first foray into the world of cybernetics by chance, when an automotive supplier client he was contracted to on a short-term basis to resolve customs issues encountered a sudden and urgent issue, namely that a short shipment from the central inventory in the United States risked causing a production line stoppage at the Liverpool plant 24 hours after the problem was identified. The application of the cybernetic principle of the VSM based on input, output, and negative feedback identified the issue very quickly, with the negative feedback stating that there was a problem. The solution arose out of discussion between various departments, including procurement, production, and logistics, and the author suggested the use of the transatlantic BA Concorde service (bearing in mind that this was in early 2000, prior to the fatal crash of an Air France Concorde just off Paris Charles de Gaulle Airport). An arrangement was made with DHL, which used Concorde for urgent priority shipments of documents and small consignments, to arrange the shipment of the semiconductors from the Indiana inventory by way of a Learjet executive jet to Newark Airport, New Jersey, where it was transferred to a bike rider courier, who took it across New York as quickly as possible to New York JFK Airport, where the consignment was transferred to a DHL courier who boarded the second eastbound Concorde service of the day, at 12:30 pm, and sat in the cabin with the consignment of boxes of semiconductors next to her. Apparently this was standard practice to ensure personal delivery, although in many cases the packages were stowed in the baggage area if space was available. The courier arrived at London Heathrow Airport, London, at 9 pm, 3 hours 30 minutes after leaving New York JFK, given the time difference, and the consignment was duly transferred to a Royal Mail flight to Liverpool shortly after. The consignment arrived at the plant in time for the start of the morning shift at 7 am, the day after the shipment from Indiana was arranged. The cost of the semiconductors was $1500, while the cost of the shipment itself was an eye-watering

$15,000. The effort was still worth it, as the consignment arrived in time to avoid the line stoppage. This cybernetic scenario related in many ways to the solutions found to supply problems in Chile in 1972, when Project Cybersyn was underway. The criteria of interdepartmental communication, addressing of negative feedback and the creation of an immediate solution based on an ad hoc control system had all been achieved, thus satisfying the criteria of the VSM and the capacity of the control system to address the challenges in their entirety.

CYBERNETIC CONTROL IN INPUT AND OUTPUT

Cybernetic control is evident in all aspects of nature and technology. It occurs when a closed system regulates itself using a feedback loop. Examples range from a body cooling itself through perspiration to a safety valve on a steam engine.

Figure 4.2 shows a simple first-order cybernetic control system in the management context.

In this case, the input would be the baseline delivery plans. Performing work, monitoring performance, and taking corrective actions are all parts of the delivery process. The output is the completed objectives according to the required standard.

This could represent a simple project, but as projects become large enough to need decomposition into individual work packages, the control

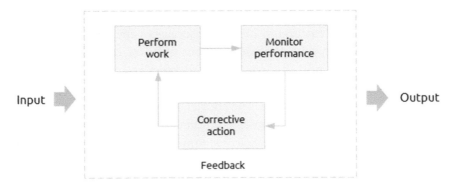

FIGURE 4.2
First-order cybernetic control 1.

system becomes second order, where one feedback loop is nested within another, i.e. where all observation and monitoring systems become part of an overall monitoring and control system, which oversees the total process. In other words, the top-level monitoring and control system controls all other monitoring and control systems beneath it, within the overall entity.

Figure 4.3 shows a second-order control system in the context of a project within a programme. The principle is the same for a project and subproject or a portfolio and a programme. At this level, the controlling system is itself observed, in order to guarantee complete efficiency and control. Not only is the delegated work function being monitored, but so too is the overall supervisory or controlling function. Indeed, this level of monitoring and control can extend right to the top of the organisation, depending upon the need for absolute corporate control. The auditing

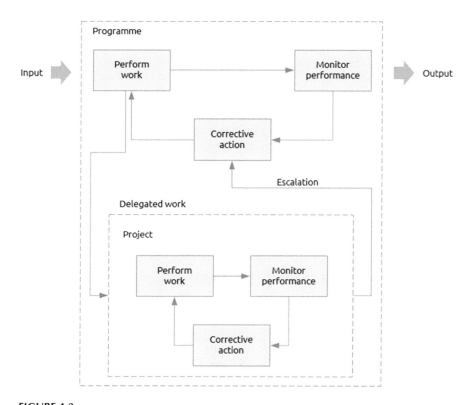

FIGURE 4.3
First-order cybernetic control 2.

process, especially that carried out by external auditors, which is an extension of System 3 in the VSM, shows that where internal auditing monitors and verifies the internal systems of a company, the external audit verifies the activities of the company from an overall, independent approach. This approach guarantees the complete impartiality of the external auditing activity and also satisfies the law of requisite variety as determined by W. Ross Ashby, whereby the controlling system must at least be as large and complex as the systems it is designed to control. An external control or auditing system fulfils these requirements to the absolute.

The system now shows that the programme manager is performing day-to-day control of the programme and is delegating work to project managers. The project managers perform day-to-day control on their projects but have triggers that cause them to escalate problems to the programme manager (who is also filling the project sponsor role in this example). The escalation is caused by the feedback indicating that the project has, or is predicted to have, breached its tolerances. The purpose of the exercise is to ensure that tolerances are not breached, lest the whole structure falls apart.

At some point, the process has to be stopped and rectified before it can continue. Part of the solution lies in the principle of statistical process control (SPC) charts, which are maintained on a frequent basis. As the data reaches criticality, i.e. that it approaches the upper or lower action limits, the process is stopped and reviewed. Any defects must at this point be resolved and rectified before the process can be restarted. In the case of a set of complex subprojects, each element must be separately and independently monitored and controlled, even if this means a temporary shutdown in the overall project owing to the interdependency of each individual subproject as part of the overall project as a whole. There are times where a remedial shutdown, however temporary, achieves better results, as it sacrifices a small amount of productivity to ensure that the overall productivity in the long term is not compromised by a problem which could, without radical intervention, exacerbate into a major breakdown, thus potentially causing long-term damage to the enterprise.

This whole approach shows the necessity of feedback as part of the DSS. Electronic systems should automatically include feedback as part of the process, by some form of sensory function. This function is part of the monitoring process and generally flags up a specific problem at the time it occurs, usually some form of impactive alert, be it a red-light system or a screen alarm. Many systems operate a "traffic light" visual display, where routine activities are shown in green, minor issues are shown in yellow or amber, while major issues are shown as red. In this way, the operator can immediately determine where the potential or actual issues lie or shut the process down until the issue has been resolved. Although shutdowns may cause a degree of delay or temporary inconvenience, they allow technicians to solve the problem as quickly as possible, thus avoiding more costly delays later on which could have resulted from serious breakdown or failure in the system.

5

Management Cybernetics and Feedback

MANAGEMENT CYBERNETICS

Management cybernetics is the application of cybernetics to management and organisations. "Management cybernetics" was first introduced by the UK consultant Stafford Beer in the late 1950s. Beer developed the theory through a combination of practical applications and a series of influential books. The practical applications involved steel production, publishing, and operations research in a large variety of different industries.

As practiced by Beer, research into operations involved multidisciplinary teams seeking practical assistance for difficult managerial issues. It often involved the development of models borrowed from basic sciences and put into an isomorphic relationship with an organizational situation. Beer initially called this "operations research" (OR) but, along with Russell Ackoff, became increasingly disenchanted with that term as the field transitioned into one in which a predefined set of mathematical tools was applied to well-formulated problems. Beer's critique of traditional OR, in part, was that it became a matter of experts in mathematics looking for situations that could be conformed to their methods. Beer insisted that what was needed for effective research into operations was to first understand the key dynamics within the situation and only then to select the theory or methods that would allow one to understand that situation in detail. Beer's *Decision and Control*, especially Chapter 6, discusses the methodology in some detail.

Viable means capable of independent existence and implies both maintaining internal stability and adaptation to a changing environment. "Internal stability" and "adaptation" can be in conflict, particularly if the relevant environment is changing rapidly, so the viable systems model (VSM) is about maintaining a balance between the two such that the system is able to survive.

The principle of internal stability versus adaptation is as follows:

1. We do nothing, so we get left behind (not an option).
2. We change radically according to external requirements but cannot cope with the sudden change, resulting in chaos and collapse.
3. We manage change, introducing it in stages to fit in with our overall long-term aspirations and objectives.
4. We support this change with extensive training and awareness, as well as the implementation of new systems to account for external changes.
5. We introduce Design Systems software and enable it to function efficiently by correctly and efficiently managing our resources.
6. We use the VSM, using and developing the five-system approach.

The VSM is a model of the structures and functions that are both necessary and sufficient for the long-term survival of a system in a changing environment. Allenna Leonard, Beer's longtime partner, suggested that the most useful way to think about the VSM is as a language. The VSM is a language of viability. The VSM is a language for diagnosing organizations and managerial teams in terms of their viability or lack thereof. The VSM is also a language for designing organizations and managerial teams that will be viable.

One of the great difficulties in managing the modern large organization is that many of the issues are far too complex for even small groups. The critical knowledge is often dispersed among a substantial number of people. Organizations are often faced with choosing between (1) very costly and time-consuming meetings of large groups or (2) making bad decisions based on an inadequate grasp of the relevant factors. Syntegration is a group method designed to solve this conundrum.

Syntegration melds a number of cybernetic principles with Buckminster (Bucky) Fuller's ideas on tensegrity. The initial "team syntegrity" format involved 30 people divided into 12 overlapping teams to deal with some broad and initially ill-defined issue. The teams and roles within the teams are arranged to achieve the mathematically optimum degree of resonance of information throughout the entire group. In practice, syntegration achieves a remarkable degree of shared understanding of the initial issue. In syntegrations intended to develop a plan of action, the implementation phase is usually very quick and effective, probably because of the shared understanding developed among the participants.

Organisational cybernetics (OC) is distinguished from management cybernetics. Both use many of the same terms but interpret them according to another philosophy of systems thinking. The full development of management cybernetics is represented in Stafford Beer's books, in particular *Brain of the Firm* and *Decision and Control*.

Organizational cybernetics studies organizational design, and the regulation and self-regulation of organizations from a systems theory perspective that also takes the social dimension into consideration. Extending the principles of autonomous agency theory (AAT), cultural agency theory (CAT) has been formulated for the generation of higher cybernetic orders. Researchers in economics, public administration, and political science focus on the changes in institutions, organisations, and mechanisms of social steering at various levels (sub-national, national, European, international) and in different sectors (including the private, semiprivate, and public sectors; the latter sector is emphasised).

FEEDBACK

One of the main issues with the management of cybernetics is that of feedback. Feedback can be either negative or positive. Knowing whether you have reached your goal (or at least are getting closer to it) requires "feedback", a concept that was made rigorous by cybernetics.

Cybernetics was derived from the Greek word for steersman, *Kybernetika*. It has many definitions, but the one that is preferred the most by various people is that it is the "study of feedback" (Littlejohn, 2001). W. Ross Ashby (1956) had a more complete definition, however; he said that cybernetics was the formal study of all possible machines and a discipline with its own foundations. This domain also touches on all traditional disciplines including mathematics, technology, and the social sciences. This is why one of the major sources for development of theory is based on a transdisciplinary study of complex systems. However, it is more specifically related to the idea of "sciences of complexity" (Heylighen et al., 1999).

The history of cybernetics can be traced to the early 1940s and 1950s when a series of meetings, put on by the Macy foundation, was called to order. The meetings were on the "circular casual and feedback mechanisms in biological and social sciences". During those meetings Norbert Wiener coined the term "Cybernetics" for the discipline and defined it as the "control and communication in the animal and the machine". This can be expanded to include society and individual human beings. It developed out of Shannon's information theory, which was designed to perfect the transmission of information through communication channels. As a later development, in 1970, Heinz von Foerster distinguished first- and second-order cybernetics, namely the study of observed systems and the study of observing systems. Its emphasis is on how observers construct model systems with which we interact.

Cybernetics focuses on how systems function and how they control their actions, and how they communicate with other systems or with their own components, thus deriving the concept of feedback to achieve this communication. Cybernetics helps give rise to some new fields such as cognitive science and neurobiology and has been useful in formulating dozens of ideas and bits of applied math. A very simple cybernetic system will consist of a sensor, comparator, and activator. The sensor is used to provide feedback to the comparator, which, in turn, decides if the machine is off basis. The comparator then gives guidance to the activator. This then provides an output or feedback, and the feedback is in some way affective to the environment. This concept of feedback is essential to the concept of cybernetics.

Feedback loops are a fundamental object of study within cybernetics in that they are accountable for the process of regulation within all control systems. Feedback loops are divided into two qualitatively different types, what are called positive and negative feedback. **Positive feedback** occurs when the system is working perfectly well, and the output data verifies this. On this basis, a process may be continued, as there is nothing to suggest that there are any problems with it. However, **negative feedback** occurs when the output data suggest that a problem exists and that it requires immediate rectification. A negative feedback loop represents a relationship of constraint and balance between two or more variables. When one variable in the system changes in a positive direction the other changes in the opposite negative direction, thus always working to maintain the original overall combined value to the system. An example of this might be the feedback loops that regulate the temperature of a machine. Different parts of a machine work to maintain a constant temperature within the machine, such as a car engine, by either conserving or releasing more heat, possibly through a fan or coolant system that is designed to operate when the heat generated by the engine increases. This is normally governed by a thermostat, whose sensors detect any uncontrolled heat generation and automatically activate the cooling system. These also counterbalance the fluctuations in the external environment's temperature. Another example of negative feedback loop might be between the supply and demand of a product. The more demand there is for a product, the more the price may go up, which will, in turn, feedback to reduce the demand. This is the most basic of economic principles and is always taught as a pre-requisite feature in any economic course.

However, some feedback systems are more complex than others. The simplest difference can be found between active and passive behaviour. For example active behaviour comes directly from the system, and passive behaviour comes straight from outside stimulation. Sneezing is a passive behaviour, but giving a friend a high five is an active behaviour. When we look further at active behaviour we can categorise it into purposeful behaviour and random behaviour. For example, moving one's hand could be just a random action. However, if the intention is to move one's hand in order to emphasise a point, or to gesticulate, then this would be a purposeful behaviour. When we look deeper into purposeful behaviour, it can be seen that this behaviour consists of different levels of complexity. In a simple system, an organism responds to feedback by turning on or off. For example a light switch only has two functions, i.e. on or off (unless, that is, it is a variable light switch). Complex systems however use feedback to determine what they will do, hence the variable light switch. It can be altered to regulate the level of light in a room. In this manner, complex systems are able to adjust and adapt. Also, complex systems can be predictive, or you cannot predict the outcome. The feedback that is determined through complex or even simple systems can also be classified in a few ways. Feedback can be negative or positive. If I kissed a girl and got slapped, then that would be negative. I would probably not do it again because my system would respond by avoiding that outcome. However, a reciprocal response would be positive, and I would probably do it again more often. This is important in system growth because it implies learning is taking place.

Similarly, if a government decides to implement a policy which causes street protests, riots, and a general election where the government loses power, then that feedback is decidedly negative. However, if a government implements a policy which induces greater wellbeing in the population and business, e.g. tax reductions, then the feedback is positive, and the government will consequently seek to enhance economic well-being by further reductions in fiscal burdens, thus inciting economic growth and consequently well-being for everyone. Again, this implies that learning is taking place.

The theory of cybernetics also touches on the concept of three feedback states. They are steady state, growth state, and change state. In a steady state when negative outcomes occur, the system acknowledges a problem and returns to normalcy to balance out the situation. An example of this may be in a classroom situation. Let's say that a teacher is receiving negative feedback from the students that the tests are too hard or that the lectures are too boring. In order for the teacher to return to a positive class atmosphere he or she might try to provide a study guide and incorporate a movie or two into the lectures. The second state is growth. In a growth state, a system begins to deviate, until a positive feedback causes it to increase in an accelerated direction. For example, let's say that a kid thinks it is funny to always make fun of his friend's weight. His friend is irritated but doesn't act as being too upset. So, the kid continues to make fun of his friend and this happens every day. What will happen is that their friendships will increasingly disintegrate, until their friendship falls apart completely. In this situation, the positive feedback was not a good feedback. Instead, it was growth, but growth in the wrong direction. Also negative feedback would be needed for the friend to express his dissatisfaction with the fat jokes in order to have their friendship system maintain balance. The third state is change. This system involves both negative and positive feedback because it is constantly changing yet adapting. This feature is both a remarkable trait of human and non-human systems. An example of this system could take place in a relationship. Let's say Ben and Susan start having problems in their relationship. Ben decides to become more supportive, and it helps their relationship. However, Susan begins to take advantage of Ben's approach, and conflicts begin to arise again. As a result, Ben decides a change is needed and decides to criticise Susan on her actions. When Susan begins to be more affectionate with Ben, he reduces his criticism. At this point, the relationship of the system has moved to a new state of somewhat less supportiveness and more scrutiny, as a degree of mutual trust and well-being may have been lost in the overall process, resulting in degrees of mistrust and insecurity. The problem is that on the one hand, the relationship may become more reconciliatory, while on the other hand, it could deteriorate to the point of divorce.

In business terms, this situation can affect the supply chain radically. Let us translate a personal relationship to a business relationship within the supply chain. For example, a logistics provider has been used for many years to transport materials between companies A and B, A being the supplier and B being the customer. However, the logistics provider has not invested in its transport fleet, and trucks start to break down. This results in delays to shipments, without any reasonable explanation as to why the delay has occurred, and no attempt to rectify the situation. Company B starts to complain that their production line is being severely compromised by these delays, and, in turn, this spills over to Company A, which has been arranging and paying for the shipments on a delivered basis to Company B. Both companies complain to the logistics provider, which starts to realise that things are not good and decides to spend much more money on an urgent basis in revitalising its transport fleet. However, its transport costs rise, and both Companies A and B complain once again because of these increased transport costs. The logistics provider starts to lose business from other customers as a result and eventually goes bankrupt. There is, of course, a moral to the tale. Instead of the adverse situation being exacerbated, if the logistics provider had spent more time earlier in recognising its weaknesses and consistently maintaining its fleet of vehicles in good order, it could have incorporated these lower costs in its overall business structure, passing on a lesser degree of these costs to its customers along with a justifiable explanation of the reasons for its cost revisions and thus could have maintained its business levels, along with its reputation, and kept its customer base accordingly. This is why algedonic feedback is vital to business relationships; because a problem is recognised early in the process and is acted upon and resolved quickly, it is much less likely to compound and exacerbate, resulting in catastrophic failure later on.

Figure 5.1 illustrates the situation where feedback influences the manufacturing process as an information flow, in the form of inputs, outputs, with goal-seeking and goal-implementing systems, referred to as 'control' systems, sandwiched between these.

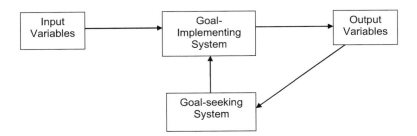

FIGURE 5.1
Feedback system.

The feedback system shown in Figure 5.1 illustrates that effective achievement of a control system can only be reliably achieved if information about the state of the system (specifically the variables which we are trying to control) is "fed back" to the goal-seeking system, represented by a control mechanism such as a thermostat. The goal-seeking system then takes appropriate action based on the difference between the output variables and the goal. This is the "feedback" based system often referred to as an "error-controlled system". The majority of electromechanical control systems designed by engineers are of this type. If the feedback is positive, the overall mechanism is working correctly and the outcome is as desired. However, if the feedback is negative, the control mechanism will detect this and will apply control procedures as required as the means of rectification.

It can be stated with confidence, even though we may not be able to identify the mechanism at work, that any system which exhibits stable patterns of behaviour over time is dominated by feedback control. The fact that trends exist (which we are able to forecast) is evidence of this. If a system was not feedback controlled, the system would be chaotic and therefore unforecastable (Figure 5.2).

Another type of arrangement is the "feedforward"-based system where, instead of waiting for error (output) information, the goal-seeking system acts on information about its potential future state with the aim of anticipating (and so avoiding) errors. Where the goal-seeking system has a reliable predictive model, this approach can provide effective control. An example of this is an automatic cut out system – a power surge is detected, and the system closed down before any damage can be done to a piece of equipment. Many quality-based systems work on this principle, i.e. incorporating anticipatory systems whereby any potential problems can

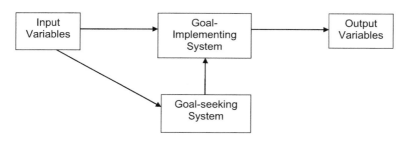

FIGURE 5.2
Feed-forward system.

be addressed before they actually occur. The Taguchi methods invented by the Japanese engineer Genichi Taguchi for the Japanese automotive industry used precisely these principles, i.e. anticipating potential problems and then resolving them before production took place, thus ensuring guaranteed quality-based production of Japanese cars. This concept is now used throughout the global automotive industry and guarantees high-quality production of motor vehicles worldwide.

While cybernetics yields many important concepts as far as the feedback process, it also has a great deal of relevance to more complex systems. An advanced system that is part of a larger more complex system or even the environment is called a subsystem, e.g. the inventory process in a manufacturing company. In a complex system, there may be multiple loops that provide feedback that forms networks. The most consistent rule of this feedback loop is that output will always return as feedback input. Cybernetics helps us explain this larger more complex model because it helps explain concepts such as self-regulation, interdependence, wholeness, and interchange with the environment. Cybernetics is a critical way of thinking that touches on key issues such as circular reasoning, not just the basic statement that one thing happens because it was caused by another thing. In the real world, what goes around comes back around like a boomerang. However, from an observer's perspective, it is often difficult to see how this pattern of cybernetics works in a system. Therefore, the phrase "Second Order Cybernetics" was coined as a tool to help explain this phenomenon.

Second-order cybernetics helps explain how the observation process itself is a system in which feedback loops are established between the observer and the observed, as established by von Foerster in 1981. The observer cannot help becoming a cybernetic system himself or herself because knowing is taken from what is learned and we learn in part from observations, which, in turn, are effected by what is seen. In second-order cybernetics, the powerful idea that a system is affected and affects the observer is an important concept. This is because humans often have a hard time accepting that we are not separate from what we observe. Another important concept is called structural coupling. This means that two systems may be affected mutually because when we observe a system, we are affected by the past and structure of that system. An example of this is when you try to explain to someone how your memory works, but right at that time, you are remembering the subject you are speaking about. So, two systems can indeed have mutual effects.

Although the theory of cybernetics can be relatively complex, it can also be evaluated at many levels. For example, a theory is a scientific account of a phenomenon. The theory of cybernetics fits this definition because cybernetics explains the phenomena of regulation and control in a system, although it also contributes in a practical way to that regulation and control. Another way to evaluate this theory is by using different criteria. For example, a theory must be capable of corrigibility, i.e. correction, so we must be able to challenge it by making observations, especially where actual situations are analysed. For cybernetics, it is easy to observe this theory and test it for corrigibility, i.e. correctness, because networks exist in every aspect of life. Therefore, we can observe networks and verify how systems adjust and change under the concept of cybernetics. Also a theory should be able to provide an explanation about the outcome of a series of events. Therefore, cybernetics must be able to reduce the uncertainty about the outcome of a system and how it gauges its effects. We can see that cybernetics as a theory does accomplish this set of criteria because it uses feedback models in place of hazy examples. Due to the existence of feedback models, one can apply a system, and it will fit appropriately into one of the models.

In the real world, this theory can help explain how a simple organism responds to feedback, in the same way that a thermostatically controlled heater switches on or off according to the temperature of a room. It can also explain more complex systems such as the relationship between a manager and co-workers. This theory is very relevant and practical at any level because it optimises the transmission of feedback through any sort of communication channel, and it explains how the system functions.

Indeed, any structure can only operate effectively with feedback. Without feedback, there is no way of knowing whether the system is operating properly or not.

Therefore, negative feedback conveys the communication that an action has resulted in a deviation, problem, or fault in the system, and that steps are to be taken to rectify that deviation and bring it back to the norm. Conversely, positive feedback conveys the communication that an action has been taken, which alters or adjusts the system to become more efficient or radical in its function, and that the function concerned has changed the overall structure of the organisation, hopefully for the better.

FEEDBACK AND RISK ANALYSIS

Feedback results from the input of information and therefore governs output. It is the only way of determining the outcome of a possible set of actions. If an action results in success, the feedback is positive; if the outcome is a failure, the feedback is negative. What is not necessarily taken into account is the relative risk of undertaking a particular action. Much to the time, risk is never appreciated until a major impact occurs, as it was never planned in advance.

Risk is the combination of likelihood and impact. These two factors are multiplied together to calculate the risk of an adverse event or result. In general, both factors of likelihood and impact are sub-divided into five levels, namely

- minimal
- low
- moderate
- high
- critical

These five levels for each factor are then multiplied together to yield the overall risk level and can be shown as part of the composite risk index (CRI).

The **composite risk matrix** works on the basis of two factors: likelihood and impact. Each factor is graduated in the form of five levels, ranging from:

Likelihood: 1=very unlikely to 5=highly likely
Impact: 1=minimal to 5=critical

Multiplying these factors together, we derive a scale of $1(1 \times 1) - 25 (5 \times 5)$. These scales then equate as follows to form the **composite risk index (CRI)**:

1–8 (low)
9–16 (medium)
17–25 (high), and are colour-coded as below

They are then arranged in the 5×5 risk matrix as shown below.

The 5×5 method can be used where data is available or a good degree of judgement can be applied to estimates of the frequency and consequences of each hazardous event in the form of a simplified matrix. This risk ranking approach allows for a normal level of accuracy and consistency in the risk estimates that can be obtained.

Note: The size of the matrix and the factor difference in frequency and consequence rankings can be altered to give the best ranges to suit a particular organisation's operation.

This solution works for any factor difference (2, 5, 10, 100, etc.) providing both the frequency and consequence ranking estimates separated by the same factor (Figure 5.3).

These CRI numerical levels and codes are used in the risk register, to show the levels of risk for each column, namely **L** (low), **M** (medium), and **H** (high).

Once the initial (i.e. raw) risk has been established, a conventional risk register will detail the **raw risk**, i.e. the initial risk at the time of the audit, and then recommend mitigating actions in order to arrive at the **residual risk**, i.e. the risk level resulting from the implementation of this mitigating action. In this way, the risk analysis acts as a form of negative or positive feedback, i.e. algedonic feedback. In general, the residual risk will be lower than the raw risk, although the degree of difference between the two may vary according to the effectiveness of the mitigating action. There is also the additional risk that is classified as inherent risk, which can be linked with both raw risk and residual risk.

LIKELIHOOD ↓	MINIMAL (1)	LOW (2)	MODERATE (3)	HIGH (4)	CRITICAL (5)
VERY LIKELY (5)	5	10	15	20	25
REGULAR (4)	4	8	12	16	20
FREQUENT (3)	3	6	9	12	15
INFREQUENT (2)	2	4	6	8	10
VERY UNLIKELY (1)	1	2	3	4	5

I M P A C T

COLOUR CODES AND LEVELS:

1-8: LOW (ALARP – As Low As Reasonably Practical)
9-16: MEDIUM
17-25: HIGH

SIMPLIFIED:

GREEN - LOW (1-8)
ORANGE - MEDIUM (9-15)
RED - HIGH (17-25)

FIGURE 5.3
Composite risk matrix.

Inherent (raw) risk: The risk that an activity would pose if **no controls** or other mitigating factors were in place (the gross risk or risk before controls).

Residual risk: The risk that remains **after controls** are taken into account (the net risk or risk after controls).

Inherent and residual risks are commonly used terms within the operational risk community, especially by accountants. While residual risk is relatively simple to define within the simple risk model (e.g. "Residual Risk" is "Risk" as used in the model), the definition of inherent risk is more problematic. For example, in the auditing community, inherent risk is defined as the risk that a financial record is incorrect absent any internal controls. In this situation, it is tempting to simply equate inherent risk to cost, since both terms refer to the importance of a process or asset to a business before controls (vulnerabilities) are taken into account. Alternatively, inherent risk could be equated to the probability that the financial record is incorrect.

There is general recognition that inherent and residual risks are connected in the following manner:

Inherent risk less than the effect of controls equals residual risk.

This implies that residual risk will always be less than or equal to inherent risk. However, any general rule is there to be challenged. Can residual risk be higher than inherent risk? To assess this, we need to understand the way in which controls modify risk, leading to a residual risk position.

A common definition of controls is "A specific action taken with the objective of reducing either the likelihood of the risk occurring and/or the consequence if the risk were to occur". This implies that residual risk must be less than inherent risk. In contrast, ISO 31000 defines a control as "measure that is modifying risk" without the implication that it is always reducing risk.

Three types of control are commonly recognised:

1. **Preventive**: Attempts to prevent the risk from occurring and therefore is aimed at reducing the likelihood.
2. **Detective**: Attempts to identify the occurrence of risk; if it is prior to the risk occurring, it reduces the likelihood, and if after the risk has occurred, it is aimed at reducing the consequence.
3. **Remedial** (reactive/corrective): Attempts to limit the damage from the risk having occurred and therefore is aimed at reducing the consequence.

We can define inherent risk be examining the factors that combine to form residual and inherent risks. These are:

- cost
- threat
- vulnerability

Residual risk $=$ cost $\times$ threat $\times$ vulnerability (after mitigating action has been implemented)

Residual risk/vulnerability $=$ (cost $\times$ threat $\times$ vulnerability)/vulnerability

These two vulnerability factors cancel out in the second part of the equation, leading to

Residual risk/vulnerability $=$ cost $\times$ threat

Residual risk/vulnerability $=$ **inherent risk** $=$ cost $\times$ threat

This therefore leads to a more accurate definition of inherent risk:

1. The risk that a process poses to the business before controls are taken into account
2. The risk that a process poses to the business based on the financial exposure if the process fails and the presence of threats that could exploit a vulnerability in that process

How then does this relate to the principle of cybernetics and feedback? Much of the principle of risk is based on perception, rather than actuality, i.e. that a project or activity could fail if certain potentiality of adverse events was not taken into account. That situation could arise if feedback, especially negative feedback, were not taken into consideration during or at the start of the process.

Risk can only be properly assessed when it is quantified, usually by way of the CRI. Once we have established the calculated level of risk, we can then determine the extent to which it may be mitigated by monitoring and auditing processes. If we input a set of information into the system, we will be able to derive a series of responses. If a specific project is working well, the feedback is therefore positive and the risk level is therefore low. If, however, there are anomalies or weaknesses in the project, the feedback is therefore more negative, and the risk level rises to either medium or high. If there are major flaws or adverse incidences, the risk may rise as high as critical. At this stage, it is necessary to terminate the project or, at very least, temporarily suspend it until the anomalies have been addressed or rectified. In this situation, we resort to the four risk options (the 4 "T's"):

- **Tolerate** (low risk)
- **Treat** (medium risk)
- **Transfer** (medium or high risk)
- **Terminate** (high or critical risk)

Much of our action will depend on the feedback resulting from observations. Where the feedback is positive, any risk can be deemed to be **low** and can therefore be tolerated. Where the feedback is more negative or conditional, the risk can be deemed to be **medium** and can therefore be treated, i.e. mitigated or transferred to a specialist entity. Where the feedback is definitely negative, the risk is much higher, namely **high** or **critical**, and avoiding action must be taken, usually to terminate or suspend the project pending further action or decision concerning future activities.

The purpose of risk and compliance is to keep companies operating between the lines so that they do not fall in a ditch on their way to mission success. To ensure that this does not happen risk and management controls are put in place to act as guardrails (protect against loss) as well as to drive processes and practices towards targeted outcomes in response to stakeholder obligations.

- **Stakeholders include** customers, suppliers, shareholders, employees, government, and the public at large.
- **Requirements** (mandatory) and **commitments** (voluntary) are derived from obligations contained within internal policies, guidelines and code of conduct; regulations and standards; contracts; and product and service specifications.
- **Obligations include** conformance, performance, achievement, and outcome based specifications.

In the field of cybernetics, there are two models of the organisation, namely *management cybernetics* and *organizational cybernetics*.

- **Management cybernetics** treats organisations such as machines and organisms congruent with the philosophy of hard systems thinking.
- **Organisational cybernetics** is concerned with management and organisations that break from the mechanistic and organistic thinking and is able to make full use of the concept of variety (Stafford Beer).

The concept of controls comes from these theories of systems. The most common form of a control process is the feedback control loop used to apply corrective actions in response to system output deviations from target values. The control loop serves to keep the system between acceptable operating limits (e.g. constraints, performance levels). Although used within almost every system (technical or sociotechnical), the audit-fix cycle is most familiar to those in the compliance function, as compliance relies on constant monitoring and auditing of systems.

Risk cybernetics is a concept comprising risk specification and risk control techniques using advanced artificial intelligence and computing technologies with circular-causal volatility feedback in a Genetic Algorithm Neural Network (GANN) framework. More generally, risk cybernetics refers to risk management techniques, which combine human and computer capabilities and functions in a circular-causal network or system. The objective of risk cybernetics is to achieve self-learning, self-enhancing, and full-automation capabilities so as to reduce accidents, errors, etc. and obtain predictable and sustainable returns which can be applied to any industry including applications in market data, financial time series, cyber security measures, production facilities, robotics, etc.

CYBERNETIC CONTROL

Cybernetic control is a system of control through which a critical resource is held at the desired level by a self-regulating mechanism. For cybernetic control to work, standards must be set, actual results must be reliably measured, standards and results must be compared, and the resulting comparison must be feedback to management for action.

Most non-business organisations (universities, schools, cities, and museums for instance, as well as utility and administrative organisations such as police, health, and government administration) do not meet these conditions, as essentially they are non-productive. The business firms that are not involved in either production, operations, or sales—research and development, advertising, personnel labour relations, engineering, legal, and accounting also do not meet these requirements. Therefore, the organisation's objectives and standards are frequently missing, unclear, or shifting, and hence, results of activities are difficult to measure accurately and reliably, and feedback information is often unavailable, neither timely nor dependable. Non-cybernetic controls and control systems are those which do not meet all of the criteria for cybernetic controls.

The concept of modern cybernetic systems only arose with the advent of electronic computing systems and the realisation of the homology between the human nervous system and its intelligent functioning, and that of computing systems and their potential for intelligent functioning. Although the work carried out by Norbert Wiener in the late 1940s provided the basis and foundation of present cybernetic functions, the entry of the electronic age consolidated this work and gave it a more complex and advanced approach and outlook. The entire foundation of cognitive science research, especially of "hard" Artificial Intelligence (AI) as created by electronic means, has been the achievement and creation of automated systems that are human-like in their intelligence capabilities, leading to the creation of Artificial Neural Networks (ANNs). The degree to which systems integration can be achieved by means of digital and electronic information processing remains as yet unknown and unfulfilled, but it is now expected to be greater than anyone now might imagine.

Providing feedback that is capable of modifying input and adjusting output on a continuous and dynamic basis forms the basis for all systems, and the degree to which this is achieved in systems should be taken as a measure of their relative complexity and sophistication. Without this feedback, there is no way of determining the success or failure of an operating system, to the point that if a breakdown in the system should occur, it will not be detected until the damage has been incurred and the entire system fails.

What is lacking from a meta-systems standpoint is a clear-cut objective theory and methodology about management cybernetic control systems in general and applied systems in particular. Such a scientific framework would progress a considerable way towards the development of a viable automated meta-system that permits the intelligent integration of systems upon multiple levels. However, it should be pointed out that there is no standardised off-the-peg solution, as every corporate entity has a slightly different structure and modus operandi, and therefore requires a different bespoke solution, be it a meta-system approach or a set of individual solutions for different levels of the entity, especially where the corporate entity operates in different countries, with each national entity requiring a specific set of solutions according to its own national needs. Although it is accepted practice that a multinational corporation uses an overall standard system of operational and management controls to manage the overall global business, it must equally accept that individual subsidiaries in different countries may require certain variations on this theme, as they may be influenced by two specific factors:

- They were absorbed by the multinational by way of takeovers.
- They were established in a specific country to cover and serve that specific market.

To this extent, specific systems pertinent to one environment cannot be imposed on another environment. The PESTEL structure illustrates this as follows:

- Political
- Economic
- Social
- Technological
- Environmental
- Legal

The operations of a specific multinational organisation are therefore determined by all the above factors, and no end of feedback will standardise this approach. Production lines in one country may well differ from those in another, as productivity and efficiency may differ, owing to a variety of factors such as machine efficiency, human labour efficiency and productivity, supply chain limitations, economic environment, national legal requirements, climate, etc. State-run companies may have completely different priorities from privately-run enterprises, as shown by the Cybersyn project in Chile in the early 1970s. Feedback from production facilities in Chile was used on a state-based level to support the state economic machine and therefore support the political aspirations of the left-wing regime, whereas in a free-market economy, feedback in an individual company is more important to its level of efficiency and competitiveness within the free market. Companies operating in the sub-arctic conditions of northern Scandinavia and Alaska will encounter different challenges from those operating in sub-tropical or tropical conditions of Africa or Latin America, and feedback will prove this.

Such control mechanisms that occur in the world take many forms. In the process of exploring different kinds of systems at many different levels of systems articulation, many interesting examples can be found of feedback mechanisms that serve the purposes of maintaining cybernetic control over systems. In highly elaborate and differentiated systems, cybernetic control itself becomes elaborated and specialised between different functions and sub-functions.

Most such mechanisms are the basis of projects that are organized within systems and their associated sub-frameworks. Many control mechanisms in the world are not publicised and are usually kept in the background. Such mechanisms tend to serve many different purposes in a complicated and increasingly diverse world.

Some of the functions relevant to the world at large include the following:

i. **Security:** Protection of people, resources, property, and information within the framework, and relating to the framework, as well as extended meta-system protection encompassing security frameworks for larger world contexts. Security includes some of the following concerns: encryption, password protection, hidden systems, backup systems, protection from attacks involving viruses, spam, hacking, various forms of fraud, vandalism, or violence or violation of personal or property rights.

ii. **System-state monitoring:** Systems that are capable of continuously or periodically providing a system-state check at critical points, including traffic flow, tracking, e-mail, linking, client feedback and satisfaction, emergent Web development patterns, etc.

iii. **Infrastructure management and development:** This includes resource availability, acquisition, organization and storage, and communication services and activities.

iv. **Network management and development:** This includes hyperlinking, submission, contacts, mailing and emailing systems, marketing frameworks, advertising, information control, image management, etc.

v. **Organisational management and development:** Organizational management involves planning, scheduling, prioritisation, human resource development, partnering and the development of affiliate frameworks, etc.

vi. **Structural management and development:** This includes production systems development, tool and technology frameworks, workstation and work centre development, and resource management frameworks.

vii. **Environmental-state monitoring:** External state monitoring systems include surveillance systems, alarm systems of various kinds, weather monitoring systems, temperature and climate control systems, habitation systems monitoring, etc.

viii. **Monitoring and management of external state development:** Management and development of feedback mechanisms mediating relations between internal and external systems and subsystems components.

Cybernetic or steering control is by far the most common type of control system. The key feature of cybernetic control is its automatic operation. Consider the following: a system is operating with inputs being subjected to a process that transforms them into outputs. It is this system that we wish to control. In order to do so, we must monitor the system output. This function is performed by sensors that measure one or more aspects of the output, presumably those aspects one wishes to control. Measurements taken by a sensor are transmitted to the comparator, which compares them with a set of predetermined standards. The difference between actual and standard is sent to the decision maker, which determines whether or not the difference is of sufficient size to deserve correction. If the difference is large enough to warrant action, a signal is sent to the effectors, which acts on the process or on the inputs to produce outputs that conform more closely to the standard.

A cybernetic control system that acts to reduce deviations from standard is called a *negative feedback loop*. If the system output moves away from the standard in one direction, the control mechanism acts to move it in the opposite direction. The speed or force with which the control operates is, in general, proportional to the size of the deviation from the standard. The precise way in which the deviation is corrected depends on the nature of the operating system and the design of the controller. There are three different response patterns. Response path A is direct and rapid, while path B is more gradual. Path C shows oscillations of decreasing amplitude. An aircraft suddenly deflected from a stable flight path would tend to recover by following pattern C, although in most cases its recovery would follow path B, i.e. a more gradual approach. An example is the international currency market. A company in one country, Company A, exports goods to a customer in another country, i.e. Company B. The transaction is conducted in US dollars, but the currency of Company A is pounds sterling. Company therefore needs to quote the price in US dollars to Company B based on a spot rate but with payment based on 30 days' credit terms. Therefore, Company B will pay Company A for the transaction 30 days following the issuing of the invoice. Company A's bank will therefore quote both the spot rate (i.e. today's exchange rate) and the forward rate (i.e. the rate calculated for 30 days' time), as well as any predicted further fluctuation between the two rates. There will, of course, be a difference between the two, as it is very unlikely that the two rates will be the same, i.e. par. In order to address the difference in exchange rates, the difference between the two rates is expressed as either a premium (i.e. an increase) or a discount (i.e. a decrease). Either of the two could adversely affect the value of the transaction to the supplier or the customer. An increase in the exchange rate means that the customer pays more for the transaction, whereas a decrease in the exchange rate means that the supplier could lose money on the transaction. The bank therefore makes the adjustment in the form of hedging to ensure that neither party loses out. It therefore subtracts the premium from the exchange rate to guarantee equilibrium, or it adds the discount to the exchange rate. In doing so, it protects the value of the transaction and therefore ensures that neither party loses out on the transaction. This whole process is in effect a variation of the negative feedback situation, in that the actual negative feedback emanates from the fluctuation of the exchange rates, and this is therefore rectified by the adjustment made by the bank to the actual transaction rate as influenced by the 30-day credit terms. Indeed, the financial markets make good use of negative feedback, as they need to cover themselves against adverse currency fluctuations, as has been seen in the recent past by way of extreme financial market fluctuations. A slight fluctuation in one market, such as the Far East, could result in a major adverse fluctuation elsewhere, such as in Europe or the United States, and this is why the issue of algedonic feedback is vital to the financial services sector. From this, it can be seen that algedonic feedback is vital in any part of the commercial sector, as it ultimately affects the whole of economic, financial, and commercial means of conducting business, be it in the overall supply chain, manufacturing and production, or services.

However, feedback must be judged by its effectiveness and its accuracy. The use of data must be very selective, as some data is unreliable and cannot be used for mitigation. Data derived from a production process is absolute, as it is derived from a production process, against established standards and norms as determined by the blueprint for that production process. For example, a machine is designed to perform a given number of tasks in a specific timeframe. If that number is exceeded, then the machine demonstrates a greater level of efficiency, and the feedback is thus positive. However, if the machine slows down or even breaks down, the feedback is negative, and remedial action must be taken to recover progress.

In terms of services or human-related tasks, the data derived is less reliable. Customer service is an area which can prove greatly inconsistent, as one customer may have a completely different opinion from another. Quality is defined as the standard of a product or service as measured against other things of a similar kind. It can also be defined as the degree of excellence of something in terms of satisfaction determined by a customer or user. However, as the old saying goes, "One man's meat is another man's poison". What may be seen as absolutely excellent by one person may be deemed mediocre by another. It depends upon the aspiration and demands of different people or organisations. Two people can catch a flight lasting 1.5 hours from one place to another by a specific airline. They receive a basic refreshment service on board free of charge. One person likes the quality of the refreshments; the other could not care less about the refreshments as long as they arrive at the airport of destination on time. The feedback in both cases will be very different, hence the value of customer surveys. Human nature will always defer to personal tastes, whereas machine-based feedback is standard because of the nature of the automated process.

To this extent, human-based cybernetics differs significantly from artificial machine-based cybernetics. Human-based cybernetics takes into account natural thought processes, where human decision is all-important, whereas artificial machine-based cybernetics is based on mechanical and artificial processes, where decisions are based solely on the information fed into the machine and how it is programmed. Machines cannot think for themselves; they can only operate in the way that they are programmed and instructed to do so. Computers may make significant in-depth decisions, but these decisions are based purely on the data which is fed into the computer and how it is programmed. Computers cannot make decisions based on assumption or perception, as these thought processes are generated by the human brain, generally in coordination with the five senses, namely

- sight
- hearing
- touch
- taste
- smell

Each of these senses triggers the human brain to make decisions based on how they affect the brain, and consequently the brain sends messages to the body to react in a particular way. If we touch something hot, we immediately recoil and back away. If we hear a sudden ear-splitting sound such as a siren close-up, we immediately put our hands over our ears to stifle the noise. If we smell something bad, we put our fingers over our nose and move away fast. If we see something, we express our feelings in the appropriate way. All these elements generate feedback, either positive or negative.

Artificial cybernetics, however, cannot take these factors into account. If a computer is suddenly jolted, it does not move away of its own accord. It still continues to function, as long as it is not damaged in the process. Extreme heat might melt a computer, but this is because it does not have the innate ability to take immediate action to avoid the source of heat. However, if a computer is linked to a set of sensors that detect a sudden movement or fault, it is designed to generate a set of messages alerting the operator. It is this scenario that can itself cause huge problems. The disaster that struck the offshore oil and gas installation *Deepwater Horizon* in the Gulf of Mexico was largely caused by a set of deficient sensors in the blow-out preventer. The reason for the deficiency was that the batteries powering the sensors were themselves deficient. The result was a massive blow-out which destroyed the installation and created a huge level of oil pollution in the Gulf. This scenario could have been easily avoided if the correct precautions and checks had been carried out by the installation operators. The same is true of the circumstances which destroyed the North Sea installation *Piper Alpha* in 1988. No provision was made for replacement control valves in the pipes carrying gas from the seabed into the installation, and when essential maintenance work necessitated the removal of both of the existing valves in each of the condensate pipes, they were replaced by temporary flanges to cover the holes, and reports were issued to the management team not to activate the pipes. These reports disappeared at the time of changeover of shift teams on the evening of the ill-fated day, and the new team that started the night shift were not made aware of the overhaul work on the valves. They activated the main pipe, and gas surged through the pipe out of control and ignited, causing a sequence of massive explosions and a resulting fireball that enveloped the installation and destroyed it in a short space of time. Over 160 lives were lost as a result. Again, this disaster could have been avoided if replacement valves had been available on the installation. This was partly human error, but also a deficiency in the system that did not allow for contingencies, a deficiency caused by the failure of artificial controls. This was a deficiency in feedback and the failure of the systematic regime which led to tragic disaster. In other words, it was a failure in the first-order system of cybernetics.

6

Economic Cybernetics

Economic cybernetics is a scientific field concerned with the application of cybernetic ideas and methods to economic systems. In an expanded and not entirely accurate sense, economic cybernetics is often taken to mean the field of science that has developed at the junction of mathematics and cybernetics with economics, including mathematical programming, operations research, mathematical economic models, econometrics, and mathematical economics. It has, in many ways, been associated with command economies of socialist regimes rather than free market economics, as it revolves around planned economies such as those found in countries such as Russia, China, and North Korea.

Economic cybernetics considers the economy and its structural and functional components as systems in which the processes of regulation and control are carried on by the movement and conversion of information. The methods of economic cybernetics make it possible to standardize this information and articulate it; to streamline the receipt, transmission, and processing of economic information; and to work out the structure and composition of data-processing equipment. It is this approach that gives research in economic cybernetics its internal unity and character. Such research serves specifically as the theoretical basis for building automated control systems and data-processing systems for the national economy.

Economic cybernetics is still in the formative stage. In many countries, such investigations are still included under systems analysis, operations research, and management science, as in the United States and Great Britain, or under information science, as in France. The term "economic cybernetics" was first used in the early 1960s by V. S. Nemchinov (USSR), Oskar Lange and H. Greniewski (Poland), and Stafford Beer (Great Britain). These scientists also sketched the main lines of development of the new science, devoting special attention to the connection between systems analysis of an economy on the one hand and logic, control theory, and information theory on the other. Many fundamental propositions of economic cybernetics were formulated much earlier, however. The notion of an economy as a system is contained in F. Quesnay's Economic Table (1758). It was elaborated and scientifically substantiated in the works of Karl Marx and Vladimir I. Lenin.

A paper entitled *Cybernetics in Economics*, produced in 1965 in what was then Communist-run Czechoslovakia by Kyn Oldrich and Pavel Pelikan, during the Soviet era, stated that as yet there was no agreement about the nature of cybernetics itself, and even less about the application of cybernetics in the economy. Some scholars and experts put the main emphasis on mathematical models and the techniques of transmitting and processing economic information. The authors believed that cybernetics in economics meant primarily a specific approach to economic problems, in which the objects of investigation were not physical processes, but exchange of information and decision-making. They concentrated on problems of organization and control in economic systems.

The authors determined the following three types of programs:

- **Closed programs:**
  Systems with a program of this type have no information inputs. The resulting decisions are determined in advance by the internal program.
- **Unconditioned reflexes:**
  Unlike the preceding program, this system has inputs that bring information from the environment, but the system always reacts in the same predetermined way.
- **Conditioned reflexes:**
  A system with a program of this type has even looser connection between the original program and the actual decision. In the preceding case, the information from the environment determined directly the decision of the system according to a fixed algorithm. Here, the algorithm itself is created through the influence of the environment and is therefore determined by the issues and challenges that are derived from that environment.

Systems with conditioned reflexes are frequently called learning systems because their programs permit learning. Since systems with programs of a reflex type are capable of continuously receiving information from environment, there need not be as much information contained in their programs. From this, the reduction of the volume of information is only a less important benefit of economic planning. It is evident that a function of the plan is to provide a program for economic activity in the future.

If it is a closed program, it must determine output of an extensive range of products in advance. Although this was for some time considered to be the only and most effective form of planning, its shortcomings are obvious. In such a case, the plan must contain an enormous amount of information, and at the same time, the stability of the economic system would be threatened by every unforeseen event, whether this were change in demand, in technology of production or in foreign markets. In contrast to this, a plan of the second category would continuously receive information about the changes in conditions and derive operative decisions that could not be made in detail at the time when the plan was set up. The particular objective would be to plan the reaction to unpredictable circumstances. A plan of the type of conditioned reflexes would mean a further improvement in these reactions. The system would learn from its successes, and mistakes are more important that not all the needed information is available initially when the system was constructed. Systems with closed programs are incapable of performing tasks that depend on unpredictable events.

The authors also concluded that it was evident that not all the real systems can be considered "goal-seeking systems". They therefore classified the concept of real system in the following three groups:

- Systems whose behaviour is determined exclusively by physical inputs. Such systems can be either deterministic or stochastic, but there is no need to use the concepts of information and decision-making in this case.
- Systems whose behaviour depends not only on physical inputs but also on information received, but there is no need for the concept of goal or objective.
- Systems whose behaviour depends on physical inputs, information received, and the goal of the system. These are "goal-seeking systems".

The third category is the structure most often found in first-order cybernetics. The purpose of the exercise is to observe the process of inputs and outputs based on information received, and the need for rectification based on feedback, especially negative feedback, as that information is processed within the system and produces outputs. The more negative the output, the greater the need to identify and examine the negative issue resulting from the feedback and provide a solution, which will make the output more positive and effective.

Classifying systems according to these criteria is to a certain extent arbitrary. Information is always carried by some physical process, but informational significance may or may not be ascribed to it. The same object can be studied either with or without concepts of information and decision-making. If one does not use the concept of information, but observes only the changes in the physical states of the system, the motions can be described as cause and effect using laws of physics. In this way, the process of the system being observed relates to first-order cybernetics, where a process is being observed. The concepts of goal seeking and causality do not necessarily contradict each other but are merely two different views of the same reality.

The authors continued by stating that the principle of natural selection is also important for the progress of human society. Social progress means the introduction of new technologies of production, new economic relationships, new forms of management and organization, better than the preceding ones. Their novelty lies in the fact that they were unknown before they were introduced. There was no information about them and therefore they could not have been consciously introduced with guaranteed success simultaneously throughout the whole society. Mutations in society are also of a fortuitous nature. No experts can guarantee correct filtration of unfavourable mutations so that only favourable remain. This is an artificial form of control, where only positive results emerge, which in reality distorts the natural image of a scenario, as in an ideal world, and does not, in reality, paint a true picture of the scenario. One simply needs to recall the gallery of scientists and inventors of genius who were not recognized by their contemporaries. Only when the emergence of random mutations is not prevented, can advantages of some new forms be demonstrated in practice and thus be extended to all of society. Every society that wishes to speed up its evolution must make random mutations possible.

The new forms must have the possibility of showing their advantages or their shortcomings in practice to be compared with previous forms. This is, of course, not easy because society should also prevent survival of unfavourable mutations that could act as cancer on the organism. The authors therefore determined that they could divide the systems with goal-seeking behaviour into regulating, controlling, or organizing systems. If a system is defined in such a way that regulated, controlling or organising systems are a part of it, then this is described as automatic regulation, control, or organisation, which was, of course, very much a feature of the Marxist system.

For a long time, Marxists believed that the automatic or spontaneous processes could lead only to imbalances and anarchy in the economy. They concluded that it would be desirable to suppress automatism and replace it, where possible, with the principle of conscious, centralised direction, as in the Stalinist 5-year plans. The authors stated that the error of this idea is apparent. Reducing automatism leads to growth in size of the central administrative apparatus, making it slow, cumbrous, and bureaucratic. In reality, this is exactly what happened in the Soviet system, and which is indeed characteristic of the structure of the European Union (EU), whose governing system is in itself cumbersome and bureaucratic, as well as being grossly inefficient (the opinion of the author of this book).

In designing the control of economic systems, it is necessary to reckon with the fact that these systems are made up of people, that is to say, elements that are themselves systems acting not only purposefully, but also consciously. However, economic systems must take into account other major driving economic factors, such as industry, agriculture, production, trade, and money. Therefore, each control directive is only one of the information inputs, used by the controlled to make a conscious decision. Controlling people means influencing their decision-making in the desired way. The harmony or conflict of interests between the controlling body and the controlled plays an important role. If both parties want to reach the same goal, it is not necessary to make the controlling directive compulsory. If such a common interest is lacking, the controlling directive must be supplemented by measures that ensure its effectiveness. Among the means employed, the most frequent is the use of force or coercion, which can be seen as undue influence and therefore not benevolent in any way. It should be remembered that in the human body, the direct comparison with an artificial control system, the brain does not operate by force; rather, it sends messages to the other parts of the body that automatically react to those messages and do not question them. The arms or the legs do not say to the brain, "Why should I listen to you or obey you?" The natural reaction, as determined by nature, is to obey the message almost instinctively. Indeed, if the human being is exposed to a sudden adversity such as crossing the road and being approached by an oncoming car, the brain picks up the message of an impending peril through the vision process through the use of the eyes and automatically sends a message to the legs, "Move quickly in reverse or run like mad!". The legs obey instantaneously to avoid an accident.

Sometimes, a deliberate distortion of information is used for this purpose. If, for example, the controlling body succeeds in persuading the controlled that carrying out the orders is in their own interest, although it may be only the end desired by the controlling person or body, people can actually be made to act against their own interests. Nationalism, chauvinism, and racism can be misused by some groups of people to induce others to actions that in reality do not serve their interests.

This line of thinking adhered very closely to the Soviet policy, i.e. a series of economic plans, especially those devised by Josef Stalin to control the Soviet economy during the 1930s, in the form of his 5-year plans. These plans could not be allowed to be affected by externalities, as such external influences could risk derailing or, at very least, compromising the 5-year plans, which, in Stalin's view, would have had an adverse effect on the Soviet economy, given that this policy was of planned economies and was subsequently extended to the Soviet-controlled states of the Eastern bloc following the end of the Second World War in 1945. The COMECON, or Council for Mutual Economic Assistance, as it was known, imposed this line of economic thinking on the countries of Eastern Europe that were invaded and occupied by the Soviet Union in 1945, and this system, for all its faults, prevailed until the fall of the Soviet Bloc at the end of the 1980s. However, this same policy was to spawn the Cybersyn project in Chile under the Marxist regime of President Salvador Allende between 1971 and 1973, when he was ousted in the military coup led by Augusto Pinochet and the project was abandoned.

The authors of the paper then address the cybernetic elements of national economics, i.e. a view of the economy as informational and decision-making structure, which in reality it is. The system created for this purpose consists of people who are interconnected by informational flows. The environment consists of other social systems and nature. In this case, nature is taken to include all the physical things relevant to the economic process, including "artificial" nature, i.e. machinery, buildings, and equipment that are the products of human productive activity.

The risk of decision depends on the amount and kind of information that the decision-making agent obtains. There is not only distortion of information as it is transmitted in the economy but also a deliberate distortion, thus giving rise to the saying: "Duff information in, duff information out". This is basically saying that if the information input into the system is inaccurate, the resulting information emerging at the output end is equally inaccurate, if not more so owing to the processing of that information within the system. This is certainly true of much of the information propagated to the UK public during the coronavirus crisis. The government was reassuring the public that hospitals and care workers were adequately equipped with preventive personal equipment (PPE), when the reality was that this was simply not true. It only emerged later that PPE was in very short supply and that medical staff were, in many cases, being asked to work with no preventive garments whatsoever. This state of affairs amounted to gross misinformation, which at best was pernicious and at worst was downright dangerous.

Systems that provide information sometimes try to use distorted information to influence the decisions taken by those who receive the information. Therefore, a theory of economic information needs more than a statistical theory of information that was elaborated primarily for the needs of communication technique, but it would be necessary to include also some considerations from the game theory.

Human capacity to receive and process information is limited, unlike a computer, which can receive and process information within a matter of seconds. No individual can handle all the types of information needed for a smooth operation of society. Consequently, the whole social control process must be subdivided among various controlling subsystems. For example, we can visualise society as a hierarchy, with the lower base formed by the output elements, and those who make the decisions are placed in upper layers over those who receive and implement the decisions. The base elements send information about the state of nature upwards to upper layers of hierarchy. Since each place in the hierarchy has a limited capacity, the amount of information must be gradually reduced. Not all the information collected below can arrive at the highest places. The problem, of course, is how to reduce information without losing what is essential for making decisions. The reduction of information on the way up means that the highest places cannot issue decisions that would contain enough information to eliminate all the uncertainty in the output elements. That is to say, each place in the hierarchy has a certain degree of freedom for independent decisions. The allocation of degrees of freedom within the hierarchy determines what is usually called the degree of centralisation or decentralisation. A high degree of centralisation requires large information processing capacity at the upper layers to reduce the risk of centralized decision-making. If there is too much centralisation, it can easily happen that the costs of transmitting and processing information would be many times higher than the most pessimistic estimates of loss that could occur with an effective reduction of information and a decentralisation of a large part of the decision-making process.

Of fundamental importance for economic cybernetics as a socialist tool were the theory and practice of national economic planning and management in the USSR and the other socialist countries, in particular, the development of a system of plan indexes and the incentives for achieving them (the analysis of information needs and content in the national economy has been done by economic statistics). In the 1950s and 1960s, special attention was devoted to applied questions of building data-processing systems. These questions included study and streamlining of data flows, coding, and organisation of data processing. Through these investigations, computers could be used more efficiently in data-processing systems; previously, they had been used for one-time calculations and had not been employed on the control level. Diagrams for the regulation of economic systems, some very abstract, were constructed as illustrations of the theory of automatic control.

All these investigations, which at first were very weakly interrelated, gradually came together to make up the problem area of economic cybernetics. As the transition was made from comparatively small-scale data-processing systems at enterprises and firms to analysis and planning information systems on the sectorial and national levels, the common features of the field emerged. In this case, information flows and data processing could no longer be considered apart from the processes of planning and controlling the socialist economy as a whole or the processes of control in the capitalist economy. The question of information supply for large-scale systems of mathematical economic models became especially urgent. Solution of the central problem of combining models of objects being controlled and models of control processes became the basis for planning automated control systems. With the solution of this problem, efficient and optimal plans that meet the set requirements of the controlling body could be developed and implemented to create an optimal control system.

It can be determined that economic cybernetics is developing along three main lines, which are being coordinated ever more closely: the theory of economic systems and models, the theory of economic information, and the theory of controlling systems. Although the free market argument states that cybernetics could be an encumbrance to the process of free market economic, in times of crisis there needs to be a cybernetic process embedded in any economic system, in order to derive order from what would otherwise be absolute chaos. The global coronavirus pandemic has seen national economic structures virtually collapse as a result of a lack of forward contingency planning. When all is well in terms of the national economy, everybody thrives and prospers. In time of national emergency or crisis, e.g. the COVID-19 crisis, everything falls apart because of a combination of factors. These can be categorised as

- lack of national coordination;
- lack of national planning;
- lack of national policy;
- knee-jerk reaction, usually far too radical;
- national panic;
- no obvious outcome or solution;
- no means of addressing major adversities as they arise;
- lack of forward thinking or strategy; and
- no internal coordination within government, i.e. lack of national control.

This shows that the strategies of Oldrich and Pelikan, and indeed Beer, which led to his Cybersyn Project, can be easily vindicated in times of crisis. As stated, a free market economy works when all is well but fails dismally in times of crisis. A command economy works on the basis of an ideal system but is controlled at all levels to ensure coordination and efficient operation, despite the fact that there are few, if any, degrees of freedom within the system owing to decisions imposed from the top. Furthermore, a command economy gives little room for free enterprise and lower taxes, thus stifling the economy to a degree. The ideal solution is a hybrid, i.e. a command and control structure to ensure a smoothly run operation, but allowing for market freedoms to guarantee liberty of operation within the controls imposed from the top on the basis of economic management. Total command economies do not give rise to overall economic prosperity, as there is no freedom to achieve it based on the burdens of state control. Even the Chinese system fails, as although there are major Chinese conglomerates in operation, they are private by name only, as they are still influenced by the state, given its communist nature. The thoughts of Chairman Mao did little to foster-free economic growth in China, and the present regime is no different. Even now, shortages of basic commodities occur, and the insatiable demand by China for overseas commodities, including iron ore, coal, and oil, has shown that the Chinese internal economic system is far from perfect, to the point of an increasing influence of China over the South China Sea in flagrant breach of international maritime conventions.

Given the concepts of economics, there is no perfect global economic system, as revealed by the coronavirus crisis. The extremities of either a total command economy or a total free market economy cannot work, as they are both imperfect and demonstrate significant flaws. A total command economy allows for no economic freedoms whatsoever, whereas a total free market economy allows for too many, with no provision for a control system of any kind. There has to be some form of middle ground, where the provision exists for a control system when and where it is needed, coupled with a policy of free market growth based on a favourable economic climate. There will always be fluctuations in any economic system, and these are generally compensated for in economic recovery from a recession. However, where a major global crisis occurs, as in 2020, then the provision must be implemented of radical command and control to physically rectify the adversity based on a series of systemic controls which operate to address the negative feedback generated by the crisis and implement a set of procedural controls to address the crisis and rectify it as soon as possible.

The immediate post-war years that had succeeded the global conflict and, even before it, the great economic depression of the early 1930s, were dominated by radical new-wave economic thinking such as Keynesian economics, which advocated state intervention to rectify economic problems and foster economic growth based on lessons learned from the 1930s. The policy implemented in the United States by President Franklin Roosevelt of "get the wheels turning" was based on state economic intervention, similar to the economic concepts of the British economist John Maynard Keynes, who advocated injecting large quantities into a system in order to make it work, usually by way of increased government spending. This enabled US industry to recover quickly and develop the national economy to the point where it was already prepared for the approaching conflict at the end of the 1930s. This policy partly resulted in the so-called "Marshall Plan" following the end of global hostilities in 1945, which gave rise to the European Coal and Steel Community (ECSC) of 1952, designed to rebuild European industry following its near-destruction as a result of the war in Europe. This model worked well for the early years of what became the European Economic Community (EEC) in 1957 with the Treaty of Rome, but it stifled economic growth of what became the European Union (EU) owing to bloated administration and uncontrolled bureaucracy, despite the idealist principle of an open, pan-European Single Market, where all internal barriers to trade would be removed, allowing for the four main principles of free movement of goods, labour, services, and capital. In principle, the concept was ideal, except for the dangers imposed by the free movement of refugees from the Middle East, allowing for uncontrolled immigration into many EU member states, coupled with a rapid spread of the deadly coronavirus, which resulted in a hurried implementation of pan-European border controls in order to attempt to stifle the spread of the virus. In the event, this sudden knee-jerk reaction failed at the point of implementation, although later it had rather more effect. This supposed free internal market policy has led to a series of dichotomies and anomalies, namely a supposed free internal market and uncontrolled international movement within the bloc, yet on the other hand a totally bureaucratic, cumbersome, and undemocratic control regime in the combined form of the European Commission, Council, and Parliament, which is democratic by name only, in that it cannot overrule decisions made by the Commission and Council, but can only amend or approve these decisions. And given that neither the European Commission nor Council is elected by the European people, autocracy rules and thus defeats the principle of democracy. This flies in the face of any cybernetic principle, as the principle of cybernetics is to establish a control system based on consensus ad idem, i.e. that all elements of the system should work in complete harmony with each other.

The theory of economic systems and models considers the methodology for conducting systems analysis of an economy, modelling the economy, and reflecting the structure and functioning of the economic systems in the models; the classification and construction of sets of mathematical economic models; economic regulation and the correlation and mutual coordination of different incentives and influences in the functioning of economic systems; and the behaviour of people and collectives. In its investigation of these problems, economic cybernetics relies primarily on political economy and general systems theory, as well as on sociology and control theory; it summarizes the results of the development of mathematical economic methods and models.

The theory of economic information considers the economy as an information system. It studies information flows circulating in the national economy as communication among its elements and subsystems. It also investigates the characteristics of information channels and the messages transmitted along them; economic measurements and symbolic systems in the economy generally (that is, the languages of economic control, including the development of systems of economic indexes and rules for calculating these indexes; these questions are singled out in economic semiotics); and decision-making and data-processing processes in the information systems of the national economy at all levels, including questions of optimal organisation of these processes. Here, economic cybernetics touches closely on information theory, research to determine the usefulness and value of information, semiotics, programming theory, and information science.

The theory of controlling systems in economics brings research in other areas of economic cybernetics together and gives it concrete form. It concentrates on comprehensive study and refinement of the control system for the national economy and for separate economic units and, in the last analysis, on their optimal functioning. Special attention is devoted to planning and directing the fulfilment of plans, including study of the methodology, technology, and organization of control functions and the use of mathematical economic models and other scientific methods in control practice; developing an internally coordinated system of economic, administrative, legal, and other incentives and norms for control and constructing organizational structures for administrative bodies; studying human factors (including social and psychological factors) in the processes of economic management and the interaction of the human being and the machine in the automated control system; and designing and introducing the automated control system. Economic cybernetics considers the automated control system not as a data-processing "addition" to particular administrative bodies but rather as the economic administration system itself, a system based on comprehensive application of mathematical economic methods and models and modern computer and information technology and including the appropriate techniques and organization for its operation. Research and applied development in these areas are under way in the USSR at all levels of national economic management, from the systems of the State Planning Committee of the USSR and the sectorial automated control systems to enterprise automated control systems.

The Twenty-fourth Congress of the CPSU (Communist Party of the Soviet Union) projected the creation of a nationwide automated system for collecting and processing information. In the ninth 5-year-plan (1971–1975), the introduction of automated control systems for enterprises and organizations in industry, agriculture, communications, trade, and transportation was accelerated.

The principal research centres in economic cybernetics were the Central Mathematical Economics Institute of the Academy of Sciences of the USSR, the Institute of the Economics and Organization of Industrial Production of the Siberian Division of the Academy of Sciences of the USSR, the Institute of Cybernetics of the Academy of Sciences of the Ukrainian SSR, the Scientific Research Economics Institute of the State Planning Committee of the USSR, and the Computer Centre of the Academy of Sciences of the USSR.

Economic cybernetics thrives in an environment of control, where economic decisions are taken nationally on a centralised governmental basis. Free market economics allows an economic structure to self-equilibrate based on prevalent market forces, such as those proposed by the eminent former Harvard Professor of Business, Michael Porter, in his study on the five forces. The five forces, as proposed by Porter, are

- bargaining power of suppliers;
- threat of new entrants;
- threat of substitutes;
- bargaining power of buyers; and
- the central element, industry rivalry.

Porter based his arguments around the principles of the free market, in a similar manner to the Austrian-British economist Friedrich Hayek, and in that respect both economists base much of their work on similar principles. The main difference between Hayek and Porter is that Hayek believed in liberal economic thinking, whereas Porter based his ideas on more directed and structured thinking.

However, while economic cybernetics do not go hand-in-hand with free market principles, which allow a form of self-equilibrium subject to these forces of supply-and-demand economics based on market elasticity, cybernetics do prevail in terms of industry efficiency and competitiveness. In other words, governments practising free market economics have no use for cybernetic control mechanisms, but the corporate environment does, in order to remain efficient, competitive, and viable. The central pivot of the five forces model is industry rivalry, where industries must increase their efficiency to remain competitive and thus economically viable, hence the importance of Stafford Beer's viable systems model (VSM).

If we study the organisational structure of most of major organizations of the present day, we will be given their "organization charts", and most of them can relate in some way to the "family tree" of some noble lineage. However, the missing link that we will always find in them is the notion of viability. Stafford Beer noted in his book *Brain of the Firm* that the last thing that corporate entities consider is the whole issue of "viability". They are more concerned with making profits and tidy sums of revenue, but they do not consider the cost of the sale on the profit and loss account or even the costs associated with their existence. Viability is the first prerequisite of an organisational structure, as otherwise it becomes an expensive "black hole", where resources are expended without any form of accountability or profitability. However, we are accustomed to asking for organisational charts, instead of inquiring into the very organisational structure itself. Stafford Beer developed the VSM of an organisation based on laws of cybernetics and the human's nervous system. He is quoted as stating that:

> The difference is that the VSM is a "whole systems" theory. Almost all other theories of organisation think in the billiardballs mode of A leads to B leads to C, and therefore miss the essence of what's really going on. They forget that A, B and C are inextricably linked with a myriad other factors, and that for any model to work it must take all of this complexity into account.
>
> (Walker, 2002)

The contemporary organisational charts do not embed the vital stakeholders and the circumstances of the organisation in which it is embedded. Indeed, stakeholder accountability is vital for any organisation, as any organisation is accountable to its stakeholders, i.e. those who benefit from its use without having invested in it. In this respect, there is more accountability required to stakeholders than to shareholders. One will never find customers, but the environment is either narrowly integrated or absolutely absent. It only defines job titles, which can mean anything as they are not necessarily fully defined. The VSM, however, has its main focus on the "organisation versus environment" or vice versa, and thus, it ensures adaptability based on natural laws. "Struggle for existence and life" lies at the heart of all natural phenomena.

> In looking at Nature, it is most necessary to keep the forgoing consideration always in mind- never to forget that every single organic being around us may be said to be striving to the outmost to increase in numbers: that each lives by a struggle at some period of its life; that heavy destruction inevitably falls either on the young or old, during each generation or at current interval.

> (*Darwin, 1859, p. 66*)

Peter Drucker (1954, p. 75) emphasises that all objectives and decisions ought to aim at providing the supplies needed for market standing (environment) and innovation (adaptability).

"COMPLEXITY", THE 6TH FORCE THAT SHAPES MANAGEMENT STRATEGY

The root of complexity derives from the Latin word *complexus*, meaning "entwined" or "embraced", which means that two or more distinct parts are joined in such a way that it is difficult to separate them. Therefore, we find here a basic duality, where these parts cannot be explained by analytical methods, since by separating them, we destroy their connection and interaction, in the same way that by cutting branches off a tree, we cannot fully understand how a tree works, as the branches derive their nourishment and existence from the tree itself. We therefore cannot understand a system by dismantling it. Complexity is not understood by analytical methods; it is understood by the notion of "ordering systems and its reality". Complexity can also be defined as influencing the emergence of order out of disorder or chaos. Complexity is the interrelation, cause, root, and status of real systems. However, the most difficult thing about complexity is its definition, since we tend to think in reductionist way, but to understand complexity, we need to change our mindset that in order for us to understand what complexity is, we need to understand what complex systems are. The best way to understand complex systems is by understanding how they are controlled. Strategists in the future ought to focus on how complex systems are kept in advance under control in a chaotic, unpredictable, turbulent, and complex environment. The strategist may not be able to predict what precisely may occur and how the system under his control may react to any given situation, but he can capture the underlying characteristics of complex systems and their dynamics by means of modelling and simulation, especially through cybernetic modelling, in order to understand and control them, thus enabling the design of measures, actions, and policies that the system can use to foster desirable developments. That said, the strategist is likely to make errors along the way which require correction. Therefore, the main function of the manager/strategist is to control complexity. The fundamental and really hard problems of management arise from the complexity of the systems that one has to construct and steer, hence the use of cybernetics as part of this strategy. Money, material, machinery, and human resources are only a part of the strategic management spectrum; the next frontier is best denoted as complexity (Beer, 1979–1994, p. 31).

Order in organisations is a well-structured manifestation and observation of absorbed complexity, in that order must prevail over chaos, especially that borne of uncontrolled complexity. In the cross-linked and interconnected world of our era, the main theme of the strategist is "to control" dynamic complexity. The strategist's challenge is not merely the construction of strategic economic and business models as in Porter's Five Forces description; it is the generation and creation of favourable circumstances and conditions for the management and control of the organisation. The revolutionary shift in strategic thinking ought to be shifted from the old concept of "construction via detail" to the "construction of a favourable reality" while relying on the behaviour and dynamic of the organization as a regulator (first order) and an observer/overseer (second order).

It is now necessary to therefore return to the conflict between controlled order and natural order. Controlled order requires everything to be put in its place and controlled from a high level, as with the centralised government principle. Conversely, natural order infers that everything will find its own balance in the global context. However, natural balance can be idiosyncratic and disparate concerning the position of an entity within an overall structure. In a world of increasing competitiveness, there is an equally increasing need for some degree of control, especially at a corporate level. This degree of control must ultimately determine the future of an organisation and its competitiveness at the global level, hence the application to cybernetics to this level of the economic structure. In this respect, economic cybernetics refers to the corporate structure, not the national or international administrative or political structure, as it affects economic viability, not profit-making or even national policy. Although the studies of those mentioned in the first part of this chapter had a bearing on their own environments, these environments were, to a large extent, artificial and cocooned, as they did not refer to the real world as defined by Western economists and strategists. With the fall of the Iron Curtain, these regimes had to change and adapt to a completely different way of thinking, and so too did their interpretation of economic cybernetics.

However, the role of the state is still a hybrid function, as the state controls various sectors, especially in the case of sectors such as the health service, the local councils, education, and defence, to name but a few. There has to be a level of controllability in all these sectors, regardless of the direction of the economy. In a command economy such as China and North Korea, the state is in charge of everything, even organisations which are supposedly "commercial" by nature and deemed to be private companies. In a free market economy, the economy is driven by market forces, not by state intervention.

During the regime of Salvador Allende in Chile in the early 1970s, the state system was in charge of the whole economy. The Cybersyn project was devised and implemented to enable the state to use cybernetic principles and techniques to direct the economy and supposedly achieve maximum potential based on feedback and rectification of anomalies and deficiencies caused by whatever circumstances. In his cybernetic notes, Stafford Beer, the instigator of the project, makes reference to the application of the VSM to the functioning of the state, and how it enabled the state to operate in a more efficient manner, as follows:

- Recursively speaking, the Chilean nation is embedded in the world of nations, and the government is embedded in the nation itself. This was understood; all these are supposedly viable systems.

- The government should be conceived as a viable system (System 5 being the President of the Republic) in which System 1 consists of the headquarters of each major function – health, education, finance, industry, and so on.
- Picking out industry as a viable system embedded in this (System 5 being the Minister of Economics), we find a set of industrial sectors constituting System 1. These include such elements as food, textiles, automotive, and so on.
- Each sector (System 5 being the Undersecretary for Economics with his appropriate committee) contains, as System 1, a set of enterprises, or firms.
- Embedded in the enterprise is the plant; within that department; within that the social unit of a working group; and within that the individual worker – viable systems all.

(Brain of the Firm, p. 249)

The paper with the above notes concentrated on the organisation of the enterprise, of the sectors, of industry itself, and of the state insofar as its relationship with the social economy was concerned. It also reinforces the principle of the recursive systems theorem detailed in Chapter 3 of this book, i.e. that every subunit of a main unit is in itself a viable system. This set of notes was later developed into the principal objective of the project, stated as follows:

OBJECTIVE

To install a preliminary system of information and regulation for the industrial economy that will demonstrate the main features of cybernetic management and begin to help in the task of actual decision-making by 1st March 1972.

(Brain of the Firm, pp. 251–252)

Looking at the objective in a simple way, the essence of the statement could be applied anywhere in the world. Any government that exerts control over any national function should be able to use this objective in terms of national management and control, regardless of the type and nature of the economy or political structure. This same approach can be used in the free market economic structure, as it still applies a tangible level of control to all government-controlled entities, right down to government departments.

The context of this project involved three indices, namely productivity, latency, and the product of both of these, namely performance. All combine to produce efficiency and viability. If performance is lacking, the other factors will suffer accordingly, and this applies to national and regional administrative levels as much as it applies to corporate level. If government cannot perform, one cannot expect a national state to perform, regardless of its corporate activity. Government is there to control and direct stable national policy. Where policy is indeterminate or at best vague and incohesive, and exercises little cohesive control, the state cannot function in a fully directed and ordered way. Decision-making is only as good as the information provided to achieve it, and if the information is vague, or even non-existent, there is no possibility for informed and rational decision-making. Government ineptitude and incompetence inevitably leads to collapse of the economy, society, and the overall state of the nation, and this is becoming prevalent as at the middle of 2020.

CYBERNETICS AND TAXATION

A word that to most people is somewhat less than palatable is taxation. It is said that the only two certainties in life are death and taxation. Death ends life, while taxation plagues it. However, taxation is a necessity in that governments tax their population to raise revenue for national requirements, such as defence, education, health, welfare, national infrastructure, and so on. Government of itself has no revenue held in vast reserves, contrary to the views of many people. It raises revenue through taxation. However, it adopts taxation policy based on its own budgets, not those of the country itself. Politics shows that governments of different political persuasions will raise or lower taxes dependent upon their political ideals. Socialism breeds a more rigorous and higher taxation policy, which can stifle the economy, based on the generation of revenue to finance expensive welfare schemes, whereas Conservatism breeds a policy of free market economics, where taxation is kept to a much lower level to encourage economic growth, where social welfare is based more on higher levels of employment.

Unfortunately, government does not consult the people or businesses when it comes to the raising of taxes. If it did, there might be a more equitable national taxation policy, where everybody wins. Some countries, such as Sweden, engage in a policy of high taxation, but the people know that this is used to ensure that everybody, including the unemployed, maintains a reasonable standard of living owing to a well-supported welfare state that looks after everybody, young, middle-aged, and old. The Chilean economic model under Salvador Allende was intended to redistribute the wealth from the extremely rich to the lower classes. It did not last long.

If a government engages in a policy of feedback, where it listens to the electorate that voted it into power, it would soon discover that high taxation helps very few people. A policy of high taxation stifles the economy and reduces productivity. It is a form of what Stafford Beer called "Eudemony".

Beer considered that there were two critical aspects to measuring the way a nation state was performing: one was the performance indicators from the basic organisations and their employees, known as S1s, and the second was the eudemonic measurements of citizens' well-being. Indeed, it could be shown that the two were directly proportional. If the well-being of the population increases, so too do the performance indicators. He suggested the use of an "algedonic" metric to measure eudemony, or how well people feel in general. The way that they felt in terms of overall well-being could thus be measured in terms of positive or negative feedback. What was used was a simple device which was given to people on the street who rotated the knob on the device until the blue and orange segments of the circle provided an indication of how they were feeling. The researcher then turned over the device and read off the two-figure digit, which provided the eudemony measurement. The system did not threaten people, as the identity of the person surveyed was kept completely anonymous and could express very simply how well they felt at a particular time. It is fairly evident that if the question was asked as to how they felt about how they were taxed, the answer would be a definite negative. Present-day surveys conducted by organisations such as Chambers of Commerce through media such as SurveyMonkey, do exactly the same job, in that they derive data from the participant through a series of multiple choice questions and then use the data derived as a measure of overall business well-being. It is fair to say that the more negative the survey results are, the more there is a tendency of unwillingness to be any more productive, as the overall feeling is that to become more productive and thus earn more money results in higher tax bills.

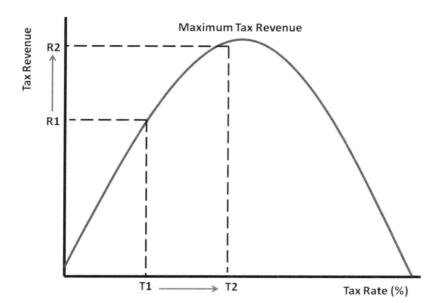

FIGURE 6.1
The Laffer curve.

The Laffer Curve, devised by the American economist Arthur Laffer, demonstrated the principle of the adverse effects of high taxation on business as a whole. It demonstrates a eudemonic approach to business confidence and productivity based on the difference between low and high taxation, using a sliding scale (Figure 6.1).

The essential principle of the curve is that up to a certain level of taxation on the economy, increasing revenue is earned by the government as a result of taxation, thus relating to a level of positive feedback from the nation in terms of the acceptability and toleration of taxation levels. However, beyond a certain level, which may be variable, the feedback turns negative as a result of opposition to taxation levels, and government revenue resulting from taxation decreases as a result of either companies transferring operations overseas to avoid such levels of taxation or simply reducing productivity resulting from a lack of incentive to be more productive owing to the taxation burdens imposed upon businesses.

One implication of the Laffer curve is that reducing or increasing tax rates beyond a certain point is counter-productive for raising further tax revenue. In the United States, conservatives have used the Laffer curve to argue that lower taxes may increase tax revenue, as there is a greater incentive towards increased productivity, resulting in higher corporate income, which, although taxable, increases the profits of the company and therefore increases the sense of corporate well-being and hence its contribution to the national economy as a whole.

In terms of corporate policy and associated taxes, the view is that increased taxes discourage higher production and sales, as the increased revenue yields higher levels of tax, especially where exports are concerned, since increased exports yield higher levels of corporate revenue. International trade therefore suffers as a result. Similarly, higher levels of imports result in higher levels of import duty payable, thus discouraging imports. In short, higher duties and taxes discourage international trade, as well as overall productivity. However, decreased taxes and duties encourage productivity and international trade, as there is a fiscal incentive to produce more, export more, and indeed import more as import duties are kept to a minimum. This will result in positive feedback and an increased sense of individual and national well-being. The new UK Global Tariff being implemented at the start of 2010 encourages the imports of many commodities, as it will either reduce or remove many import duties from a variety of commodities and thus stimulate and foster higher levels of international trade. However, if other countries do not lower their import tariffs, there is still less incentive for the United Kingdom to export elsewhere. The European Union, on the other hand, maintains a higher level of import duties on many products as part of an overall policy of protectionism, despite the number of free trade agreements that it has with many countries. Indeed, it could be argued that the policy of high import tariffs is to deter trade with specific countries. This can prove detrimental to a national economy, as some economies require a vigorous import policy to ensure the availability of various commodities on the domestic market. Policies of Import Substitution, which meant that the imposition of high import duties on the import of many commodities in order to encourage local production, regardless of the fact that local production was both inefficient and expensive and thus drove prices of such products much higher, was seen as detrimental to the national economy. Such a policy equally adversely affected exports, as the export price of products produced locally rose accordingly because of such production weaknesses and disadvantages. Feedback from consumers in such cases was negative and did little for the national support of governments implementing such policies. Only with free trade agreements and the encouragement of the import of commodities at lower prices would feedback become more positive, and international trade would be stimulated and increase as a result.

To this degree, there is a fine balance in terms of eudemony, economic well-being and confidence, and incentive. Higher taxes reduce these factors, whereas low- or medium-level taxes increase them. Taxes are a necessity but should be balanced in terms of economic fortunes. In times of economic depression or crisis, high taxes will do nothing to bolster the economy and need to be reduced accordingly. In times of economic boom, taxes should be managed in such a way that government revenue is guaranteed for national policies but should still enable businesses to grow and flourish. Negative feedback from business will not stimulate government; it will destabilise it. Where businesses suffer, revenue suffers accordingly. If business revenue suffers, the taxation derived from that revenue decreases. That means less revenue for the government, which therefore cannot meet its national policy obligations. Where businesses flourish, revenue increases, and so too does tax payable to government. This would imply that if a government is to achieve higher yields from taxation, it needs to reduce the tax burdens on businesses and individuals and thus collect higher levels of taxes based on lower levels and rates of taxation. Such a policy encourages more positive algedonic feedback and also increases the viability of both government and industry in terms of the VSM, hence the importance of feedback in terms of taxation and its effects on the national economy. One of the requirements of government is to heed feedback and act upon it if that government is to remain in power. We all have to pay taxes, but we like to know where the money is being spent, and if it is being spent wisely in order to stimulate economic growth. It is pointless trying to help the workforce in terms of welfare when the businesses that employ such workforce are suffering because of increasing tax burdens, lower levels of productivity, and decreased sales owing to higher prices contributed to by – guess what – higher levels of taxation; a vicious circle, indeed. If we pay lower taxes, we have more disposable income, which means we spend more. We have a more comfortable lifestyle, and our individual well-being is increased – eudemony at its best. If we have an increased well-being, we are more productive, and we contribute to a more productive environment which produces more and earns more as a result. Similarly, in the productive sector, if businesses pay lower levels of taxes, they too have more disposable income, and they can spend more on materials and thus produce more. The more they produce, the more they export, and the more they can supply to the market in general. The more they supply, the more revenue they earn, which can be put back into the business as well as more tax being paid to the government. This is a win–win situation for the whole economy as well as reinforcing the VSM and the decision support system, as algedonic feedback is likely to be positive. Where there is no incentive to be productive, the algedonic feedback is negative, and the economy suffers, whereas if the incentive exists and algedonic feedback is positive, productivity increases, and so does the national economy. Positive thinking makes an economy thrive, and cybernetics proves it.

THE COVID-19 PANDEMIC

This text has been written at the time of the COVID-19 pandemic and its effects specifically in the United Kingdom. It has become evident over the course of 2020 that the UK government was woefully ill-prepared for the pandemic and did not implement anywhere sufficient procedures to protect the staff of the National Health Service (NHS) with PPE to avoid the possibility of contraction of the virus by medical staff. Instead of implementing a seriously flawed national lockdown policy which led to economic and social disaster, and which certainly failed in protecting many people from the harmful effects of the virus, more effort could have been made in heeding the algedonic feedback from the country as a whole and limiting any lockdowns to the areas more severely affected, such as the major populated areas of the country. There appears to have been a failure to procure the right materials and resources and even manage their distribution to the point of need. In the European Union, steps were taken to engage in mass procurement of the appropriate materials and resource, and to use them effectively where required. This is surely a case where cybernetic controls as detailed earlier could have avoided much of this mess and address the issues at the time and place of the point of need. This is equally a case where the VSM would apply at its best and proves that a failure to implement such a policy leaves the government in a state of woeful ineptitude. The essence of the Cybersyn project, namely to transmit the crucial indices of performance in every region to the central point of control by way of electronic links, could have been used to maximum effect in the present scenario in the United Kingdom, but it has not even been considered. Such means of control, i.e. feedback, would enable the authorities to distribute materials and resources anywhere in the country where they are needed. The equivalent system used as part of the Cybersyn project was known as Cybernet (cybernetic network), and it enabled factories up to 3000 miles away from Santiago to transmit performance details on a daily basis by way of telex machines linked to the central computer system in the capital Santiago. Today, this can be achieved by fully electronic transmission of databases, by e-mail or by electronic upload.

The same can be done for economic monitoring and control. It is estimated that the UK economy will shrink by as much as one-third because of the crisis. If the same rationale can be achieved as per the Chilean project, the government would soon realise the adverse effects of the crisis on the UK economy and hence take more tangible steps to address the issues at stake rather than some ethereal strategy which has little substance, i.e. pledging financial support which is so conditional that it might also never have been mooted in the first place. Economic deficiencies need to be reported from all the regions to central national government, as well as to the regional councils, so that appropriate remedial action can be taken in terms of protection of the small businesses that are vital to the regional and national economies.

In an age of crisis, radical control action is necessary. That is why we have national government to ensure that controls are implemented to avoid national economic and social chaos. It is true that the Cybersyn project never had the chance to fully flourish, given the sudden coup d'état that toppled the President and his regime in September 1973 and led to the abandonment of the Cybersyn project. However, the short time during which the Cybersyn project functioned allowed the project's managers to achieve significant results to attempt to stabilise the economy. Would that it could be revived elsewhere when and where it is most needed.

7

Neural Networks, Connectivity, Varieties and the Rationale behind the VSM

Oh I don't know how I got here last night,
And I've a feeling that something ain't right.
It's hard for me to get off the chair,
And I don't know how I'll get down the stair.
Clowns to the left of me, jokers to the right,
Here I am, stuck in the middle with you.

Gerry Rafferty: Stuck in the Middle with You

The song may seem familiar, but it actually highlights a serious problem concerning neural networks and control mechanisms. Just getting off the chair seems to be a big problem for Mr. Rafferty, and he wasn't even on Baker Street at the time!

Humour apart, the issue of neural networks and connectivity figures greatly in terms of corporate management and how it relates to the neural system. This relationship was examined by the Father of Cybernetics, Norbert Wiener in his book on Cybernetics of 1948, where he related the control of the machine to the neural system in animals and humans.

Imagine a normal day in the author's household. I am sitting in front of my computer in my office, typing a text. My wife shouts from downstairs that lunch is ready in her usual way: *Vem comer*, which is Portuguese for "Come and eat". I arise from the chair, and head downstairs (my office occupies what was originally the smallest bedroom in the house). Several neural events have occurred in that short space of time. My visual sensors (eyes) have focused on the computer screen, while my brain transfers that information to my hands and fingers, which operate the computer keyboard and touch the keys in a chronological manner to create a text which appears on the screen. My brain has therefore transmitted signals from one part of the body via its control centre to other parts of my body. These signals are interrupted by my hearing sensors, i.e. my ears, which pick up a spoken message from downstairs. This message takes priority over my visual sensors, as the brain (the control centre) tells me that something else must take priority, i.e. the nourishment of my body. My brain, therefore, tells me to arise from the chair by using my leg muscles, walk down the stairs, and go to the kitchen where my nourishment (food and beverage) awaits. The coffee is especially useful early in the morning!

NEURAL NETWORKS

Neural networks are networks linking the control centre with a variety of functions to ensure that these functions work in an efficient way. They can be either natural (animals and humans) or artificial (machine-based or corporate). The whole purpose is that the control centre (the brain) controls, stimulates, and activates each part of the neural system to work independently but also interdependently, with each element of the structure communicating with the other elements of the structure as required. In terms of cybernetics, they can be used to model complex relationships between inputs and outputs or to find patterns in data as part of the decision-making process. Therefore, my body acts as an integrated neural network, transmitting messages form my brain to other parts of my body on an input/output basis.

The utility of Artificial Neural Network (ANN) models lies in the fact that they can be used to infer a function from observations and also to use it. Unsupervised neural networks can also be used to learn representations of the input that capture the salient characteristics of the input distribution, i.e. the receipt of information as an input, and then generating an output based on the processing of that information. My brain tells me that I need to refresh, so I stop work and relax. This recharges my body (rest) and enables me to sit down and relax. My body has generated a message saying "tiredness", which reaches my brain as an input. The brain then instructs my body to reduce its physical activity as an output message, and my body obeys. Several hours later, a message from my brain tells the body that it is time to wake up again, and the daily physical process starts anew. This all occurs as a series of natural actions and reactions and continues throughout the body's working life.

Neural networks can be used in different fields. These can be biological, physical, mathematical, corporate, and psychological. Their commonality is that they all cover the essence of control mechanisms over different elements, all of which can be independent and inter-connected. Some of the books *Brain of the Firm* and *Decisions and Control* by the cybernetician Stafford Beer deal with these issues and should be studied in detail to understand the complexities of such issues.

A Simple Neural Network

The relationship between the inputs and outputs is represented by a hidden layer, which can be the brain, in the case of the human body, or an artificial control system, such as a homeostat or an electronic control system. An artificial control system is known as an ANN (Figure 7.1).

ANNs or **connectionist systems** are computing systems vaguely inspired by the biological neural networks that constitute animal brains. Such systems "learn" to perform tasks by considering examples, generally without being programmed with task-specific rules.

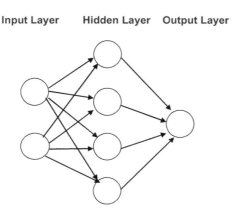

Input Layer   Hidden Layer   Output Layer

FIGURE 7.1
A simple neural approach.

An ANN is based on a collection of connected units or nodes called artificial neurons, which loosely model the neurons in a biological brain. Each connection, like the synapses in a biological brain, can transmit a signal to other neurons. An artificial neuron that receives a signal then processes it and can signal neurons connected to it. Typically, neurons are aggregated into layers. Different layers may perform different transformations on their inputs. Signals travel from the first layer (the input layer), via the hidden layers, to the last layer (the output layer), possibly after traversing the layers multiple times.

ANNs are composed of artificial neurons which retain the biological concept of neurons, which receive input, combine the input with their internal state (*activation*) and an optional *threshold* using an *activation function*, and produce output using an *output function*. The initial inputs are external data, such as images and documents. The ultimate outputs accomplish the task, such as recognising an object in an image. The important characteristic of the activation function is that it provides a smooth, differentiable transition as input values change, i.e. a small change in input produces a small change in output.

A simple diagram of an ANN is as shown in Figure 7.2.

Note that in this case, there is a binary output function, comprising two possibilities, i.e. positive or negative. This amounts to feedback, and

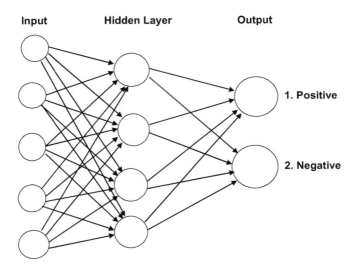

FIGURE 7.2
Artificial neural network.

therefore is seen as reaction to the input information. It can be expressed in a more human form as the brain saying: "I like it", or "I don't like it". In management terms, this can be translated into "successful outcome" or unsuccessful outcome", i.e. failure. This is vital in terms of project management, as it determines the success of a failure of a project depending upon the information provided to the system during the project, e.g. costs, delivery of materials, quality of manufactured products, and customer satisfaction. However, the output layer can be increased, based on decision criteria. For example, rather than a simple positive or negative, there could also be a conditional outcome, initiating the requirement for amendment or rectification prior to resubmission of the data resulting in a positive outcome.

Translating this into corporate strategy, convert the input layers into a set of corporate functions, e.g. finance, procurement, production, logistics, and sales. Each function submits information to the hidden layer, i.e. the control function, representing the brain of the organisation. The hidden layer processes the information provided and emits a set of signals to the output layer, namely either positive or negative, which then emerges as feedback. If the outcome is positive, the process continues to its intended conclusion or objective. If, however, the outcome is negative, the process is either stopped, amended, or rectified as the need requires.

The ANN approach and structure can also be applied to a risk assessment index system (RAIS). The conventional risk matrix combines the elements of likelihood and impact, and categorises the results in a 5×5 composite risk matrix, as follows.

The **composite risk matrix** works on the basis of two factors: likelihood and impact. Each factor is graduated in the form of five levels, ranging from:

Likelihood: 1=very unlikely to 5=highly likely

Impact: 1=minimal to 5=critical

Multiplying these factors together, we derive a scale of 1(1×1)−25 (5×5).

These scales then equate as follows to form the **composite risk index (CRI)**:

1–8 (low);

9–16 (medium);

17–25 (high), and are colour-coded as in the following.

They are then arranged in the 5×5 risk matrix as shown in the following.

The 5×5 method can be used where data is available or a good degree of judgement can be applied to estimates of the frequency and consequences of each hazardous event in the form of a simplified matrix. This risk ranking approach allows for a normal level of accuracy and consistency in the risk estimates that can be obtained.

Note: The size of the matrix and the factor difference in frequency and consequence rankings can be altered to give the best ranges to suit a particular organisation's operation.

This solution works for any factor difference (two, five, ten, one hundred, etc.) providing both the frequency and consequence ranking estimates separated by the same factor (Figure 7.3).

The term ALARP means As Low As Reasonably Possible, and refers to the concept or reducing any perceived risk to the minimum level of risk that can be achieved. These CRI numerical levels and codes are used in the risk register, to show the levels of risk for each column, namely **L** (low), **M** (medium), and **H** (high).

A study by Hossein Sabzian, Ehsan Kamrani, Seyyed Mostafa, and Seyyed Hashemi of the Department of Progress Engineering, Iran University of Science and Technology, Tehran, Iran, into the application of a neural network to the Pharmaceutical Industry used the neural network

	I M P A C T				
LIKELIHOOD ↓	MINIMAL (1)	LOW (2)	MODERATE (3)	HIGH (4)	CRITICAL (5)
VERY LIKELY (5)	5	10	15	20	25
REGULAR (4)	4	8	12	16	20
FREQUENT (3)	3	6	9	12	15
INFREQUENT (2)	2	4	6	8	10
VERY UNLIKELY (1)	1	2	3	4	5

COLOUR CODES AND LEVELS:

1-8: LOW (ALARP)
9-16: MEDIUM
17-25: HIGH

SIMPLIFIED:

GREEN - LOW (1-8)
ORANGE - MEDIUM (9-15)
RED- HIGH (17-25)

FIGURE 7.3
Risk matrix.

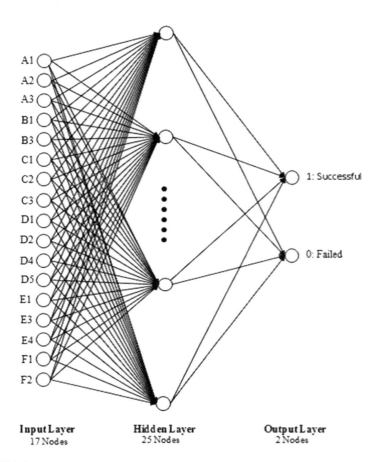

FIGURE 7.4
Artificial neural network.

structure in the context of a RAIS to determine how each level of risk could influence the viability or success of a specific project, which, in the case of the study, applied to the pharmaceutical sector. However, the same reasoning can be applied in any commercial sector, as the overall structure applies to most corporate disciplines. First, a table is created of all the pertinent risks associated with the project, as shown in Figure 7.4.

The ANN proposed by the study is illustrated in Figure 7.1. Note that all the factors detailed in Table 7.1 appear as neurons in the input layer. All of these contribute to the signals passed via the hidden layer to the output layer, comprising two outcomes, namely positive and negative, thus denoting the success or failure of the project.

TABLE 7.1

Risk definitions table

Risk Contents	Risk Variables
A: R & D risks	A1:The financial resources availability
	A2:Capable human resources
	A3:Knowledge resources
B: Technical risks	B1:Technical maturity
	B3:Technology advantage
C: Production risks	C1:The standardisation degree of the production tools
	C2:The standardisation degree of the production process
	C3:The supply capability of the raw material
D. Marketing risks	D1:Market prospects
	D2:Substitute products
	D4:Product competitiveness
	D5:Possibility of new entrants
E. Management risks	E1:The degree of managers' technical competencies
	E3:The scientific weights of decisions
	E4:The quality of managers' behaviour
F. Environmental risks	F1:The quality of conformation to cultural norms
	F2:The degree of governmental support

Note that the Marketing Risk section bears a great resemblance to Porter's Theory of the Five Forces.

The ANN would therefore have two possible outcomes; either success or failure, depending upon the impact of the risks detailed in the previous table, and would therefore determine the success or failure of the project concerned.

Application areas of ANNs include nonlinear system identification and control (vehicle control, process control), game-playing and decision-making (backgammon, chess, racing), pattern recognition (radar systems, face identification, object recognition), sequence recognition (gesture, speech, handwritten text recognition), medical diagnosis, financial applications, data mining (or "knowledge discovery in databases"), visualisation, and e-mail spam filtering. This is particularly useful, as it profiles incoming messages against the recipient's security requirements and blocks any messages that do not fit those requirements. From this, it is possible to create a semantic profile of users' interests emerging from pictures trained for object recognition. It also recognises user profiles to the extent that, using user profile characteristics, it filters promotional material perceived as beneficial to the user based on historical purchasing trends and is only amended by way of an algedonic function when the user submits a negative feedback message by clicking on the advertisement and deleting it as no longer applicable. This negative message tells the system that there is a need for rectification, and the system adjusts accordingly.

However, the main application of the neural network for this purpose is the issue of corporate control, and why it is essential for the efficient operation of any organisation. The brain of an organisation is the control centre, and works around a corporate management system. Or at least it should. However, the corporate structure of many organisations works on an ad hoc basis, only responding to adverse events as and when they happen, often with the result that there is no control system in place to anticipate these issues, and the corporate system falls apart. The COVID-19 crisis of 2020 has shown how most Western systems have been unable to cope with the rapid spread of the virus and have virtually collapsed as a result. This is where contingency planning is a wonderful thing, as companies that have emergency structures in place, including distance-based communication and operations, have been able to react in a positive way to the virus and the governmental lockdown policies without major upheavals. Elsewhere, panic has struck, and much economic damage has been incurred as a result (Figure 7.5).

In order for the whole system to operate properly, there has to be a full interconnected relationship between the sensory elements and the motor elements, as illustrated in Stafford Beer's book *Brain of the Firm*, page 143. The diagram is as shown in Figure 7.5.

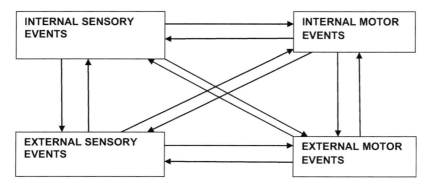

FIGURE 7.5
Sensory and motor interconnectivity.

Connectivity and communication are vital in this process. It is pointless having a neural network if the various elements involved cannot communicate with each other. Let us imagine a scenario where a part of the human body is impaired. This compromises the efficiency and smooth-running of the body as a whole. Convert this into the supply chain. For whatever reason, a manufacturing company cannot receive supplies from its suppliers or (as in the case of the coronavirus pandemic) does not have the personnel available to manage the supply chain process. The company will cease to function properly and runs the risk of complete collapse. Not only does the manufacturing company suffer, but so too do its customers.

Beer points out that every corporate management (of the body or the organisation) must maintain continuous compatibility over all six couplings of these four major areas of concern in order to function correctly. "Sensory" means awareness or perception, and "Motor" means movement, action, or activity. Motor-based activities therefore depend on sensory activities to operate. A gas-measuring instrument, for example a blow-out preventer on an offshore oil drilling platform, uses a series of sensors to detect the sudden upward movement of oil or gas and deploys the prevention valves to prevent an explosion or a sudden egress of oil or gas, thus safeguarding the drilling operations. It was a failure of these sensors in the blow-out preventer on the offshore platform "Deepwater Horizon" in the Gulf of Mexico that caused the explosion, which ultimately destroyed the platform. In the case of the tragic and disastrous explosions on the "Piper Alpha" platform in the Northern North Sea in July 1988, the removal of the control valve in a pipe facilitating the transmission of gas from the subsea wellhead to the platform itself led to the sudden surge in gas and the resulting explosion which ripped through the platform and ultimately destroyed it. In both cases, these were tragedies which could have been avoided, had the correct sensory procedures been maintained. This implies the need for constant connectivity between all four elements if the whole structure is to function properly. The brain therefore controls all these links and connectivities (Figure 7.6).

Let us now consider a series of elements, all independent and indeed dissimilar, in that they all constitute different functions and have different properties. However, they are all part of the same overall entity. In the human body, these could be arms, legs, toes, fingers, and internal organs such as the heart, bladder, liver, kidneys, and arteries. They all work independently of each other but are coordinated by the brain to work

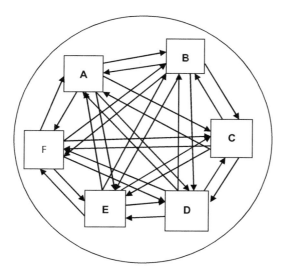

FIGURE 7.6
Hub and spoke network.

interdependently, as each element supports and is supported by the others. This can be shown in Figure 7.5.

This diagram is called the **systematic assemblage of dissimilars** and is a development of the assemblage of dissimilars. It can be found in Stafford Beer's book *Decision and Control*. This assemblage becomes a **dynamic system**, in that not only does it exist, but it operates and actually does things. Not only are the six elements coherent, and their relationship patterned, but they are unified in a definitive whole, i.e. the entity itself as represented by the circle enclosing them. They are unique, in that they exist as sub-entities, and yet they are interlinked as part of the whole entity. Their dynamism functions as an interdependent set of operational activities, where each element functions within itself, but also as a part of the whole unified entity. The link between each sub-entity is reciprocal, represented by arrows in each direction between the entities. They constitute the variety of the assemblage (i.e. the unit as a whole), and this is represented in mathematical terms as

$$[n(n-1)]/2, \text{where}$$

n represents the number of sub-entities, $n-1$ represents the number of sub-entities connected to a single sub-entity, and the division by 2 represents the single unified link between each sub-entity, as the link is reciprocal, represented by the arrows in each direction. Thus, for the purpose of this exercise, the variety of the assemblage enclosed in the circle is:

$$[6(6-1)]/2 = (6 \times 5)/2 = 30/2 = \mathbf{15}.$$

The variety represents the total set of sub-entities within the full corporate entity. Control over this entity is defined by Ross Ashby's Law of Requisite Variety, which states that the control over the varieties can only be obtained if the variety of the controller (or control mechanism), and consequently all the parts of the controller or control mechanism, must AT LEAST be as great as the variety of the situation to be controlled. In cybernetics, the number of distinguishable items, i.e. the sub-entities within the total entity, is called the "variety". However, the other aspect of the dynamic system is that it is susceptible to and capable of change. Rather than remaining inflexible, it can operate under a series of changes, depending upon how radical and far-reaching these changes are. Some change is good for an organisation, especially where the organisation makes significant advances as a result. Such change would result in positive feedback, which, from previous chapters, states that the implemented change or adaptation has resulted in greater efficiency and satisfaction, thus enhancing the venture.

However, the greater the number of entities within the framework, the greater the likelihood of uncontrollable complexity. Suppose there were 40 sub-entities within the framework. There would therefore be

$$40 \times 39 = \mathbf{1560}$$

communications at any time, which means that the risk of a breakdown in the system is far higher. It would also mean that the control over all these varieties would have to be far more complex and manageable, which then enters the realms of complex electronic ANNs, as well as additional checks and balances to ensure efficiency and continuity at all times. The challenge is to ensure that all the sub-entities concerned operate at equal efficiencies alongside each other at all times and maintain that efficiency throughout.

The other scenario is the hub-and-spoke network, where the central activity relies on the spoke function for supply by its satellites, each of which are not inter-connective, i.e. they do not communicate with each

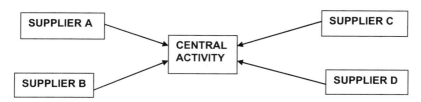

FIGURE 7.7
Supplier hub-and-spoke structure.

other but only communicate with the central hub. This is especially true of companies involved in the supply chain, where each supplier functions completely independently from all other suppliers. The structure can be represented as shown in Figure 7.7.

In this case, there is no inter-connectivity between suppliers, and hence if a problem occurs between the central hub and one specific supplier, there is no effect upon the connectivity between the hub and the other suppliers. The rectification is required solely for the problem concerning the single supplier. However, if the problem is insurmountable, such as bankruptcy or other functional problem with the supplier, replacement suppliers must be found. This is an issue which relates to supply chain risk management, is a problem experienced on a regular basis, and requires a strategy of maintaining a contingency with regard to access to substitutes, i.e. alternative suppliers.

However, not all change is beneficial, and change caused by adverse externalities can inflict significant damage on the organisation, as in the coronavirus pandemic of 2020. Negative feedback as a result of such change will inform the controller that rectification is required, and that may mean either a need to change operational practices, engage in greater quality management, or restructure either a department or the organisation as a whole. That is, not to say the resistance to change is an ideal solution. During the Industrial Revolution, the so-called "Luddites" tried to resist advances in technology, as they feared losses of jobs, but in time that resistance waned as the inevitable happened and the new technology was progressively embraced by the industrial sector benefitting from it. Similarly, the container revolution met with fierce resistance form the dockworkers who vehemently opposed it, fearing extensive job losses. However, containerisation was here to stay, and although it resulted in many docks being closed as a result of an inability to adapt to the changes, new port facilities emerged which led to a much more efficient form of vessel loading and unloading on a global scale.

Economic downturns, more aggressive governmental fiscal policies, sudden technological change, or even Porter's Five Forces, can cause adverse effects on any organisation. It is the ability and capacity of the organisation to adapt to sudden or progressive change that influences the ability of the company to remain viable.

Let us consider the entity as a corporate entity such as a manufacturing company. Within this company, we have several sub-entities, or departments, namely

- production;
- quality control;
- finance;
- sales;
- procurement;
- inventory; and
- logistics.

i.e. 7 in all. Using the aforementioned formula, we derive the variety of assemblage in this case as being 21, i.e. $(7 \times 6) / 2 = 42/2 = \mathbf{21}$. Any control mechanism would have to account for all these possibilities, hence the application of Ashby's Law of Requisite Variety.

We also have the Board of Directors, i.e. the control mechanism, which could loosely be described as the "Brain of the Company". We also have a computer system linking all these sub-entities through a corporate database system known as ERP (enterprise resource planning). The ERP system contains data pertaining to each department and provides data-based information to the Board. However, it does not control the organisation as a whole. That is left to the interpretation of the database figures by the directors and hence their referral of these data to the overall Board for consideration and decision-making. However, this does not amount to a control mechanism, as it does not directly rectify anomalies or shortcomings generated by negative feedback form the department concerned, which a cybernetic system based on the viable systems model (VSM) would. Databases do just that; they store data in a common base. On its own, those data are useless, as it tells no stories. Use an interpretative or even statistical form of analysis, including the Six Sigma approach, and you derive a much more powerful story.

It can therefore be deduced that this same approach using the VSM can be applied to the sub-entities themselves at a microlevel.

Finance includes

- accounts payable;
- accounts receivable;
- credit control;
- budgets; and so on.

Sales may include

- domestic;
- Europe;
- Middle East;
- Far East;
- North America;
- South America; and
- Africa.

Procurement may include

- raw materials;
- components/sub-assemblies;
- imports;
- services; and so on.

To a degree, externalities can affect much of this structure. Supply and demand, competition, import duties and taxes, quality standards, compliance requirements, authorised economic operator (AEO) status, customer demands, and government policy can all place additional requirements on the organisational and operational structure, as well as requiring the organisation to adapt to such influences and changes.

There has to be an internal synergy within each department for it to function properly, as well as the inter-departmental synergy required to operate the company in a fully coordinated manner. If a department cannot function properly, this will ultimately have an adverse effect on the functionality of the organisation/company as a whole. In this respect, there is no priority or special status for any company department, as all these elements must function efficiently at the same level of quality in order to ensure the smooth and efficient functioning of the company or organisation as a whole. Indeed, this functional process is biblical. The apostle St. Paul writes in his first letter to the Corinthians, Chapter 12, that "The **body** is a unit, though it is made up of **many parts**; and though all its **parts** are **many**, they form **one body**…As it is, there are **many parts**, but **one body**".

Syntegration

Gunter Nittbaur of Malik Management, St Gallen, Switzerland, conducted an extensive review of Stafford Beer's works, including his final book on the subject of team syntegrity, effectively the study of cybernetic synergy. Over some 40 years almost up to his death in 2002, Stafford Beer published a steady stream of seminal books and papers in which he applied cybernetic science to organisational problems. In all of these, he explained underlying principles, developed new theories, and recorded a great variety of practical applications. In his last book, published in 1994, entitled *Beyond Dispute: The Invention of Team Syntegrity*, he presented a cybernetic approach to knowledge management within large groups of about 30 people, called *syntegration*, composed of the words *synergy* and *integration*. Syntegration is a structured, non-hierarchical process for highly effective and efficient dialogue that leads to much faster, much more informed outcomes and aligns people behind the resulting decisions, messages, and action plans with a high chance for implementation. Since its invention, this powerful method has been very successfully applied more than 200 times in the organisation of normative, directional, and strategic planning and other creative decision processes. The underlying model is a regular icosahedron. This has 30 struts, each of which represents a person. Each of the 12 edges represents a topic that is being discussed. An internal network of interactions is created by a set of iterative protocols. A group organised like this is an ultimate statement of participatory democracy, since each role is indistinguishable from any other. There is no hierarchy, no top, no bottom, no sideways. Beer illustrates how continued dynamic interaction between persons causes ideas and resolutions to hum around the sphere, which reverberates into a kind of group consciousness. Mathematical analysis of the structure shows how the process is determined by the even spread of synergy. The aim of this chapter is to present to managers and their advisors a new planning method that captures the native genius of the organisation in a non-political and non-hierarchical way. That produces the best possible results in the shortest possible time from the largest possible number of people, by making optimised use of the knowledge these people have. It is, to all intents and purposes, knowledge management and synergy at its best.

This icosahedron model has no hierarchy, no top, no bottom, and no sideways and can be regarded as a highly pragmatic and innovative tool for knowledge sharing, consensus building, and conflict resolution whenever a large number of people are involved, i.e. in business, in politics, and in every societal body, panel, or committee. Hence, the syntegration can serve as an effective driving belt for the transfer of Agora-style thinking into contemporary planning and decision-making (Figure 7.8).

The Agora was the heart of ancient Athens, the focus of political, commercial, administrative, and social activities; the religious and cultural centres; and the seat of justice. Dating back to the 6th century B.C., the Agora has witnessed countless convocations and uses, reflecting the true meaning of democracy, of governance by the people, which indeed led to the principle of basic socialism, where the people's influence prevailed, a principle seen in the titles of several countries where modern socialism prevails. Politicians, philosophers, and citizens have gathered to discuss issues of common interest and relevance. Dialogues were held, and disputes were fought. But the Greeks were at a huge advantage in comparison with modern day interlocutors as they convened against the background

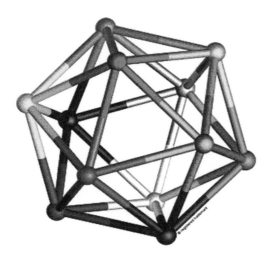

FIGURE 7.8
Synergy Icosahedron.

of a world much less complex than the one which is host to our present global village. Political, economic, and societal systems and their subsystems were by far less interlinked and embedded in each other, whereas the removal of limitations of today's systems and subsystems has become more and more obnoxious and unacceptable.

Complex problems require complex thinking in order to find accurate, holistic, and sustainable solutions. The cybernetician W Ross Ashby proposed in 1952 that only variety can absorb variety; hence, control in a system can only be obtained if the variety of the controller is at least as great as the variety of the system to be controlled. This is a process of logic, as a system cannot be controlled unless the control mechanism takes into account every element of the system that it is controlling. In practice, this requires the integration of the entire knowledge of a system that is concealed in the brains of its members with a minimum amount of time and management. Syntegration therefore offers a highly intelligent design that combines the effectiveness of small groups with the efficiency of large gatherings in terms of knowledge dissemination, as the small group is in effect a subset of the overall large gathering. A major conference or convention always has sub-groups addressing and discussing specific issues, and once the issues have been addressed and decisions have been made, the subset groups reconvene and the outcomes are submitted to the convention as a whole for discussion or approval.

In Beer's Syntegration model, effective communication is implicit in the structure on which the communication is based. It comes into being automatically and necessarily if the syntegration structure is used. The participants in a syntegration (derived from the words synergy and integration) are free to discuss what in their view needs to be discussed. The structure, however, lays down for them who discusses what with whom, when, for how long, and in what role.

The revolutionary idea that Beer had was to use this same structure for efficiency and robustness in communication. He placed the topics for discussion at the 12 vertices of the icosahedron and the people at its 30 struts. With this model, 30 brains are, as it were, networked together in such a way that they operate as one joint brain that is that much more powerful. Each of the topics that relate to an opening question is covered by a group of the optimum size of five people. In this case, the topics are networked via the people, because each person is involved in a number of topics. As well as his or her role as a team member for two topics, each person also performs in two other roles: as critic for two other topics and as observer for four others. This means that each topic is not only discussed by five members but also added to by five critics and observed by up to ten observers.

Prior to the start of a syntegration exercise, an opening question must be formed that represents the issue upon which participants will focus their best thinking, discussion, and debate. An example could be: "What must we do to become a highly efficient and effective organisation and benchmark for our industry?" Indeed, this is one of the primary aims of this overall text. The participants in a syntegration (usually a group of between 15 and 40 people) are typically selected to represent a broad group of stakeholders within an organisation or among organisations. Participants represent different levels within the organisation and can be subject matter experts, leaders, managers, employees, partners, customers, and clients. The participants provide the "requisite variety" and critical mass of individuals necessary to make much more informed decisions.

The syntegration, designed as an intensive workshop of a given timeframe, has no predetermined agenda. The participants themselves set the agenda at the very beginning of the syntegration as no one of the group would be able to define what everybody else finds relevant to discuss in regard to the opening question. This agenda setting requires about half a day and consists of different steps within an *importance filter* that leads the group via brainstorming, marketplace, and consolidation from some hundred individual statements down to 12 key agenda items.

The specific number of topics is important – not too many to lose track of things during the discussions and not too few to underrepresent the complexity of the opening question. Then each participant is being asked to bring these topics into an order of preference against the background of the question to which topics one can contribute the most. Finally, a computer program based on an algorithmic calculation selects among some 10^{40} possibilities of allocation of participants and topics within the icosahedral structure the best option.

Each participant is being assigned member in two topic teams, critic in two other topic teams, and observer in up to four more topic teams. Whereas the members are responsible for their topic and have the task to arrive at clear actions in regard to their topic by the end of the syntegration exercise, the critics are responsible for criticising the content that is being developed by the members and for making the process a self-managing one.

Observers, finally, may not intervene at all during the discussions and may only listen. They play, however, an important role as networkers of knowledge: They take on what is being discussed in the teams they observe and carry the new insights and ideas into their own groups if that information is relevant for the discussions. And, because they are not allowed to speak during the time that they are gathering this information, observers filter their own thoughts and responses instead of speaking them aloud immediately. These different roles of members, critics, and observers ensure that everyone has the same rights and opportunities to participate in the debate: positional, hierarchical, or rhetorical dominance that prevails in the organisational context and often inhibits equality of thought is not being totally neglected but is being dampened very effectively through the protocol.

When a topic team meets, there is at least one representative of all other 11 topic teams present in the meeting room. This *reverberation* ensures that every thought, every new idea, is being transferred automatically to all other topic teams via the short-term memory of the participants and also via the statements that are being written by trained facilitators who take notes during the discussion, monitor the adherence of the participants to the "rules of the game", and support the group in arriving at clear solutions.

Each group meets for three times during a syntegration exercise with the same constellation of people. In the first meeting, the group defines the status quo in regard to their topic and the relevance for answering the opening question. In the second meeting, the topic teams discuss how the ideal situation would look like and what would be done in a "Greenfield approach". The third meeting of each team finally focuses on the actions: "What do we as Topic Team… propose to the board of directors for implementation"? One run of all 12 topics (which requires usually a full day) is called *iteration*. A syntegration exercise necessarily consists of three iterations because only after each topic team has met for three times and has networked with all other teams, a dissemination of relevant knowledge of some 90% can be realised and the proposed actions fit together like the pieces in a jigsaw.

Results are achieved through a syntegration exercise on four different levels:

- A clear action plan has been developed that integrates the best knowledge of all participants.

- The participants share a strong commitment for implementation of what has been jointly developed.
- The participants are highly networked after a syntegration, team building has occurred.
- Participants learn from each other and better understand the other participants' positions and constraints.

Organisations of any kind face an extremely high internal and external complexity which they need to manage in order to survive in their specific competitive environment. According to W. Ross Ashby, they can only do so if the directive and regulatory mechanisms that are in place can cope with the complexity they need to manage, i.e. if the variety of the management is at least equal to the variety caused by the organisation and its environment. This could be achieved, if the entire knowledge that is available in the organisation were combined. But as a matter of fact, organisations consist of an accumulation of scientists and specialists that have undergone different types of education in different areas and now occupy highly focused niches of expertise within their organisations. The word science has its etymological roots in the Greek prefix ski as in schizophrenia or schism and means to separate or to distinguish. Hence, science itself separates reality into different areas and looks at our world from a mathematical, a biological, a psychological, or a theological point of view. Transferred to the context of organisations, we have a marketing perspective, a sales perspective, a R&D perspective, a quality management perspective, and a customer or supplier perspective But only by integrating the knowledge and experience of these specialists in a way that they can network into one large biological brain, the necessary variety is being assembled that is required in order to manage complex organisations in their complex environments.

- The syntegration method can be applied to all kinds and sizes of organisations regardless of their level of internal competence, communication culture, or industry. Two prerequisites, however, need to be observed in order to make a syntegration exercise a success: The topic of the syntegration, reflected in the opening question, must be of high relevance for the organisation, and the participants must be selected very carefully: Whom do we need for knowledge generation (the experts) and whom do we need for the implementation of the actions proposed (the "drivers").

- Areas of application are commonly: strategy definition or implementation, project kick-off, post-merger integration, change management, or conflict resolution.

Organisations need to make every effort to integrate and to network the knowledge which is available in the organisations, i.e. in the brains of its collaborators. Syntegration can be regarded as an effective catalyst for knowledge generation and dissemination. The methodology raises organisations to a new level of communicative competence and operative effectiveness. It thus opens the door to a new world of competitive advantages achieved by speed, accuracy of targeting, strength of consensus, and organisational intelligence. Thus, syntegration depicts the genetic code of effective communication and epitomises the ideal management team, based on the principle of consensus ad idem.

Organisational Synergy

Let us now consider another sector to which the discipline of synergy can apply, namely the airline/aviation industry.

We have the airlines themselves. These operate on the basis of internal synergy and therefore are subject to the structural disciplines of the VSM. The captain of each passenger aircraft is responsible for the crew and the passengers on board the aircraft, as well as in-flight management, catering, baggage, and fuel. Therefore, there has to be an internal synergy among all concerned on board the aircraft, from the moment that it is loaded at the airport of departure to the time that it is unloaded at the airport of arrival. These would be covered by Systems 1–3 of the VSM. The airline itself is responsible for the smooth operation and management of all its flights and therefore has a duty of care to its stakeholders, including its passengers. Any breakdown in the system, including delayed flights, has a direct knock-on effect on the rest of the operations. Given that a flight delay can be caused by any number of adverse circumstances, the whole of the varietal synergy, from the assemblage to the individual elements of that assemblage, is severely compromised.

There are also the externalities, accounting for System 4 of the VSM. These include, but are not limited to, the following:

- airport management;
- air traffic control;

- runway maintenance;
- flight catering services;
- baggage handling;
- check-in;
- cargo handling;
- aircraft maintenance;
- pushback and apron services; and
- refuelling.

If any of these elements goes wrong, the whole system collapses. This is clearly evident as a result of air traffic controller strikes, baggage handler strikes, and, for that matter, the coronavirus crisis.

System 5 of the VSM controls all the elements above, and applies therefore to not only the functioning of the airline but also the airport itself.

From this, we can deduce that the whole assemblage process, and therefore the application of the VSM, can apply to any sector, whether fully commercial or administrative. The functionality of the VSM revolves around the whole concept of varieties and the extent to which those varieties are taken into account as part of the VSM process. It should be also pointed out that externalities also include the concept of stakeholders. A stakeholder is anyone who has an interest in the venture, project, or operation. Airline passengers are stakeholders. So too are freight forwarders and shippers of goods. Where shareholders have a vested interest in the venture, i.e. for pecuniary gain, stakeholders do not, yet they are still committed to the operation, and ultimately stand to be severely inconvenienced in the event of breakdown or collapse in the system. That said, a passenger who purchases an airline ticket is an investor in the company and therefore expects that he/she will be satisfied by the company's service and performance. The cybernetic approach to the airline industry ensures this expectation.

We can therefore state that the dynamic and varietal assemblage system, as well as the VSM, can apply to the following:

- Direction and management of the organisation as a whole
- Departmental organisation and control
- Inter-departmental organisation and control
- Externalities

- Provision for and monitoring of these externalities
- Overall corporate strategy

All of these elements encompass the management of the organisation, and how it functions and performs. To this extent, the application of management cybernetics to this whole spectrum enables the organisation to function far more efficiently and cost-effectively.

The other factor which can influence the issues detailed above is well tried and tested SWOT (strengths, weaknesses, opportunities, threats) analysis. The SWOT approach enables organisations to assess their own status based on these elements.

Strengths:
- Competence
- Staff awareness
- Internal documented procedures
- Existing control systems
- Quality control
- Previous operational research work carried out
- Facility and ability to adapt to change
- Strong market position
- Operational flexibility
- Use of benchmarks and key performance indicators (KPIs)

Weaknesses:
- Lack of competent staff
- Lack of awareness or education
- Lack of internal procedures
- Lack of internal controls
- Failure to observe externalities
- Resistance to change

Opportunities:
- Adoption of changes to various activities
- Emphasis on quality and control procedures and mechanisms
- Expansion through efficiency
- Investment in new systems and structures
- Use of analysis tools such as cybernetics

Threats:

- Global change
- Competition
- New technology
- Government interference

An organisation which is self-protective, resistant to change, and incapable of adaptation is one which is destined to failure. It is likely not to have any knowledge of analytical tools available, nor is it likely to understand the needs for change or for self-improvement. In many cases, lack of internal control mechanisms results in chaos and eventually breakdown of the organisational structure. Lack of coordination of internal structures means that the integral structure explained earlier will fail because of an inherent lack of synergy. This amounts to an inherent breakdown in internal communication, or even an inherent lack of internal communication in the first place. Many company failures have resulted from a failure to accept any of the above issues. The attitude of "my grandfather did it this way, my father did it this way, and I will do it this way because it hasn't failed yet" is typical of many organisations. This results in a failure to accept changes to the external and internal environment, and the inevitable issue referred to earlier in the book of isolation and inevitable demise.

Business Control

The control of business using cybernetics solutions is of great importance, as long as the business has a self-organising system as part of its strategy. To rely on a laissez-faire approach, i.e. to employ a strategy of unregulated operation, reveals gross inadequacies and anomalies. The paradox that emerges is that even in a free market economy, where regulation is kept to a minimum, controls still remain necessary, and in this respect, a cybernetic approach is very definitely required to ensure management and operational control of the organisation, whether it is industry, business, administration, or government. Indeed, government in itself needs a degree of regulation, in order to render it fully accountable to the electorate. And yet, government and its administration are self-perpetuating and are reluctant to adapt to global changes, despite their relevance to national administrations. In this respect, regulation flies in the face of democracy, and the two definitely do not mix. Command economies differ radically from free economies, as shown by the Cybersyn experiment in Chile under the Marxist administration of President Salvador Allende between 1971 and 1973. Cybersyn was designed to control and regulate Chilean industry and, to a degree, achieved significant success until its abandonment following the military coup d'état which toppled the Allende regime in September 1973.

The paradox of regulation versus free market can be easily resolved once an understanding of management cybernetics has been obtained. The use of management cybernetics controls the enterprise, not the national economy, although the enterprise contributes to the economic well-being of the nation. After all, an enterprise which is better controlled and regulated from within is more able to prosper based on the internal controls which maintain its stability, on the grounds that its viability and commercial stability is enriched by an internal regulatory approach. Homeostats, i.e. machines capable of adapting to a given environment, which comprise a large number of inter-related sub-systems, will not work unless they are richly and comprehensively interconnected. An example of this is the homeostat constructed by the cybernetician W. Ross Ashby for Barnwood House Hospital at Gloucester in 1948. It comprised a set of control units, with inputs, feedback, and magnetically driven, water-filled potentiometers. It illustrated his law of requisite variety, automatically adapting its configuration to stabilise the effects of any disturbances introduced into the system by way of rectification of negative feedback. It was, in effect, a synthetic brain designed by man, as reported in a *Time* magazine of 1949.

It is very possible to superimpose a hierarchical organisational structure upon a self-organising system, as this structure will serve to exercise control over the organisation as a whole by way of imposing a control regime over the organisational structure itself. This gives rise to the cybernetic validity of a control system based on the objective assessment of effective results based on feedback which can be analysed and used for the purposes of positive regulation. This also means that an experienced manager needs to work on the basis that the system to which he has become conditioned actually does work, or at very least to think outside the box, in other words, not to simply accept that which he has been told in the past but to analyse for himself how a beneficial regulatory system actually does work. This is why many management consultants or new company CEOs or chairmen have been too keen to destroy a centralised management structure in favour of branch-autonomous structures, which cannot communicate with each other and therefore cannot be controlled by a centralised structure. This is why there is the inherent need for horizontal or vertical management. Vertical management works on the basis of a hierarchical structure, where the control system emanates from the top and works towards the bottom, with feedback emanating from the bottom upwards. A horizontal structure, however, works on the basis of an assumption that organisations working in parallel will adopt the same control structures throughout the network. However, business experience shoes that this is not the case, as similar enterprises function in different ways depending upon their national location, even if they are ultimately controlled by the same overall global corporate headquarters. Multinational corporations such as Procter & Gamble, Johnson & Johnson, Mondelez, General Motors, and Ford have a different modus operandi depending upon the location of the national representative offices and production plants. It is impossible to apply the regulatory environment and regime of one country to another several thousands of miles away. The US ethic, for example, would never work in China or Europe, as the culture of each country is entirely different from the other, although in countries such as Japan and South Korea, the US culture runs in parallel to the local cultures. In Europe and the United Kingdom, there is more sympathy towards the US culture, whereas the Latin world insists upon the prevalence of its own ethics. However, in cases where the organisational structure is limited to one country in the form of vertical integration, the chances of total control are far greater owing to a commonality of structural and control regimes. Simply assuming that any semi-autonomous branch of an organisation based in one country will operate exactly in the same way as a branch in another country is very unwise, and at worst pernicious, as this assumption cannot be made.

The richly interconnected homeostat, i.e. an entity which self-corrects and self-adapts according to prevalent needs, thus constituting the self-organising system, must take priority as the only means of obtaining any form of coherence, as it is designed to maintain this self-organisational structure and equip itself against any form of threat or unexpected change. Secondly, the hierarchical system which is superimposed upon it, i.e. the chain of command, is designed to elicit quick responses in the event of negative feedback or any form of breakdown or failure, e.g. problems with production or shortfalls in inventory or delays in inward delivery of raw materials which might affect production schedules.

It is fairly evident, even to the layman, that the purpose of the exercise is to have an enterprise which can attain a goal or a series of objectives which are formulated, or planned, in advance, hence the importance of forward and contingency planning, i.e. the notion of Plan A plus a back-up Plan B in the event of adverse conditions or unexpected problems. This is based on organisational design. The purpose of the exercise is to modify the structure without destroying the self-organisational properties of the system. This is illustrated by the cartoon of the garden swing, where the user simply wanted a piece of wood with two rope supports attached to the branch of a tree. The designers ended up chopping half the tree to bits to come up with an unusable complex design which would never have worked. And the moral of the tale is... keep it simple! That makes it evident that the goals achieved, seemingly by accident, which were the ones only recognisable after the event, turned out to be the goals that were originally envisaged by the management – this is exactly what was supposed to happen. Well, we told you so! Isn't hindsight wonderful?! In the world of policy-making, the expert manager, be it government minister or company director, knows intuitively that this is what he is supposed to do. The paradox being, of course, as vividly expressed in the film *The Italian Job*, as expressed vividly by Michael Caine, that "You were only supposed to blow the bl**dy doors off!!!". And since the whole of the mechanism by which he operates is verbal, i.e. unwritten, inter-personal, and political, he is able to achieve his objectives, i.e. do as I say, not do as I do. The global coronavirus pandemic illustrates this very well. Written directives have been few and far between as policy has been implemented "on the hoof", with decisions made almost on an *ad hoc* basis. The only problem is that personal charisma and presence often holds sway over objective rationale and that personal politics rules the roost. The classic example of this was Germany in the 1930s, when the personal charisma of Adolf Hitler weighed over rationale and ultimately swept him to power as Chancellor in 1933. Unfortunately, this can get in the way of objective and rational thinking. Personal loyalties often conflict with clear thinking and decision-making, which can severely compromise the route to operational efficiency. This is the way the chairman wants it, so this is the way in which it will be done, regardless of whether it is the best way or not. It is this ethic (if that is what one can call it) that so often clouds the intention of optimising the system by way of tried and tested methodology. To this extent, internal politics often overrules logic.

A classic case of this was the British passenger airliner VC10, which was designed to the specifications of a combination of the RAF and BOAC, which is largely why it never sold in large numbers elsewhere in the world. Its intended predecessor was the Vickers V1000/VC7, designed as a four-engine jet transport, which was cancelled at the point of an advanced stage of production of the prototype in November 1955, largely owing to spiralling costs and doubts by the airline BOAC and the Royal Air Force as to its ultimate suitability and value for money. The VC10 was primarily designed as a commercial airliner to operate in "hot and high" conditions, where air was less dense and runways were somewhat shorter than elsewhere, and were thus less suitable for airliners such as the Boeing 707, which required denser air and longer runways. These specifications did not necessarily meet the needs of most other airlines, despite the fact that the aircraft turned out to be very successful in its operational performance and capacity, as well as being a very attractive aircraft to observe. It also satisfied the needs of the Royal Air Force, which used the airliner as its main troop and VIP transport, even to the extent that the RAF VC10s became the official air transport for Prime Ministers and members of the Royal Family. This gave rise to the conundrum of the airline tail wagging the aircraft designer dog, or vice versa. The US aircraft company Boeing may have had several airlines in mind, including United Airlines, when it designed the famous and big-selling Boeing 707, 737, and 777 airliners, but it was not governed by the specifications of these airlines. The aircraft were designed for the needs of those airlines wanting a high-density long-range passenger aircraft, and they got such an aircraft. Again, we have the paradox between supply-push versus demand-pull. And we safely return to inter-departmental synergy, this time the conflict between design and sales departments. As Henry Ford is reputed to have said about his Model-T Ford automobile, "You can have any colour you want, as long as it is black". In government, each ministry is set up and arranged to deal with a specific aspect of affairs, as if it could cope with that aspect on its own in a vacuum, whereas in reality, no one single aspect can be supervised without the collaboration of all the other departments, hence regular cabinet meetings to determine a *consensus ad idem*, in a way a form of syntegration, although in both government and the corporate entity, there will always be a defined leadership, i.e. a Managing Director/ Chairman, a President, or a Prime Minister. In industry, this is why we have directors of production, sales, finance, engineering, and research, for whom the same argument applies. They each have their own departmental responsibility, and work independently of the others, but convene regularly at board meetings to determine collective company policy and overall decision-making. In this sense, the company directorate equals the government cabinet in its role.

However, the most elementary analysis of self-organising systems shows that the interactions obtainable at this highest level, if they are not mirrored and executed all the way down to basic operator level, are powerless to produce the cohesion and collective will of the entire enterprise which is essential to its efficiency and ultimately its prosperity. Cybernetic research shows that the totality of the organisation needs to be composed of building blocks that can be referred to as *quasi-independent (semi-autonomous) domains.* This is the compromise located between de facto independent domains (decentralisation) and no independent domains at all (centralisation). These domains have a degree of local autonomy and may claim to be entirely autonomous. However, they are not autonomous in the metalanguage (overall embracing language) of the whole system, which monitors their activities according to the laws of cybernetics. This approach is true of local and regional government as opposed to national government, especially in a national federal system, where regional government holds a degree of autonomy, as in the case of the United States or Canada, for example in issues of taxation, but still defers on national policy to the central government in Washington DC or Ottawa respectively. In the United Kingdom, Scotland may have its own quasi-national government at Holyrood, Edinburgh, but still must defer to national UK government in Westminster on most major issues.

The same is true of commercial enterprises. Each department exercises its own degree of semi-autonomy, but as a corporate venture, it still defers to the board of directors for overall policy and decision-making. If this overall command structure did not exist, the enterprise would explode and collapse. This is not to say that the only answer is state control, although, in the case of several UK train companies, their inability to exercise complete autonomy, especially in the case of the inefficient running of their networks and resulting bankruptcy, resulted in their takeover by national government in the form of the Department for Transport. Two cases of this were East Coast Trains, originally run by a consortium of Stagecoach and Virgin, and Northern Rail. The issues became so acute that in each case the UK government stepped in and effectively nationalised them both, with East Coast becoming LNER (London North Eastern Railway) in its new government-run guise. As at mid-2020, whether the nationalisation of Northern Trains will result in a new operating name only time will tell. Certainly, the introduction of new, more efficient trains on many routes has, to a degree, enhanced the network. However, cosmetic surgery does not necessarily change the interior. There is still the question of the overall efficiency of the rail network, and whether this will radically improve. You can introduce as many new trains as you wish, but if they are still delayed by lack of train crews or line congestion then little has changed. In this way, any attempt to achieve overall control in a centralised way would turn the interaction of localities into a self-defeating mess and is inherently obvious when the control mechanism goes woefully wrong. Indeed, under such conditions, any attempt at cosmetic improvement might as well not have been carried out at all.

Therefore, the design of the control that is required for commercial enterprises lacks hat could be deemed to be a central nervous system, as would be found, for example, in the human brain, hence the need for some kind of neural system. What can be seen concerning control "systems" in industry is in reality a collection of separate and specialist functions. These can include the following:

- Order processing
- Sales allocation
- Demand forecasting (often susceptible to demand amplification because of inaccurate forecasting or time-series analysis)
- Forward planning
- Procurement
- Plant programming
- Machine loading
- Stock control (inventory)
- Order progressing
- Production control
- Dispatch sequencing
- Just-in-time management
- Financial control
- Information technology
- Invoice processing
- Cost accounting

- Budget control
- Quality control

In reality, each of these activities, however non-sensically, could lay claim to being the most pivotal and important activity in the company, as well as being the key mechanism of managerial control. The reality is that although they may independently, they still rely on each other and collaboration with each other to contribute to the central management of the enterprise. However, there is no common or substantial thread, similar to a central nervous system in a human body, to all these activities. Instead, they are characteristic of a central control system which does not actually exist (Figure 7.9).

However, whichever activity is being addressed, a simple cybernetic process can be used for each function. This refers back to a previous chapter, but if we revisit it, we arrive at the following diagram, which represents a first-order cybernetic process, i.e. the control mechanism over an internal corporate process in the management context.

Performing work, monitoring performance, and taking corrective action are all part of the delivery process. The output is completed objectives. In some ways, Figure 7.9 relates to the Six Sigma principle of **DMAIC**, which is

Define
Measure
Analyse
Implement
Control

However, the cybernetic principle expands these areas, as it defines the control mechanism more precisely, and implements a more solid means of continuous control, in the form of monitoring.

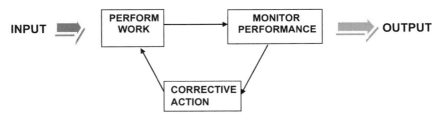

FIGURE 7.9
Project workflow.

The delivery process itself is also an area which requires significant cybernetic control. Let us take a look at this process in more detail.

The delivery phase of a small project may comprise only one stage; the delivery phase of a programme may comprise only one tranche. Most projects and programmes will comprise multiple stages or tranches that are conducted in serial or parallel.

Whatever the context, managing each stage or tranche will follow a basic "Plan, Do, Check, Act" cycle, sometimes known as the Shewhart cycle, named after its proponent, Dr. Walter Shewhart, and developed by W. Edwards Deming.

In the delivery process:

- "Plan" becomes "authorise work"
- "Do" becomes "coordinate and monitor progress"
- "Check" becomes "update and communicate"
- "Act" becomes "corrective action"

The goals of delivering a project or programme are then to

- delegate responsibility for producing deliverables to the appropriate people;
- monitor the performance of the work and track against the delivery plans;
- take action where necessary to keep work in line with plans;
- escalate issues and replan if necessary;
- accept work as it is completed; and
- maintain communications with all stakeholders.

The cycle will be repeated for the duration of each stage or tranche until a boundary or limit is reached, or the project is finally completed. The management team will operate the cycle within their defined authority, i.e. while the work remains within agreed tolerances. If tolerances are exceeded or are predicted to be exceeded, then issues will be escalated to the sponsor for guidance, supportive action, or, in extreme cases, a decision on the continued justification of the work. In some ways, this process is also carried out as part of the statistical process control (SPC) methodology, although the principle of SPC is that a process must be stopped if it exceeds the upper or lower action limits (UAL/LAL) at any stage in the process. The process

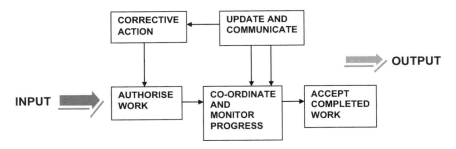

FIGURE 7.10
Advanced project workflow.

can only restart if and when the problems are rectified and the recorded data remain within the defined and predetermined limits.

The plan, do, check, act cycle and the activities described below are shown as discrete steps in a workflow. In reality, a project or programme manager's day will involve elements of all of these activities that are connected in ways not shown in the diagram, and the delivery process can be illustrated thus in Figure 7.10.

Authorise Work

Much of the planning work will actually have been completed in the definition process (if this is the beginning of the delivery phase) or in the boundaries process (if this is the second or subsequent stage or tranche), represented by the output.

At this point the previous planning will need to be expanded or enacted depending upon the context. For example:

- A stage in a smaller project may be broken down into work packages that comprise a number of products. These work packages may then be assigned to teams of internal resources.
- A stage in a larger, more complex project may be divided into sub-projects that follow technical specialities, such as groundwork or electrical services in a building project. These sub-projects may be performed by external organisations under contractual terms with associated formal initiation.
- In a programme tranche, the delivery will include projects and business-as-usual work. The authorise work activity at programme

level could then equate, for example, to the identification process at project level. The project team will then be given a project brief from which to continue the rest of the project life cycle.

The exact nature of this activity will vary considerably according to the context of the work. However, the basic principles are the same: the stage or tranche is broken down into manageable sections which are documented and delegated to individuals, groups, or suppliers.

Delegation requires that those who are being assigned the work are clear about the objectives and how the work will be coordinated and monitored. Clear specifications for the delegated work should be accompanied by relevant extracts from the governance documents to ensure that those managing and performing the work understand how the relationship will operate.

Coordinate and Monitor Progress

On all but the smallest of projects, different individuals and teams will be working on different aspects of the project or programme at any one time. This requires coordination to ensure that different work packages or sub-projects within a project, or projects within a programme, can coexist. It may be that two teams in a project need to work in a single physical space; two projects in a programme may require common, but limited resources; two work packages may impact on a common deliverable.

The management team may be able to avoid many potential conflicts in the initial planning and in the way they authorise work. However, there will always be a lot of work conducted in parallel. The greater the complexity, the more closely the work needs coordination from the management team. Each delivery team will provide the management team with regular progress reports but must also have clear lines of communication that allow them to escalate issues or ask for guidance at any point.

Progress information may be in the form of regular time-based progress reports or periodic event-based progress reports. The management team must consolidate these reports to understand the overall status of the project or programme. In the process of that consolidation, the management team will need to feed information back to delivery teams where they may be affected by progress in other parts of the project or programme. This activity will utilise many of the specific steps of delivery procedures such as assessing change requests, implementing risk responses, engaging with stakeholders, and so on.

Depending upon the complexity of the work, the responsibility for monitoring and consolidating progress may be given to a separate support function to free time for the management and delivery teams and probably ensure greater consistency in reporting.

Update and Communicate

This element constitutes the feedback that is an integral part of cybernetic control. Documentation will be updated on a regular basis as specified by the relevant management plans. Some documents, such as schedules, will be very dynamic with frequent updates. Others, for example, the business case, will be reviewed at significant points such as stage or tranche boundaries.

Of course, the routine update and review documentation should be supplemented by ad hoc reviews governed by the experience and judgement of the management team. For example, if there is a significant combination of schedule, risk, and financial updates that cumulatively impact the business case, the management team must not wait until the next routine review.

Progress will be routinely communicated with stakeholders in accordance with the communications plan. Where any aspect of the work exceeds, or is predicted to exceed, the agreed tolerances, then this must be escalated to the sponsor.

Corrective Action

Some degree of corrective action will be happening all the time. This is the essence of coordinating work and may be as simple as rescheduling meetings or assigning a task to another person due to illness.

This corrective action activity is about more significant action constituting a deviation from the baseline plan. The range of examples of what constitutes corrective action is vast and how it is handled is primarily down to the experience and judgement of the management team.

Two defining characteristics are as follows:

- **Which aspects of the work does the corrective action involve?**
  The action needed may relate to any or all of the fundamental project components in any combination. It could be very tangible in that

a product has failed its quality control test (scope), material delivery is delayed (schedule), or resources have been underestimated (resource and cost). It could be less tangible where, for example, new risks have been identified that significantly increase the overall risk, or influential stakeholders have changed their position with regard to the work.

It is important that the way the fundamental components of the work inter-relate is understood. How does a need to discard a product and rebuild affect the schedule; how does a change in schedule affect risks and resource availability; which stakeholders are affected and how; what are the effects of the revised schedule on the funding arrangements? – and so it goes on.

An understanding of these complex inter-relationships comes from thorough planning and maintenance of the delivery documentation. In short, if the work was inadequately planned, it will be very difficult to control.

- **How severe or radical is the corrective action?**

  The first and most obvious distinction for severity comes from the tolerances set out in the management plans. When delivery plans are updated with progress, they should be able to not just identify that tolerances have been exceeded but predict that tolerances may be exceeded at some point in the future.

  If appropriate techniques have been defined and implemented, then escalation should occur on the basis that an issue is likely rather than an issue has occurred. The corrective action is therefore something that can be discussed and agreed between the manager and sponsor through the escalation part of the process before implementation.

  Even with the best planning and control procedures, it is always possible that events will occur that had not been foreseen or anticipated. The failure of a vital piece of equipment, delivery delays, or the insolvency of a supplier can have an immediate and unpredictable effect, and both can amount to supply chain risk. In these cases, the corrective action needed may involve significant replanning. Delivery plans may not just need to be adjusted but reworked. These are referred to as exception plans and are simply new delivery plans that show how issues will be overcome. Exception plans should be submitted to the sponsor for authorisation.

The ultimate consideration is the effect on the business case. Can the plans be reworked so that the project or programme remains justifiable? If not, the corrective action may be to prematurely close the project or programme to prevent further investment that will not generate an adequate return.

ACCEPT COMPLETED WORK

At some point during the coordinate and monitor progress activity a delivery team will say to the management team "this piece of work is finished". Depending upon the context, the delivery team may have performed quality control and simply present the results as evidence that the work is complete or it may be that the management team is responsible for quality control and must now test the results of the delivery team's efforts.

This can range from straightforward inspection of standard components to extensive testing and formal, contractual sign-off. Whether formal or informal, acceptance signifies the transfer of ownership of the work and its products from the delivery team to the management team.

Once work has been accepted, delivery documentation should be updated and, if required, the acceptance should be communicated to relevant stakeholders.

Projects and Programmes

Small projects may simply apply the delivery process, but as the complexity of the work increases, it becomes necessary to break it up into manageable pieces. This decomposition takes two main forms: horizontal and vertical.

What may be called "**horizontal**" decomposition involves splitting the delivery phase into stages or tranches. These help the management team by enabling techniques such as go/no-go control and rolling-wave planning, i.e. ongoing planning on a continual basis.

"**Vertical**" decomposition involves delegating packages of work. This can take the form of sub-projects or work packages within a project or projects within a programme.

This decomposition requires additional processes. Where stages and tranches are created, there are boundaries between them. These are managed through the boundaries process. Where work is delegated through vertical decomposition, it is managed through the development process.

However, management per se is often so limited in its scope or thought process that it becomes a variety reducer, in that it limits its own scope and possibility of expansion because of weaknesses or limitations in its own mindset.

The areas of limitation, as set out by Stafford Beer, are given in Tables 7.2–7.4.

TABLE 7.2

Structural

Name	Meaning	Danger
Divisionalisation	By factories or products	Loss of corporate synergy and central control
Specialisation	By market segments	Loss of market synergy, limited market potential
Functionalisation	By profession or service	Loss of collaborators' surplus; reduced multiskilling
Massive delegation	Top people free to think, delegation of responsibility to lower levels	Withdrawal symptoms; the "cop-out"
Utter involvement	Immediate problem-solving	Loss of wider opportunities

TABLE 7.3

Planning

Name	Meaning	Danger
Short-term horizon	Ignore distant future	Lack of continuity/investment
Long-term horizon	Let immediate problems solve themselves	
Setting priorities	Sequential attention	Destroy systemic interaction
Very detailed planning	Well-oiled machinery; activities operate like clockwork	Obsession with trivia
Management by objectives	Decide where we are going, or where we intend to go	Loss of adaptability; too much single-mindedness

Note: The sections on short-term and long-term horizons are commonplace in the commercial world. They are best described as "The sacrifice of Long-Term Investment for Short-Term gain", i.e. tactical rather than strategic. In any commercial organisation, long-term strategy is as important as short-term action, given that there must be a long-term plan, however much it may be adjusted along the way owing to prevalent issues arising at the time, such as economic recession or boom. The two horizons must therefore be balanced.

TABLE 7.4

Operational

Name	Meaning	Danger
Management by exception	Ignore routine chance results	Using wrong model
Close administration	Cut down argument and anomalies	Curbs freedom to react
Averaging/ aggregating	Taking 1 year with another, etc.	Unassailable optimism; Does not take into account residuals or outliers
Sacking Innovators	Prevent "rocking the boat" or any form of dissent	Creeping paralysis; Loss of initiative
Management Auditing	Maintain a continuous check	"Big Brother" approach; Stifling initiative

Source: Brain of the Firm.

PLANNING

Planning for any venture determines what is to be delivered, how much it will cost, when it will be delivered, how it will be delivered, who will carry it out, and how all this will be managed. It occurs broadly at two levels: governance and delivery.

The goals of management plans used in governance are to

- describe the principles that should be used to manage the work; and
- provide consistency with flexibility across multiple projects and programmes.

The goals of delivery planning are to

- describe the objectives of the project, programme, or portfolio;
- define the work required to achieve the objectives and describe how it will be performed;
- estimate the resources and finance needed to perform the work; and
- document the plans and update them throughout the project life cycle.

At the governance level, a series of management plans sets out the principles of how each aspect of the work will be managed. These plans include documents such as the risk management plan, scope management plan, and financial management plan.

These governance-level plans set out policies and procedures for each aspect of management. They list preferred techniques, including templates for documentation and defined responsibilities. These plans ensure the quality of the project management processes and deliverables. Therefore, developing the governance-level plans could also be termed "quality planning".

Delivery plans address seven questions:

- **Why?** Everyone involved in, or affected by the work should understand why it is being done. At the highest level, this would be a vision of the key elements and benefits of the work. As more detailed information is developed, the question is answered in the business case.
- **What?** The work will have objectives that are determined in requirements management. These will be described as outputs, outcomes, and/or benefits in documents such as a specification, blueprint, or benefit profile.
- **How?** There are often different ways of achieving the stated objectives. Solutions development determines the best way, and this is stated in the business case and embodied in many other detailed delivery plans.
- **Who?** This covers the management organisation and the delivery resources as defined in organisational management and resource management, respectively. Who will do the work is clearly closely associated with how the work is done and is also addressed in the detailed delivery plans.
- **When? Schedule management** determines the timing of milestones, stages, tranches, work packages, and individual activities.
- **Where?** While many projects are located in one physical location, more complex projects, programmes, and portfolios are spread across many locations and often time zones. The impact of this needs to be reflected in all delivery plans.
- **How much?** Naturally, the cost of the work is an essential component of the business case.

Financial management determines how much the work will cost and how it will be funded, as well as the extent to which the project generates revenue and thus earns profit, beyond the breakeven point.

The life cycle of projects and programmes is designed to answer these seven questions in stages. Outline documentation is developed during the identification process and, subject to approval through the sponsorship process, is used to produce the detailed delivery plans during the definition process.

All delivery plans originate from estimates. These will be based on whatever data are available together with expertise in their interpretation and application. The more the information available, the more accurate the estimates. Inevitably, in the early phases of a project or programme, there is less information available than in the later phases. This results in a funnel where the range of estimates narrows throughout the life cycle. The estimating funnel below covers a normal life cycle, but the same principle applies to extended life cycles (Figure 7.11).

This inherent uncertainty in plans is often ignored or misunderstood by key stakeholders who interpret estimates in line with their personal requirements rather than practical realities. That is why techniques such as the Monte Carlo Analysis in scheduling and the use of reserves as part of budgeting and cost control should be used as evidence of the effects of the estimating funnel.

The project manager owns the management and delivery plans, but they should be developed with the wider team. Some specialist planning expertise may be provided by a support function. This removes ambiguity, sets expectations, and develops commitment to the plan.

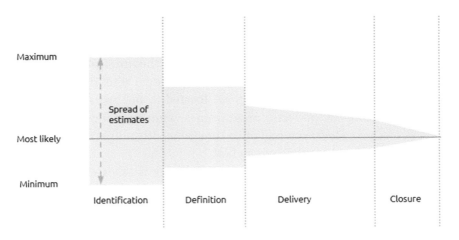

FIGURE 7.11
Project funnel.

Once agreed at the end of the definition process, delivery plans provide baselines which are periodically reviewed and updated. These form the basis of reviews during the boundaries process where the continuing justification of the work is assessed.

Projects, Programmes, and Portfolios

Small projects rarely have the opportunity to invest in the development of management plans. Good management practices will depend on the skill and experience of the project manager. In a more mature organisation, there may be standard management plans available that can be tailored to suit.

Where a project is part of a programme or portfolio, the parent body should provide management plans and guidance on the production of delivery plans. The exception to this is where a standard portfolio comprises contracted projects for different clients. Each client may specify the use of the own standard approaches. The portfolio management team must therefore concentrate on supporting management teams in their use of varied documentation standards.

Too much planning can be as damaging to a project as too little. All planning documents must be tailored to the context of the work. For example, a simple stakeholder map or risk register is far better than none at all, but time spent making them overly complicated can be a distraction.

On larger projects and all programmes, it is unreasonable to develop detailed delivery plans for the entire life cycle. Later tranches or stages of work will be subject to change as a result of altered requirements and performance in the earlier stages. It is common to apply the principle of rolling-wave planning where earlier stages and tranches are planned in more detail than the later ones.

Programmes and portfolios will have central plans and delegated delivery plans. For example, a programme may have a high-level schedule where each project and change management work package is represented as a single bar in a Gantt chart. Each project with them has its own detailed schedule. The challenge for planners is to enable information to flow between the higher and lower levels of plan while preserving the planning autonomy of the project manager and business change managers.

Cost reduction and increasing revenue are not achieved by considering only manufacturing processes but must also take into account service processes. Services occupy a significant share in today's markets. A business

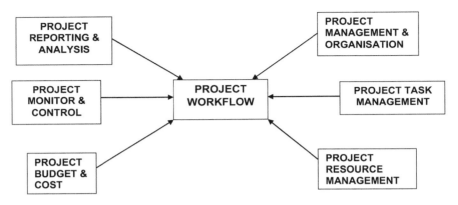

FIGURE 7.12
Project workflow hub-and-spoke.

does not run simply because of the provision of a product but also because of services, such as internal and external services in a company.

It should be noted that all these elements influence the project workflow and how it functions. Each element contributes to the overall project, and the project itself relies on all these elements for complete functionality. However, each element is entirely separate from the others and only leads to the central overall activity. There is, on this basis, no interconnectivity between each of the individual elements themselves. Any deficiency or shortcoming in any of these elements does not therefore affect the functionality of any of the other elements but does affect the overall flow of the project as a whole.

If a project of any kind is to be considered, be it short-term or long-term, then all aspects of that project must be taken into account at the same time. The section in the early part of this chapter concerning neural networks and the application of the RAIS covered some of this concept and therefore helps to explain the project as a whole as well as all its dimensions and contributory parts. A typical project workflow can be considered as in Figure 7.12.

CONTROL

Control involves monitoring performance against approved baselines, updating delivery documents, and taking corrective action as necessary.

Control is required throughout the life cycle, but this explanation is primarily aimed at controlling the delivery process, as cybernetic control is focussed on the delivery process.

The goals of control are to

- review performance against baselines;
- evaluate the effect of actual performance on future plans; and
- take action as required to achieve planning targets or agree revised targets.

Control techniques fall into one of three broad categories: cybernetic, go/-no-go, and post.

Cybernetic control is part of the day-to-day management of the work; go/no-go control is applied at the key decision points in the life cycle; post control is concerned with learning from experience so that P3 management is continuously improved.

As explained from the very outset, the term 'cybernetic' is derived from the Greek for helmsman, and a project manager uses, or should use, cybernetic control to "steer" the project, programme, or portfolio on a day-to-day basis. The work of the project manager is, strictly speaking, first-order cybernetic control, and the relationship between the project manager and sponsor is second-order cybernetic control.

The key element of cybernetic control is feedback. A system is monitored, and feedback is provided and compared to a norm. Action is taken to align the system to the norm. In project management, the baseline plans are the norm; monitoring provides the feedback on performance, and the project manager takes action to adhere to the baseline plans.

Tolerances are acceptable deviations from the baselines. If performance is outside, or predicted to be outside, the agreed tolerances, this is classed as an issue that must be escalated to the sponsor. The sponsor and manager will then agree on the appropriate corrective action. If the result is a major change to the work, then a new baseline may be agreed against which future performance is monitored.

Go/no-go control is used at key decision points built into the life cycle. These are typically found at the end of a phase, stage, or tranche of work and involve a major review of what has been delivered. At these decision points, the sponsor considers the available information and decides whether to proceed with the remaining work. In extreme cases, a project, programme, or possibly even portfolio may be terminated because it is no longer justifiable.

Post-control is entirely retrospective. It is concerned with learning from experience through, for example, post-project or post-programme reviews. Specific control methods are used according to the nature and complexity of what is being controlled, and examples are as follows.

A common method of illustrating schedule performance is RAG Reports (Red, Amber, Green). Green status means performance is within tolerances and predicted to remain there. Amber is within tolerances but predicted to exceed them. Red indicates performance has exceeded tolerances.

All six components of delivery need to be controlled. Some techniques, such as change control and quality control, are specific to one of the elements, i.e. scope. Others, such as earned value management (EVM), bring together multiple elements (i.e. schedule and cost).

In the context of creating outputs, control of scope is effectively the same as quality control. It has the most diverse range of techniques, covering inspection, testing, and measurement. It verifies that the deliverables conform to specification, are fit for purpose, and meet stakeholder expectations. Example techniques include crushing samples of concrete used in the foundations of a building, reviewing user interfaces of computer applications, x-raying welds in a ship's hull, and following the test script for a new piece of software. Inspection often produces empirical data, and tools such as scatter diagrams, control charts, flowcharts, and cause-and-effect diagrams all help to control the quality of deliverables.

Controls can also be regarded as event-driven or time-driven. Go/no-go and post control are event driven, and events could be life cycle based (the conclusion of a phase, stage, or tranche) or feedback based (when tolerances are exceeded).

Time-driven controls are more typical of cybernetic control and involve weekly or monthly reports, periodic reviews, or regular progress meetings. It is the project manager's responsibility to collect progress data and prepare reports, highlighting areas that need attention. In some cases, this work will be done by a support function, freeing the manager to concentrate on decision-making and implementing corrective action.

No work will ever progress strictly according to plan. A good plan will contain elements of contingency and management reserves that will cushion the effect of issues. Some of these reserves will be in the control of the project manager and others within the control of the sponsor.

The 3 "P's" – Project, Programme and Portfolio

The way progress data is collected and reported will depend on the planning techniques used to develop the baseline. On a small project, the schedule baseline may have been prepared and presented as a simple Gantt chart, in which case schedule progress may be shown as a slip chart, i.e. each stage of the project on a line-by-line basis and spreading across the chart on a timescale basis.

As projects become more complex and schedules are based on network diagrams, these models can be used for more sophisticated control techniques such as EVM or critical chain.

The more sophisticated the method of recording and analysing progress, the more accurate the predictions of future performance. For example, where a simple slip chart based on critical path analysis may not predict a future breach of tolerances, a forecast based on EVM will show a breach. This is because critical path analysis assumes future rates of progress will be in accord with the original plan, whereas EVM assumes future rates of progress will be in accord with historical rates of progress. Control systems for traditional projects tend to focus first on time and cost, and then on areas such as quality and accountability, as well as ongoing progress according to fixed schedules.

In programmes and portfolios, there will be multiple levels of cybernetic control. A project manager on a project will gather regular feedback on progress and take corrective action as required. Where the project is part of a programme, the programme manager may take the role of project sponsor and provides the second level of control.

If the programme is part of a portfolio, then there is a similar relationship that introduces a third level of control. This does not mean that there are three people controlling the project on a day-to-day basis. Each level of control deals with a different degree of detail and has a different span of control. Within larger projects or programmes and portfolios, the control system (possibly laid out in a control management plan) must, for each level, explain how

- tolerances will be set;
- progress data will be gathered and reported;
- interdependencies between different plans will be monitored;
- progress information will be consolidated upwards; and
- decisions will be communicated downwards.

As the work becomes more complex, it is vital to focus on KPIs rather than monitor everything in great detail. The role of a PSO (project, programme, or portfolio support office) will be indispensable as complexity increases and managers need timely and accurate information to make good decisions.

DOCUMENTED PROCEDURES AND AUDITS

One of the key areas of monitoring and control lies in the existence of documented procedures and mechanisms. All too often, tasks are carried out on the basis of continuity, i.e. *this is the way we have always done it*, and indeed in the case of **recursion**, this is a policy which is self-perpetuating, as recursive action continues on a constant basis without interruption. However, this is of no use if there is some form of discontinuity, i.e. illness or absence of staff, or even an inherent weakness that is revealed through glitches in the system or some form of unexpected operational failure. Any failure forces a rethink of the system and, in many cases, issues a serious challenge to the principle of automatic continuity. We can take too much for granted, and when a major crisis occurs, we are forced to re-evaluate our views on various aspects of life. The coronavirus pandemic of 2020 has forced a radical rethink of socialising, and the security and safety of meeting in larger numbers. This could lead to a major review of activities such as sporting events and indeed major concerts, whether indoor or outdoor. Indeed, unexpected failures in a production environment may lead to a complete review of procedures, especially given a potential compromise to the supply chain. Such reviews will ultimately test or prove the ability of the corporate entity to adapt to any necessary changes in the system or in accepted procedures, often requiring a complete review and rewrite of those procedures, leading to extensive retraining or awareness seminars, as well as a change in mindset and outlook. Anybody new to a role needs to comprehensively learn that role before they can be expected to carry it out without any means of regular supervision. For a seasoned operative, recursion is an inbuilt way of thinking, as it has become ingrained within that person's mindset, and is therefore an automatic function from which the operative cannot and does not diverge. In any cybernetic function, monitoring and supervision are essential to the control process, but it is expected that the staff involved in each of the project tasks have an acceptable degree of professional competence in their roles. This is why there is a need for a set of documented procedures for each function to ensure that all members of staff know how to approach a task or role with confidence, methodology, and accountability, as well as ensuring that the job is carried out without any errors and with the minimum need for rectification as part of the process.

The other reason for documentary processes is for audit purposes, both internal or external. Audits as a whole are the means of checking the extent to which company strategies and operations are achieving their objectives, as well as ensuring that all operations are compliant with regulatory requirements. Internal audits are an expected part of the monitoring and control process, as they identify any potential weaknesses or shortcomings in the system, as well as identifying areas that are well controlled and manageable. These can then be rectified as part of the ongoing control process. External audits, carried out by independent consultants or officials of authorities such as accountants, customs, or revenue departments, exist to provide an impartial view of the state of the company's activities in a true and fair view manner. The process of the Trusted Trader/AEO (Authorised Economic Operator) application process demands not only a review by the Customs/Revenue Authority but also a full account of the operations and *modus operandi* of the company concerned. Much of the self-assessment process for this application revolves around a questionnaire comprising a series of detailed questions, all designed along a cybernetic approach, right down to quality control measures for all quality and operational control systems. The whole purpose of these questions is to establish if there is a cybernetic-related control system in place, and if so, how it is managed on a regular and frequent basis in accordance with regulatory requirements. The purpose of this process is also to discipline the company into adopting a cybernetic approach to its management, thus encouraging complete reviews of its modus operandi, with a view to making its entire integrated structure and systems more manageable, robust, and efficient.

There are many occasions where systems are only examined and amended because of audits. If a government department, such as the revenue service, or external Sarbanes-Oxley auditors notify an organisation that they intend to carry out an audit in the next few weeks, a massive effort bordering on panic ensues to examine all the organisational systems and rectify any errors or anomalies prior to the audit taking place, as otherwise the audit would identify and highlight these issues, leading to a negative report against the organisation. A cynical view of this might suggest that the audit is deliberately designed to find errors, but, erring on the side of caution, the audit is designed more to analyse all financial activities, and, if it should detect or discover errors, to report them in such a way that rectifying action can be taken as soon as possible. The Enron scandal showed to extent to which an organisation could deceive authorities by simply shifting anomalies from one department to another without resolving them. This was in effect a systematic abuse of the VSM, as well as a blatant disregard for an algedonic system. Had the algedonic process been used properly, any anomalies would have been identified at the time of their recognition and could – or should – have been resolved at the time. Instead, they were covered up and only proved impactive when the organisation filed for bankruptcy in 2002. By that time, it was too late, and the repercussions not only ensured the complete demise of Enron but also its management consultant Arthur Andersen. Of course, it also led to far-reaching US legislation in the form of the Sarbanes-Oxley Act, also of 2002, which has now ensured that corporate anomalies cannot be covered up but must be addressed at the time they occur, with the implementation of a full detailed reporting system stating exactly the state of the company's affairs and the clarity and transparency of all the information and data therein. Not only does this apply to US companies, but also their overseas subsidiaries. Effectively, the long arm of the Sarbanes-Oxley regime spreads all over the world. It effectively uses the VSM to ensure that not only is a company transparent, but it is also completely viable and controllable.

And yet, considering this radical tightening up of the US system, such measures have not been implemented as standardised procedures on a global scale. There appears as yet to be no equivalent of the Sarbanes-Oxley legislation anywhere else in the world, and this would suggest a collective reluctance by many authorities to implement similar controls in their own countries, which is in reality the same approach to the use of the VSM. It also shows that a completely free market approach to business and economic affairs leads to fragmentation and lack of standardisation, which flies in the face of cybernetic management, which advocates full control from either a corporate or national perspective. Ultimately, there has to be a regime of control in any organisation, and this must be seen as transparent and manageable throughout the whole operating and management system.

8

Cybernetics and the Supply Chain

The supply chain is, at best, a complex set of inter-relationships between a variety of organisations, namely commercial enterprises which exist to serve the market. These organisations supply either products or services, and in some cases both. The processes involved convert raw materials to finished products which are ultimately sold to individuals or other companies. In the case of individuals, these are the consumers of the products for their own benefit, such as food, household appliances, or even cars. In the case of companies, these may be retail businesses or even end-users, which use the products concerned for use in specific sectors such as the offshore oil and gas sector, the transport sector, or even the defence industry. However, in each case, the end product is manufactured or processed from a variety of raw materials, be they animal, vegetable, or mineral in their basic state. These raw materials undergo several processes before becoming the end product and therefore must be converted at a particular stage in the process and then transported to the next stage in the production process.

The management of the supply chain, whether national or international, is a specific field of general management covering production and services systems. This specific kind of management is required to be able to adapt to the nature of the industrial evolution and development, and plan accordingly. Given that industry may be distributed around different geographic locations, the production and distribution plan must be adapted and arranged according to these locations.

CYBERNETICS AND INTERNATIONAL TRADE

Before delving into the complexities of the supply chain, it is worthwhile to examine the application of cybernetics to the field of International Trade. International Trade is the relationship between sellers in one country and buyers in another country, or several countries. The theory of international trade goes back centuries, when empires traded with each other, before biblical times. The poem "Cargoes" by John Masefield:

> Quinquireme of Nineveh, from distant Ophir,
> Rowing home to haven in sunny Palestine,
> With a cargo of ivory, apes and peacocks,
> Sandalwood, cedarwood, and sweet white wine...

sums up much of the romanticism and imagery of the principle of international trade, and in general, the essence of international trade has never changed, other than the creation of various theories by economists such as Adam Smith and David Ricardo. The Ricardian principle of comparative advantage stated that two commodities can be both produced in a country, but the efficiency of the production of one product will be better in one country than another. Therefore the country less efficient in the production of a particular product will buy from the country where the production efficiency of that product is greater, and therefore the price of that product is lower as a result, and hence the available quantity of that product is greater. The Harvard professor Michael Porter went much further to propose the theory of competitive advantage, in which he stated that the advantage lies with companies that are more competitive by way of efficiency and cost, and as a result, they will be able to capture greater levels of market share, especially concerning international markets.

However, international trade can be viewed at two distinct levels, namely global strategy, which is largely governed by the principles of international relations and political economy at a governmental level, and the practicality of international trade, which is the pragmatic element of the buying and selling of goods on an international basis at a commercial and corporate level. Companies trade internationally in goods, while governments govern the flow of international trade by the use of duties, taxes, quotas, sanctions, and restrictions. Control over international trade can therefore be divided into tariff barriers and nontariff barriers. Consider the following diagram, Figure 8.1.

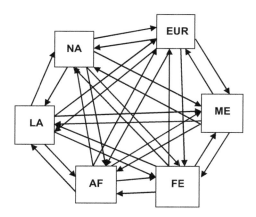

FIGURE 8.1
Neural trade diagram.

Each box represents a trading bloc based on geographic location, as follows:
NA – North America
LA – Latin America
AF – Africa
EUR – Europe (including Western Russia, Ukraine, the Balkans, and the EU).
ME – Middle East
FE – Far East (including Australasia)
(Note that this is a simplistic view of global trade and does not detail all of the main individual trading blocs).

If we are to consider the diagram as a form of neural network, we can see that all the blocs are contained with the global **systematic assemblage of dissimilars**, as described in the previous chapter. This assemblage is a global dynamic system and brings all the blocs together in the form of a single united neural network. They are unique, in that they exist as independent national and supranational sub-entities, and yet they are interlinked as part of the whole entity, i.e. the global trading network. As described in the previous chapter, their dynamism functions as an interdependent set of operational activities, where each element functions within itself, but also as a part of the whole unified entity. This network operates as a global trading network, where each bloc trades with the other blocs on an equal basis, albeit governed by international trading rules such as the WTO (World Trade Organization) Tariff structure and the WTO Trade Facilitation Agreement (TFA), along with other global trade facilities such as the UNCTAD (UN Conference on Trade and Development).

However, in the case where specific trade sanctions are applied by one country (e.g. the United States) against other specific countries, e.g. China, Iran, and North Korea, mainly for political reasons, the integrity of the overall neural network is significantly compromised concerning that axis of trade and therefore does not function properly. Similarly, if an economic crisis besets any specific countries, or applies to a specific part of the world, part of the global neural network is equally compromised. On the worst scale, if a global pandemic such as SARS-COVID suddenly breaks out, or there is a massive global conflict, the whole of the neural trade network is significantly compromised or even paralysed. There have been several cases where the UN trade organisations such as the WTO have failed to resolve international trade disputes, and this has inevitably led to trade disruptions in various parts of the world. Indeed, the failings of the original GATT (General Agreement on Tariffs and Trade) led to the creation in the 1990s of the WTO, which in itself is still challenged by global trade disputes. In this case, if this scenario is translated into a human neural network, the brain is no longer able to control the rest of the body. This is largely why the WTO exists to facilitate and stimulate world trade, especially between the fully developed nations and the lesser-developed nations, which is why the UNCTAD was originally conceived and established.

International trade, with its theories of Absolute and Comparative Advantage, is also subject to various cybernetic principles based on feedback and viability. The Viable Systems Model (VSM) of Stafford Beer can be used significantly in the function of the international supply chain, as explained later in this chapter, but the issues of positive and negative feedback are equally important in the study of both international economics and international trade. International trade is based on the basic theories of supply and demand, and the principle of the trade triangle, where excess supply of goods for the domestic market extends into the supply of the same goods into overseas markets based on overseas demand for these products. Such trade is both export-driven and demand-driven. Often, a proactive approach on the part of the exporter leads to the creation of overseas markets, i.e. supply-push, while the reactive demand of the potential buyer in overseas markets for products from overseas leads to the creation of overseas supply markets, i.e. demand-pull. Much of this principle is based on feedback. If the overseas demand for a product is based on positive feedback, the product will sell overseas much more significantly. If, however, the demand results in negative feedback, often relating to the PESTEL formula, the products concerned will not generate much success, and the supply overseas must be terminated. Given, therefore, that international trade is based on international supply and demand, the use of feedback is crucial. Equally, the ability of the supplier to meet the demands of overseas customers is crucial. A customer relies on the supplier to produce and send goods to them and therefore needs to be sure that the supplier is viable and therefore capable of supplying overseas demand. This is borne out by the five supply and purchasing characteristics, namely:

- Price
- Quantity required
- Capability of production by the supplier
- Capacity by the supplier to produce
- Quality required

These can be expanded to show the 10 "C's" as expounded by Dr Ray Carter, director of DPSS Consultants. These are as follows:

1. Competency
2. Capacity
3. Commitment
4. Control
5. Cash
6. Cost
7. Consistency
8. Culture
9. Clean
10. Communication

As long as these conditions can be met, international trade will prevail. As is often the case, a supplier may gain a customer, only to find that the customer requires much more of the product concerned over a period of time, which may constrain the supplier in terms of the capacity to produce and deliver the quantity required. Other factors may also prevail such as transport costs, Customs import duties, and sales taxes. To this extent, the ultimate delivery price to the customer will significantly increase, sometimes as much as an additional 30% of the cost of the goods concerned.

Externalities such as duties and taxes are issues which are covered by System 4 of the VSM. Where Free Trade Agreements between countries exist, these will generate positive feedback, as free trade stimulates international trade in the form of the Vinerian principle of Trade Creation. However, the reverse is true where quotas and trade restrictions such as Import Duties, especially Countervailing Duties, exist. Such measures are designed to restrict trade and cause the opposite Vinerian principle of Trade Diversion, especially in cases of trade within economic blocs such as the European Union, which seeks to encourage Trade Diversion to within the bloc. This therefore places constraints on trade with other countries outside the bloc and therefore generates negative feedback. Indeed, such is the scenario concerning the full withdrawal of the United Kingdom from the EU Customs Union and Single Market at the end of 2020. The EU is imposing strict frontier controls on all imports from the EU as from 1 January 2021, which could be construed as being a trade diversion measure against the United Kingdom. Many UK companies have been told that their EU customers would not be prepared to accept additional costs through import duties imposed on UK goods, thus implying negative feedback. The UK suppliers would either have to absorb any EU import duties in their selling prices or would have to lower their selling prices in order to account for any additional EU import duties. Either way, in this case the externalities within System 4 of the VSM would create significant problems for UK suppliers to the EU. The net result could be a decrease in trade between the United Kingdom and the on the basis of the EU policy of trade diversion, which in reality is a very introspective view of international trade.

International trade is also governed by economic conditions, such as growth and recession, and again much depends upon the cybernetic approach, as determined by the Anglo-Austrian economist Friedrich Hayek. Hayek explained that markets are self-determining and self-governing. They adjust themselves according to prevalent economic conditions and therefore determine the extent to which international trade occurs. If economic recession prevails, trade will decrease, whereas if economic growth prevails, trade will increase. However, if we apply the VSM, trade cans till increase owing to corporate efficiency and the resulting decrease in product pricing because of such efficiency. In many cases, demand always exists for essential products owing to basic societal demands, and this will never change because the international market is inelastic. Hence, the conclusion that the greater the market elasticity, i.e. sensitivity to price, the greater the need for corporate viability to satisfy the market demand. The phrase "when the going gets tough, the tough get going" applies very much to this scenario. Stafford Beer's VSM proves that the more a company is structurally and economically viable, the more likely it is to maintain market share and, indeed, increase this share. The national lockdowns and subsequent market chaos of 2020 proved that some commercial sectors fared better than others. The service sector, especially travel, tourism and hospitality, suffered badly, as did associated industries such as aviation and automotive, while general manufacturing came off lightly and in some cases prospered, especially in the supply of medical products. Every cloud has a silver lining…

The overall conclusion is that feedback, be it positive or negative, influences markets on a global basis. However, so too does the principle of corporate viability, especially with relation to externalities. If a corporate entity can adopt externalities such as international influences and global trade trends, then not only does it survive but also prosper. The theories of the former Harvard professor Michael Porter in his Five Forces model effectively include the issue of corporate viability in dealing with competition and rivalry. The Five Forces are as follows:

- Competitive rivalry
- Threat of new entrants
- Threat of substitutes
- Supplier power
- Buyer power

The greater the efficiency and viability of a company, the more likely it is that the company concerned can be more competitive and therefore maintain its market share and hence the need for the use of the VSM in determining this level of viability, even in times of global economic recession.

THE SUPPLY CHAIN

This chapter describes, from a systems science and cybernetics perspective, the management of the nature of industrial processes, in particular within the supply chain as a means of communication and supply. It is based on a paper by Isaías Badillo, Ricardo Tejeida, Oswaldo Morales, and Abraham Briones but delves further into their basic principles of cybernetics in the supply chain. Their main argument is that in cybernetics, there is one management principle, namely to understand W Ross Ashby's Law of Varieties, namely "the variety of ability to respond to industrial processes and the environment change should be greater than the variability of industrial processes and of the environment", in other words, the control system must be as complex as or more complex and embracing than the systems being observed and controlled.

Figure 8.2 illustrates the principle of how a typical supply chain should or can work.

1. The Suppliers at **2nd Tier level** supply those **1st Tier level** with Raw Materials.

THE INTEGRATED SUPPLY-CHAIN NETWORK MODEL

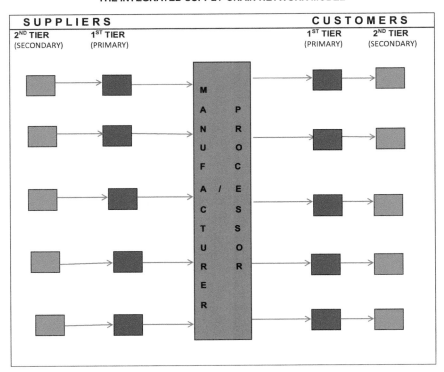

FIGURE 8.2
Integrated supply chain network.

2. The **1st Tier Suppliers**, in turn, supply the Manufacturer/Processor with semi-processed Components for incorporation in the finished product.
3. The Processor supplies the Finished Product to the **1st Tier Customer**, which, in turn, may act as a Distributor (or as an onward Processor) and supply the finished product to the End-Customer, or the End-User, located at **2nd Tier level**.

At each stage, different enterprises convert these materials and then despatch to the next stage down the line. Each stage acts as a defined element within the supply chain and therefore is a unit within the overall network, as defined by the neural network, as are the links between each unit, since these links represent the logistics elements of the supply chain and therefore fulfil and contribute to the maintenance of the whole chain. Without the logistics functions, the chain would fragment and fall apart. At each physical stage, a process occurs and is therefore an integral part of the supply chain network. If a problem should occur at any of these stages, it reflects negatively and adversely on the rest of the supply chain network and hence the need for a control mechanism to oversee the whole network and ensure that all problems, be they actual, perceived, or potential, can be rectified without causing damage or problems to the rest of the supply chain. This depends upon feedback from each element of the chain, including the supply and provision of the logistics function. Any problem needs to be communicated to the next stage along, thus giving that stage time and the ability to find alternative solutions, including the use of other suppliers. The other solution is for the supplier where the problem lies to rectify that problem as soon as possible and thus maintain the integrity of the supply chain. If the problem lies in the logistics process, the need will then exist to determine the nature of the problem and, where necessary, use alternative logistics providers. This was one of the issues that confronted the team involved in the Cybersyn project in Chile in the early 1970s, when the Chilean truckdrivers went on strike in 1972, threatening economic collapse of the country. The Cybersyn structure identified the problem quickly, thus enabling the team in the central control function to locate drivers who were not on strike, draft in others, and thus circumvent the problem before it adversely affected the economy in a serious way.

The authors of the paper state that to describe accurately the principle of Supply Chain Management (SCM), it is necessary to use the concepts of the American Production and Inventory Control Society (APICS) Dictionary, namely "The design, planning, execution, control, and monitoring of supply chain activities with the objective of creating net value, building a competitive infrastructure, leveraging world-wide logistics, synchronising supply with demand, and measuring performance globally". However, this can be easily compressed into what are known as the five "Rights", which are

the **Right Product** at
the **Right Price** at
the **Right Place** in
the **Right Quantity** at
the **Right Time**

This nicely sums up the whole supply chain process. If any part of this process fails, the whole operation fails. If all these elements can be maintained simultaneously, the balance is maintained, and the whole supply chain process functions according to plan.

There are several functions included in the definition of SCM which are represented in cybernetics by Stafford Beer's VSM. For example, the functions of **scheduling** and **execution** are the main elements of System 1 of the VSM. The function of internal **control** is the task of component number 2 of the VSM. The **monitoring** and **auditing** functions are the task of component number 3 of VSM. The **planning** and externalities functions comprise System 4 of the VSM. The creation of **net value, and effectively the overall company policy and strategy,** is the main task of System 5 of the VSM.

The **design and diagnosis** of the full SCM system is the main function in the VSM. All the five System components of the VSM interact inside by information systems called the Enterprise Resources Planning (ERP) system, exemplified by examples such as SAP and ORACLE. These systems were used to great effect by companies such as the US conglomerate DuPont in overcoming economic and financial problems in times of recession, using ERP systems as well as other concepts such as Kaizen, Lean Management, and Six Sigma. Once the strategy of low-cost sourcing was added, SCM was a natural follow-on. DuPont management started its SCM system with ERP systems, implementing several modules such as Materials Requirement Planning (MRP), Customer Relationship Management (CRM), and so on.

In accordance with the nature of this section, it is pertinent to revisit some basic systems concepts, as follows.

Cybernetics: The study of the flow of information around a system, and the way in which this information is used by the system as a means of controlling itself or being controlled.

Environment: The set of systems incorporating the system of focus.

Function: The main activities performed by the system to reach the overall purpose, aims, and objectives, as well as the overall outcome.

Human activity system: A specific system composed mainly for functions performed by human beings, based on the neural system.

Recursion (a level of): A level at which a viable system is in operation as an autonomous part of a higher-level viable system and contains within itself parts which are themselves autonomous viable systems, i.e. systems and subsystems.

Subsystem: A component which is embedded in a superior system.

System: A set of interrelated components with a purpose whose boundaries are defined by the observer.

Systems science: A scientific field to research taxonomies, concepts, theories, and methodologies.

Variety: Number of possible states that a system is capable of exhibiting.

Viability: The ability of a system to maintain a separate autonomous existence.

VSM: A set of systems within an overall entity capable of maintaining a separate existence, and equally capable of maintaining its identity and operating independently.

Systems science uses the construction of models to represent real systems; for example, the VSM was elaborated by Stafford Beer to represent human activity systems in artificial systems such as SCM.

As detailed in Chapter 3, the VSM is a recursive model that represents viable organisations, and the viability of this model is based on five functions or subsystems. A viable organisation is integrated by way of separate but interactive viable sub-organisations, which at the same time are embedded within the overall organisation itself. In the VSM, there are five interactive systems. In order for an organisation to survive changes in the environment, and consequently adapt to these changes or externalities, it is necessary to satisfy the five subsystems of the VSM. Changes in the environment, especially the external environment, could include new socio-political laws and regulations, changes in the global economy, government fiscal policy, as well as the main elements of the PESTEL structure, i.e. **Political, Economic, Social, Technological, Environmental, and Legal.** The five subsystems are designated in this chapter as follows:

1. Departments and Operations;
2. Co-ordination and Communication;
3. Plant/Internal Corporate Management, including auditing & monitoring (3*);
4. Externalities and Environment; and
5. Overall Management Strategy.

All the five subsystems should be interconnected by management information systems such as ERP. There are several information systems on the market, and the selection of any one of these depends on the characteristics of each SCM.

The following diagram of a simplified production system shows three basic components, namely the environment system, operating system, and the management system. These three basic components are interrelated by information channels, as shown in W. Ross Ashby's Law of Requisite Variety, which establishes that the variety of the management system should be greater than or equal to the variety of the operating system. The variety of the operating system should therefore be larger than or equal to the variety of the environment system, and, in turn, so must the management system which relates to both of the other two systems (Figure 8.3).

Corporate organisations, including government, are much more complex than one would imagine, and in reality, organisational charts do not necessarily show how the organisation really works. Indeed, real-world systems have a variety or set of varieties which are effectively almost infinite.

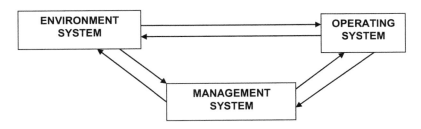

FIGURE 8.3
Law of requisite variety.

The VSM, however, has the ability to maintain its identity according to the general purpose on the organisation. The VSM model could be used to design new organisations or diagnosing issues within current organisations. This can be applied not only in the management of manufacturing industry, e.g. the explanation of the general production management model of the ERP systems, but also in the financial management and service sectors as well.

Figure 8.4, as derived from the texts of Stafford Beer, shows a SCM Model based on the VSM concept connected with a typical ERP system. Each internal system, i.e. Systems 1–5, is shown as a separate function within the organisation as a whole, with each system connected to the others using the internal network of varieties:

$$N(n-1)/2.$$

where N=the number of departments, or components, of the organisation itself, and (n−1) represents the degrees of freedom, i.e. the number of reciprocal movements between all the departments.

This formula can be found in a previous chapter and represents the number of varieties which can be found within a defined network.

System 1 represents the component of a production system that performs tasks which produce what the system is designed to do. Some of the tasks performed by System 1 are facilitated by ERP modules, such as those shown in Table 8.1.

All the components of the supply chain are interconnected between themselves and to an overall management supra-system, similar in principle to the neural network system, where there is command and control function based on feedback, be it positive or negative. In order to facilitate the management of variety, screens to receive instructions and to report performance are used. The organisational viability of the total system and its components are inherent to the VSM. This includes communications of decisions according to the Master Production Schedule. The ERP system reduces the bullwhip effect, with the help of one of the modules of ERP called Distribution Requirement Planning (DRP). The algorithm of this module avoids the quantitative subjective process of planning order receipts. It should be noted that the bullwhip effect is a distribution channel phenomenon in which forecasts yield supply chain inefficiencies. It refers to increasing swings in inventory in response to shifts in customer

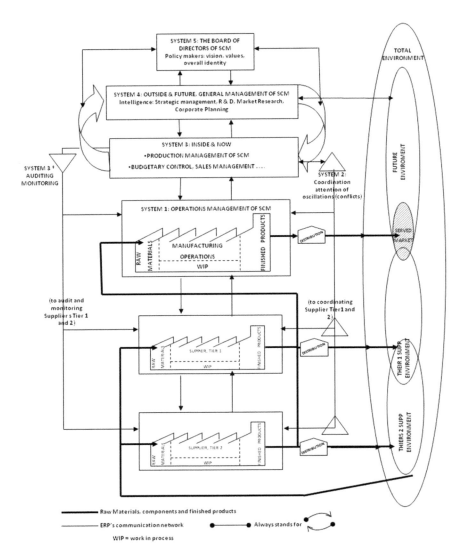

FIGURE 8.4
Viable systems model.

demand as one moves further up the supply chain. However, customer demand can be seen as a form of algedonic feedback. If the customer signals a lower demand, the supply chain must be adjusted to reflect this and supplies of material decreased accordingly. This represents a form of *negative feedback*. However, if the customer signals an increased demand,

TABLE 8.1

ERP Standard Operating Procedures (SOPs)

1. Sales and operation management (SOP) to develop tactical and strategic plans to achieve competitive advantage	2. Customer relationship management (CRM) to understand and support existing and potential customers' needs
3. Quality function deployment (QFD) to ensure that all major requirements of the "voice of the customer" are incorporated in the product or service	4. Master production schedule (MPS) to reflect the anticipated production schedule
5. Materials requirement planning (MRP) and informatics algorithm that processes data from BOM, IM, and MPS	6. Capacity requirement planning (CRP) to determine in detail the amount of labour and machine resources required to accomplish the MPS
7. Bill of material (BOM), an organisation of the product structure	8. Bill of processes (BOP), an organisation of the processes of manufacturing
9. Shop floor control (SFC) of manufacturing activities	10. Production activity control (PAC), control of manufacturing activities.
11. Supplier relationship management (SRM), relationships with vendors	12. Total quality management (TQM)
13. Maintenance management (MM), preferably total quality maintenance	14. Distribution requirement planning (DRP), to improve logistic of parts and finished products

supplies of material and production are increased accordingly to meet that demand, and this represents *positive feedback*. The risk is a phenomenon called demand amplification. This occurs when forecasted figures based on historical trends suggest an increased demand based on forward predictions, by either extrapolation or time-series forecasting, without requesting actual projected customer demands for a given forward period. The demand amplification is therefore based on perceived demand, rather than actual demand, and the resulting gap between the two can prove costly in terms of excess production to meet a perceived demand which does not actually exist. In some ways, this also relates to the bullwhip effect, where the customer requirements do not equate with expected production levels. Given that cybernetic rules state that negative feedback must lead to rectification of the issue, whereas positive feedback encourages the continuation of a particular strategy, the whole functioning of the supply of the supply chain depends upon these principles. This is why the process of communication, both internal and external, is equally vital to the whole supply chain process.

TABLE 8.2

Production Scheduling SOPs

Production Scheduling (MPS)	Quality Control of Raw Materials
Work Procedures/Bills of Processes/Standard Operating Procedures (BOPs/SOPs)	Maintenance Management
Supply Chain Event Management (SCEM)	Manufacturing and Operational Auditing/Monitoring

System 2: This is a system that coordinates the activities of various production departments, in order to avoid conflicts between them when using common resources of services. This coordination activity avoids any problematic situations that might occur. Coordination activities are based on what is seen as the best solution for the whole entity.

Systems 3 and 3*: System 3 activities are the command and control of the operations of System 1, with the help of information from System 2 and the monitoring or auditing information from System 3*. The main activities of System 3 are supported by the modules of the ERP systems as shown in Table 8.2.

The work of the accounting and finance function is facilitated by electronic data communications, and the collection of electronic data is performed by way of one module within the ERP structure. Any resulting free time on the part of the accounting function is now dedicated to assist management in the execution and performance of System 3. In addition to this free time, the accounting function could be used to improve management performance (System 3). Real-time data will be filtered to adjust variety of System 1.

As a result, the auditing/monitoring process coordinates the control element of System 1 through some ERP modules, such as

1. Advanced Planning System (APS);
2. Availability to promise and capable to promise functions (ATP);
3. Production Activity Control (PAC); and
4. Inventory Management (IM).

All of these are standard modules of any ERP system.

However, it should also be noted that the auditing/monitoring system as engendered by System 3* is also the control tool for the audit and control of the whole corporate function, as it has to embrace all elements of the corporate entity. This function is embodied in Ashby's Law of Requisite Variety, which states that the controlling system must be at least large and complex enough to embrace and control the corporate system as a whole, hence the purpose of both internal and external audits. Taken to the absolute limit, the auditing system must be able to address every item within the corporate structure, right down to the smallest and least important items purchased for the purposes of administration, including paper-clips, correction fluid, etc. This may seem somewhat pedantic, but given the repercussions of the Enron collapse, the knee-jerk reactions in the US corporate and fiscal world led to some of the most far-reaching preventive legislation in the form of the Sarbanes-Oxley Act of 2002, which has revo-lutionised financial thinking and structures in many corporate entities around the world.

System 4: System 4 performs strategic planning and interpretation of polices elaborated by System 5. Some of the tasks of System 4 are sup-ported by modules of ERP shown in Table 8.3. System 4 is the point where internal and external information can be brought together and integrated as part of the overall corporate strategy. In reality, System 4 relies significantly on externalities, such as global trends, government policy, and trade patterns, to integrate with internal corporate policy. Indeed, System 4 also encompasses the supply chain, as it takes into account issues such as suppliers and customers, logistics facilities, taxes, and the basic principles of supply and demand. Indeed, to this extent, System 4 does much to influence all the other systems within the VSM as a whole. After all, individual sections or departments detailed in System 1 are still affected by the supply chain, especially procurement, sales, logistics, and finance, as they all need to be aware of externalities relating to the supply chain, especially in terms of Supply Chain Risk Management (SCRM).

Other Modules/Functions for Systems 3 and 3* include

- Human Resources (HR);
- Advance Planning System (APS);
- Product Life Cycle (PLC);
- Long-Range Forecasts (LRF);
- Legal and Fiscal Planning; and
- Business Planning under various scenarios.

TABLE 8.3

ERP Modules for Systems 3 and 3* of the VSM

Shop Floor Control	Financial Business Modules
Manufacturing execution system (MES) (to control and monitor plant-floor machines and electromechanical systems)	Activity-based costing (ABC) to obtain real cost of finished products or services
Input-output control and production activity control (PAC) (to control details of production flow)	Accounts payable (AP)
Human resource management (HRM) (for payroll, time management benefits administration, etc.)	Accounts receivable (AR)
Plant and equipment management (FA) (fixed assets management)	General Ledger (GL)
Cost Accounting of BOMs and BOPs (CA)	Financial Supply Chain Management (FSCM)
Manufacturing execution system (MES) (to control and monitor plant-floor machines and electromechanical systems)	Payroll (PR) for salary administration
	Profit and cost centre accounting, etc.

The database of the human resources module (HR) helps to build a portfolio of human resources, by identification of employees. System 4 uses modules of ERP as shown above. This system maintains procedures to forecast future changes of equipment in other resources, for example new technology for use in the production environment.

System 5: System 5 keeps the identity and congruency of the enterprise or organisation with its environment. This system is integrated by the top-level management, e.g. the board of directors. One of the main outputs of the board of directors is to issue general management policies for the internal operation system as well as the interrelation with the environment and also relies on the other element of the cybernetic approach, i.e. feedback, to achieve this.

It should be noted that the application of this concept is not simply for one element of the supply chain; it should encompass all elements of the supply chain, from Secondary and Primary Suppliers through the Processors to the Primary and Secondary Customers. Simply having one element of the supply chain adhering to the above principles will not solve any of the supply chain issues, as the application for one element must apply to the application for all elements, as defined by the typical neural system, where an overall control system encompasses all the parts of that neural system. The same must, therefore, apply to all artificial network systems as well. If one element of the supply chain does not work properly, the whole of the chain malfunctions, resulting in chaos. Hence the reason for the network capabilities of any ERP system. For example, SAP works in such a way that it can be applied not only to one corporate establishment but also to the entire supply chain network associated with that establishment. That means that the SAP system in one company can easily communicate electronically with the SAP systems in all other associated companies, regardless of their location, be they suppliers or customers, thus facilitating a fully effective supply chain. This also implies that the process is global and is not limited to a specific country or region.

However, ERP lacks appropriate modules for the control activities of System 5, and in this respect, this issue is an opportunity to improve the functionality and effectiveness of any ERP system. ERP does not necessarily equate with management, especially at the highest levels. At present, there are no modules of ERP to facilitate the activities of System 5, since System 5 refers to the overall decision and policy-making processes which result from the use of ERP. For example, to improve decision-making on consensual agreements, corporate strategies and policies could be based on methodologies such as Syntegrity or Interactive Management. In the case of critical situations, the algedonic channels, in the form of feedback, communicate these situations directly to System 5 and thus initiate the decision-making process.

Another area of control where the cybernetic concept works well is the Process Flow of a Customs Order process. The feedback system determines the success or failure of the process, as positive or negative feedback will influence the progress of the process and the extent to which it fulfils customer requirements.

The Process Flow Diagram (PFD) is as shown in Figure 8.5.

The decision loops initiated by each lozenge represent a feedback stage where the input information leads to either positive or negative feedback, and this effectively constitutes a decision-tree process based on either positive or negative feedback.

The first feedback element occurs at the point of the creditworthiness check. In the case of negative feedback, the process is immediately terminated. If positive feedback is recorded, the process continues. This

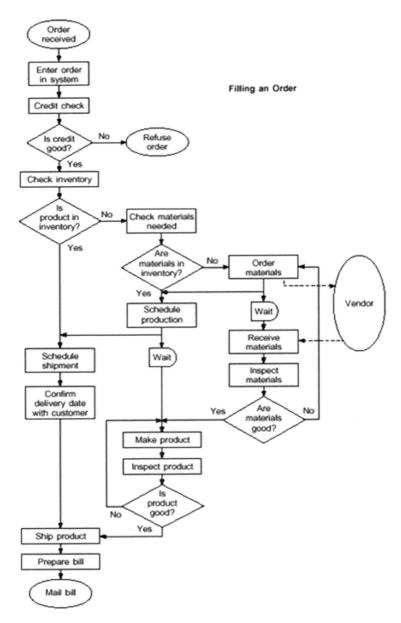

FIGURE 8.5
Process flow diagram. (www.ASQ.com.)

feedback translates into Risk. The higher the risk, there is more chance that the feedback for each stage will be negative.

In this way, the four Risk Options (The Four "T's") are also fulfilled, as follows:

Tolerate

The Risk is **Low**, if not negligible, and the process continues (**Positive Feedback**)

Treat

The **Risk** is Minor or **Medium** and is accepted on the condition of mitigating or remedial action being carried out (**Positive Feedback**, but based on conditional qualifications).

Transfer

The Risk is **Medium/Medium High** and should not be borne by the producer but should be transferred to a specialist (i.e. Insurance, Product Inspection) (**negative feedback**, but conditionally qualified).

Terminate

The **Risk** is too **High** and should be eliminated or **Terminated** (e.g. Credit Risk) (**negative feedback**).

It should be noted that all risks are based on a combination of **Likelihood** and **Impact**. For example, Credit Risk suggests that a customer may not be good at paying the supplier on time, if at all, or indeed, may be in an uncertain financial status. This would infer High Risk for the supplier and would automatically result in a customer order being refused.

The main issue concerning risk is that it should be reduced in any commercial process. Indeed, much of the purpose of cybernetics is to reduce risk and therefore costs associated with risk. This is borne out by the any neural network. For example, in a human neural network, the brain registers a particular perception or action and acts accordingly to reduce the risk associated with that action or at very least provide a warning against an action being taken. For example, if I deliberately put my hand in a fire, my hand will be burned, causing damage to the skin and severe pain. The pain is a result of the nerves in my hand being affected by the fire, and sending out alarm signals as a result. If, however, I put my hand close to a hot plate on a cooker, the warmth generated by the hot plate registers with my brain and results in my moving my hand away from the source of the heat, thus reducing significantly the risk of my hand being burned.

Similarly, in a production environment, the purpose of cybernetic management is to reduce the level of actual or perceived risk by way of feedback at several stages in the production process, and in reality generate a robust planning strategy, in the form of procuring materials in advance where the production contract demands the ongoing production of a batch of products. Risks can be incurred at any stage in the order fulfilment process, hence the need to engage in a cybernetic process to analyse the risk at an extremely early stage in the process and take appropriate remedial action in order to avoid major adversities later in the process. Although the modern concept of Control Theory addresses some of these issues, it does not account for the whole commercial process, be it production, financial, or administrative. This is why a full cybernetic process which addresses the VSM, the Law of Requisite Variety. and the principle of feedback accounts for much more in terms of project or system control. Indeed, the application of the decision tree throughout any process in terms of the Process Flow Diagram allocates a control mechanism at several different stages in the process by way of the feedback mechanism, and thus ensures that the correct route is taken as a result of such feedback, thus resulting a smooth and problem-free route to ultimate fulfilment of the project or process concerned.

The next feedback stage occurs at the point where the inventory is checked for the product itself. If the product is already in inventory, the system registers this status, and the feedback is positive. As a result, the order fulfilment process continues in a direct manner based on stock availability, where the electronic system allows a suitable item of stock to be removed and packaged ready for delivery to the customer. However, if the product is not in inventory, the system registers this, the feedback is negative, and the instruction is issued to manufacture a new item. Checks are therefore required to determine what materials are required for the production of the item concerned according to the Bill of Materials. The materials are therefore procured and are checked prior to production scheduling, although this process necessitates a set of lead and production times according to the company's production schedule, which will obviously result in longer times required for the delivery of the new item to the customer. A sub-stage in the feedback process allows for the inspection of the materials procured. If they are of acceptable quality, the feedback is positive, and the production can be scheduled. If they are below quality, i.e. sub-standard, the materials are rejected and the Vendor is informed, leading to costly delays and the need for replacement material, often under warranty. In such circumstances, it is essential to inform the customer of the timescales involved concerning the difference between the item already being in inventory and the need to manufacture a new bespoke item, which in reality may well cost more than an item already being available in the company's inventory. Indeed, a full cybernetic application would already have established whether the inventory already contained specific items, so that an order could be fulfilled without the need to procure materials specifically for the production of the item on demand.

The principle of **Runners, Repeaters,** and **Strangers** applies to this process, and this concept is summarised as follows:

- **Runners** – Products or materials regularly in large demand, resulting in an appropriate range and quantity of products and materials held in inventory accordingly in anticipation of this demand.
- **Repeaters** – Products or materials often but more sporadically in demand, but not sufficiently to require large stocks being held in inventory.
- **Strangers** – One-off products or materials that are occasionally required, but not in quantities or volumes that require regular stocks in inventories.

The cybernetic approach is to examine and analyse the feedback associated with such requirements, and to arrange and control the stock inventory accordingly. This also involves the VSM, as communication between functions within the company will determine customer demands against production needs and the consequent requirements for procurement and inventory. In this respect, the VSM must be applied to ensure that no breakdowns in communication occur and that the reputation of the company for quality and timely production and delivery is maintained. The risk is that present customer requirements could be inaccurately extrapolated, and the phenomenon known as **Demand Amplification** occurs. This is where present customer demands are assumed to apply and indeed increase according to predicted trends, and procurement of materials determined according to these predicted increases. The reality, however, may be that customer demand decreases according to economic conditions, diminished sales orders, increased prices, or other prevailing circumstances such as market conditions or economic downturns, resulting in excess inventory or production of items which cannot be sold because of the downturn in market demand.

The approach by the Austrian economist Friedrich Hayek, in his article *Competition as a Discovery Procedure*, published in 2002, addressed these phenomena by understanding, as he put it, the "self-organising or self-generating systems" called markets, thus analysing market conditions in advance and more accurately predicting market trends by the use of cybernetics, based largely on the feedback mechanism derived from information concerning market demands. This ensured less inaccuracies concerning market requirements in the short, medium, and long terms and enabled economists to make "pattern predictions" based on more accurate market information. The market, as interpreted by Hayek, is a "communication system" and an "efficient mechanism for digesting dispersed information". However, where Hayek differed from other cyberneticians such as Norbert Wiener and Stafford Beer, is that he did not incorporate a neural network in his analysis; rather, he allowed the market to function as an entity without an overall control system, in that his definition of the market did not allow for a mechanism determining market regulation in any way. His perception of the market engendered a free, unregulated market, subject to increase and decline, based on self-determining market forces, where cybernetics simply accounted for peaks and troughs in the market and consequently determined contingencies for such events, without seeking to intervene in market adversities, in direct apposition to the Keynesian approach, which advocated increased government in times of economic crisis, in order to kick-start and hence re-activate the economy through government support. The Keynesian approach is more in line with the Cybersyn project, initiated by Stafford Beer in Chile between 1971 and 1973, where government intervention sought to activate the Chilean economy, and address and rectify economic adversities as they arose through a control mechanism based on an Artificial Neural Network (ANN).

The third feedback stage occurs at the point of product inspection following the production stage. If the product inspection is positive, the feedback is positive, and the product can be shipped to the customer. If, however, the inspection is negative, the consequent feedback is negative, and the product is either rejected and a new product is manufactured, generally at extra cost, or remedial action is taken to replace specific parts or rebuild the product.

The final feedback stage, not shown of the above diagram, occurs at the point of receipt by the customer. Products can be damaged or lost in transit, and this compromises the supply chain further. If the customer has any reason to reject the consignment, the supply chain process must be investigated and rectified in order to achieve customer satisfaction.

Much of this process is controlled by Artificial Intelligence in the form of electronic ANNs. Present-day computer systems are designed to fulfil the process flow by way of algorithms and electronic structures and architecture, and incorporate complex control systems as part of their structure. Any problems register immediately with the system and generally initiate remedial action on an automatic basis without the need for human intervention. ERP systems fulfil much of this in terms of database management and account for any problems as they arise, be they delays in the delivery of materials, quality control, system failures, unforeseen price rises, etc. As long as the computer is programmed and populated in the correct way, the overall process can be managed efficiently and smoothly.

Another element of the supply chain which requires cybernetic management is the issue of costs incurred as a result of the supply chain itself, in particular logistics costs and import duties. International shipments require a combination of international logistics and Customs controls, where import duty and VAT/Sales Tax are liable. These costs add to and augment the overall supply chain costs and cannot be absorbed in the production process; they must be accounted for in the overall cost of the product to the customer or end-user. The cybernetic approach concerns the feedback mechanism concerning the delivery of the material at each stage and its cost to each element of the supply chain. In the international supply chain mechanism, there are Import Duty Relief facilities to avoid or suspend the liability for Import Duty on the basis of the process of importing materials for inclusion in a product which will be re-exported, including Inward Processing Relief and Customs Warehousing, where the imported materials are held in Customs-controlled storage under import duty and tax suspension until removed into either another Customs Duty Relief regime or are re-exported. This removes much, if not all, of the Duty and Sales Tax/VAT liability on such materials, as the majority of the products concerned may well be re-exported, thus removing duty and tax liability. Similarly, logistics costs can be managed accordingly, to ensure that the costs of transport and storage are planned ahead to take advantage of any discounts offered by the international carriers and logistics providers. In this respect, Ashby's Law of Requisite Variety is fulfilled in its entirety, as the overall control mechanism accounts for every activity in the entire Process Flow for the Order Fulfilment process.

The cybernetics perspective provides a framework to better comprehend the SCM system. This approach describes how to equate the VSM and ERP in most corporate environments. The bullwhip effect is a phenomenon experienced by supply chains when demand at the top tends to exhibit more variability than demand at the bottom, leading to anomalies in the system. Customer demand can fluctuate radically from one period to another, and this must be taken into account throughout any project or process. Just because demand for products or services can be assessed at the beginning of the project, hence the need for the project in the first place, this does not necessarily mean that the initial demand will remain the same throughout the product. This reflects in the product life cycle, which embraces the following four factors:

- Introduction;
- Development;
- Maturity; and
- Decline.

Equally, the BCG (Boston Consulting Group) Matrix translated the above into the following factors:

- **Problem Child/Wildcat** (initial uncertainty as to the overall value and outcome of the project);
- **Star** (Increasing Value of the Project);
- **Cash Cow** (still making money but no increased development); and
- **Dog** (going nowhere and time to terminate the project).

In many ways, initial market research is easily the driver in algedonic feedback. If a market exists, or is perceived, for a product, then this in itself is the major driving force in the initiation of the project. It is pointless initiating a project if there is no demand for it, in the form of supply-push. Demand-pull provides a far better guarantee for the success of the project concerned, and this is the essential element of positive feedback and algedonic response. In this respect, the cybernetic structure of inputs and outputs works extremely well. The input is the information gained from an exploratory survey. The internal process converts this data into a manageable form of statistics, which then results in output, i.e. the decision-making process leading to the initiation of a project, or conversely, the decision not to initiate a project.

The algedonic feedback at all these stages would determine the extent to which the project has a future, and for that matter, how much time, effort, and resources should be devoted to the project, including the supply chain which maintains it. Assuming negative feedback, there is no point in investing resources in a supply chain, which is no longer necessary. Assuming the development of a project, the supply chain must be maintained in equal increase, to account for the need for the supply of materials, increased production, and hence the supply of finished products to the customer in accordance with the customer's increased requirements.

Some recommendations to maintain the above framework are as follows:

1. Improve trust and reliability of communications between the components of the supply chain.
2. Implement a comprehensive decision support system (DSS).
3. Implement ERP modules in supplier and customer information systems.
4. Train suppliers and customers in the basic modules of ERP, namely MPS, MRP, BOM, IM, CRP, DRP, and S&OP.
5. Implement the same cybernetic systems and principles throughout the overall supply chain.
6. Some future research could include knowledge of system dynamics, complex systems, and other systems concepts to improve understanding and diagnosis of systems.

In today's markets, companies often design their products in one country and purchase raw materials in a second country, production is done in a third country, and the finished products are distributed in many countries, using both vertical and horizontal supply chains. Logistics mutually connect these substantially different business processes and enable more effective and efficient management of the long supply and distribution chains. In realising such a task, the intensive use of information technologies that provide timely transaction processing and give support in decision-making process is especially important, hence the application and use of DSS in this process.

Strategic decisions imply that the design of a distribution/logistics network is complex because it involves significant commitments in resources and the development of networks over several years. Strategic logistics planning, including required customer service levels, aims to minimise the inventory-related costs which are combined with producing and storing products from manufacturers to customers, as stated by G. P. Moynihan, P.S Raj, J.U. Sterling, and W.G. Nichols in their paper on DSS for strategic logistics planning. As a result, the logistics strategy is significant for long-term competitive advantages in business, especially in a logistics distribution network which is important in transportation and inventory cost. Furthermore, it is crucial to customer satisfaction regarding logistics response. Previous researchers in this field focused on the importance of IT to support decision-makers to achieve more efficient decisions and to enhance their effectiveness. Specifically, previous surveys focused on the benefits of using computer-based systems to support logistics management, especially in the areas of transportation and warehousing. G. P. Moynihan also writes that limited surveys have been conducted in the areas of inventory and product forecasting, although these studies are still embryonic and to date have not produced significant far-reaching results. Indeed, the whole application of the combination of ANNs and DSS to the logistics sector appears to be very new and has not been given a large area of priority and support.

A DSS is defined as

> an interactive, flexible and adaptable Computer Based Information System which uses decision rules, models and model base as well as a database and the decision makers apply decisions in solving problems which would not be willing to manage visualization models per se
>
> *(J. Waxlax, 1993, An object-oriented DSS for strategic management. Computers & Industrial Engineering).*

Another definition is based on the view that a DSS is an interactive and adaptable computer-based information system which helps non-organized management problems (Alyoubi, 2015; Moormann and Lochte-Holtgreven, DSS and Knowledge-based Strategic Management, 1993).

The essential element of this approach is that the whole of the supply chain benefits from this concept. In order for the whole supply chain to work properly, every part of the chain must adhere to the same principles and standards, hence the need for some form of standardisation within the supply chain, partly through the use of the VSM, and partly through a common standard use of ISO global standards, which require all participants to adhere to the same framework of globally established benchmarks. The use of the VSM within this framework also ensures that all elements of the supply chain are in complete harmony with each other and use the model to ensure that feedback is exercised effectively and that it leads to not just the rectification of potential or actual problems, but an overall synchronised operation which operates cost-effectively and efficiently to the optimum levels of quality and reliability.

GLOBAL VALUE CHAINS

A further element of supply chain cybernetic synergy is the Global Value Chain (GVC). GVCs refer to international production sharing, a phenomenon where production is broken into activities and tasks are carried out in different countries. They can be thought of a large-scale extension of division of labour dating back to Adam Smith, a famous 18th century Scottish economist who developed the economic theory of Absolute Advantage, and who in some ways is considered to be the father of present-day economics. In the famed example attributed to Smith, the production of a pin was divided into a number of distinct operations inside a factory, each performed by a dedicated worker. In GVCs, the operations are spread across national borders (instead of being confined to the same location), and the products made are much more complex than a simple pin.

Cross-border production has been made possible by the global liberalisation of trade and investment, lower transport costs, advances in information and communication technology, and innovations in logistics (e.g. containerisation and the use of 3PLs). While cross-border production itself may not be new, it has expanded rapidly in many industries in recent decades. This development has largely been driven by Transnational Corporations (TNCs) in industrialised economies, which continuously restructure their businesses and reorganise or relocate their operations for reasons of competition. The manifest example of relocation is the offshoring or outsourcing of labour-intensive stages of production from industrialized economies to low wage, labour abundant developing countries. Business operations are, however, also reshuffled among industrialised economies.

In addition to activities being divided up and dispersed geographically, one feature that distinguishes GVCs from earlier waves of cross-border production is that production activities are also increasingly being undertaken by third parties with no equity links to the TNCs in what is otherwise known as international outsourcing. To this extent, they are external sub-contractors and hence external independent suppliers. In this regard, TNCs have consolidated their international operations in segments of industries reflecting their core strengths. They have also grown more powerful by controlling and coordinating their international production networks which consist of multiple companies. One estimate suggests that GVCs which are "governed" by TNCs such as the automotive and food giants account for 80% of world trade each year as part of the overall global supply chain.

Countries can participate in GVCs by engaging in either backward or forward linkages. Backward linkages are created when country A uses inputs from country B for domestic production. Firms in country A can source inputs from country B through direct as well as indirect imports, i.e. inputs are either supplied by local affiliates of TNCs from country B or by locally owned firms that import inputs from other countries. Being able to source foreign inputs is particularly advantageous if the inputs required for production are either not available locally or available but deficient in some aspects (e.g. quantity, quality, and price).

Producing and supplying inputs for production can be especially important for developing countries seeking entry into new industries and markets, and learning to produce items for export markets. It is equally important for industrialised economies which supply complex, specialised, and possibly high-value inputs.

Forward linkages are created when country A supplies inputs that are used for production in country B. The goods produced in foreign countries may be final products (for local consumption and investment) or intermediate products which are exported further elsewhere for use as inputs. Being able to produce and supply inputs for production to firms in other countries can be especially important for developing countries seeking entry into new industries and that are in the process of learning how to produce goods (however simple) for export markets. These inputs are, however, equally important for industrialised economies that supply complex, specialized, and high-value inputs. This constitutes part of the international supply chain and is in itself an integrated dynamic system. Each successive part of this chain is dependent upon the previous element and therefore requires the whole system to function flawlessly.

Products and materials cross several borders in GVCs in different stages of production before they are incorporated into finished products. These materials start as raw materials (secondary goods), which are transported to the next stage in the production process, and are then processed into intermediate materials (primary products), before being transported to the place of final production, where they are processed into the finished product. As such, trade in intermediate goods, which require further processing and are used as inputs for production, e.g. sub-assemblies – is often used as a proxy measure of GVCs. Since 1995, intermediate manufactured materials have consistently accounted for around 50% of manufactured exports and imports at the global level, providing evidence of the existence and importance of GVC trade. However, the value chain does not end at the final production stage, as the products concerned will then be shipped to distributors and, ultimately, consumers.

To this extent, global value chains are essential neural networks, operating as individual dynamic systems. This also infers that each international supply chain, regardless of its applicable industrial sector, is *per se* an individual dynamic system, with its own specific individual entities within the system. Within this type of dynamic system, all the elements are unique and operate as distinct independent autonomous or semi-autonomous entities, but also operate as part of the overall integrated unit. If one element of this unit, i.e. an individual element, fails or malfunctions, the whole dynamic system malfunctions given the interdependency of all the entities contained within the dynamic system.

The application of cybernetic synergy to the principle of the GVC is that unless the whole structure is controlled by way of synergy and communication within the framework of an extended version of the VSM, there will be no way of accounting for feedback, especially in the domain of the VSM and, for that matter, the application of the neural network. If on element of the GVC fails, the whole of the chain fails given the definition of the GVC as a pivotal element of the global supply chain. This is why there is a need for the overall control of GVCs and overall supply chains on an international basis. The principle of feedback states that if the feedback is positive, the process is functioning properly and is therefore totally efficient. If, however, the feedback is negative, there is a problem somewhere in the system which requires immediate rectification if the supply chain is to be maintained properly. In this way, each element of the GVC must be constantly monitored and audited for the purpose of maintaining this efficiency. Any issue must be quickly identified and resolved. In many ways, this was the basis of the original Cybersyn project conceived by Stafford Beer and implemented in Chile in the early 1970s. In this way, not only is overall control required by the TNCs involved in the GVC but also the relationship between the TNCs and their independent suppliers, to ensure that there is no compromise or risk of breakdown in the overall system. Where potential problems emerge, the supplier or service provider must inform the TNC that such a problem may exist, and the decision is then taken to either switch the supply of goods or services to another supplier, or to ensure that the existing supplier rectifies the problem as soon as possible in order to avoid potential delays or stoppages. This can only occur through the process of negative feedback and any resulting mitigating or rectifying action, which, in its essence, is the basis of essential supply chain cybernetics.

A BRIEF CASE STUDY

In order to understand how a cybernetic-based solution can work in practice, the following case study based on topical prevalent issues can be used as a practical example.

A major manufacturer produces essential FMCG products for the consumer retail sector. Its products are an essential element of household consumption and are supplied to all the national retail locations via a series of distribution centres (DCs). As well as procuring materials nationally, the company imports materials on a regular basis from around the world and processes these into the finished products.

The Challenge

A major crisis has hit the country in the form of a major pandemic, and lockdowns have been imposed across the country by the national government. In anticipation of the inconvenience of these lockdowns, there has been a spate of panic buying, and many retail outlets, especially in the concentrated urban areas, have quickly run out of stocks. In the lesser-populated areas, however, it is discovered that stocks of the products concerned are still relatively plentiful owing to lower levels of demand. The policy up to the present is that all DCs should receive equal levels of stock regardless of location and demand.

The Suggested Solution

If we use the cybernetic synergy approach as applied to the Chilean economy in the 1970s, we need to ensure that the production company has a central control function dealing with its logistics operations and is capable of responding to feedback from each DC on an immediate basis and is therefore capable of reacting on an equally immediate basis.

We can assume that production is constant and that the pandemic has not affected the inward supply of materials. We can also assume that the production force within the company has a special dispensation to continue with production levels as normal. We also devise a system where each DC reports in daily to the central control function with its projections for demand and its existing stock levels.

Each DC is exactly the same size as the others and therefore has exactly the same storage capacity as the other centres. The demand level therefore accounts for the percentage capacity per DC on a standard basis.

We therefore derive the following data from each DC for a specific day based on present stock levels based on percentage capacity and anticipated (actual) demand, which represents positive or negative feedback:

DC 1: Stock level 10% capacity; demand level 50% capacity
DC 2: Stock level 0% capacity; demand level 60% capacity
DC 3: Stock level 80% capacity; demand level 20% capacity
DC 4: Stock level 75% capacity; demand level 40% capacity
DC 5: Stock level 5% capacity; demand level 50% capacity
DC 6: Stock level 70% capacity; demand level 30% capacity
DC 7: Stock level 60% capacity; demand level 30% capacity
DC 8: Stock level 20% capacity; demand level 70% capacity
DC 9: Stock level 80% capacity; demand level 15% capacity
DC 10: Stock level 50% capacity; demand level 40% capacity

If we analyse the data, we can deduce that DCs 1, 2, 5, and 8 are severely low or critically low on stock levels, with capacity at high level (negative feedback). However, DCs 3, 4, 6, and 9 are plentiful in stock levels (positive feedback).

Discounting the normal daily/weekly supplies to each DC, we can therefore take steps based on feedback from each centre to immediately redress the balance to a reasonable degree. Discounting the costs of transport, we can therefore transfer stock from some DCs to the others, where stock levels are critical. Specifically, we carry out the following measures:

TRANSFER FROM:
DC 3: 20% Stock
DC 4: 15% Stock
DC 6: 10% Stock
DC 9: 20% Stock

TRANSFER TO:
DC 1: 15% Stock
DC 2: 20% Stock
DC 5: 15% Stock
DC 8: 10% Stock

Balance: 5% Stock as a cushion remaining.

DCs 7 and 10 – manageable stocks based on existing capacity.

It should be noted that these figures are purely hypothetical but loosely represent a mitigating strategy. However, the principle is the same. Feedback is required to assess the situation as it exists and to take the appropriate steps to rectify this situation based on demand requirements.

Because technology now applies to the whole process, we also use the principle of the DSS, in particular the Strategic DSS (SDSS) to control the whole DSS process and enable top management to make informed and balanced decisions. SDSSs are a means of helping managers understand strategy and its implications, by way of the use of a series of subordinate Decision Control Systems. SDSSs contain many general DSS features and are intended for senior managers. An example is as shown in Figure 8.6.

Note that each element is inter-communicative, in that each subsystem communicates with the other support systems, and all the support DSSs

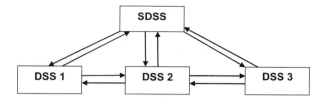

FIGURE 8.6
Typical decision support system (DSS).

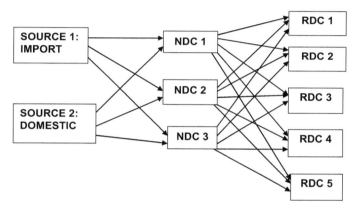

FIGURE 8.7
ERP application.

N.B. The number of RDCs has been compressed for the purpose of the exercise, but the overall principle remains the same. It should also be noted that as well as the movement of materials between the NDCs and the RDCs, the RDCs provide feedback to the NDCs in terms of material requirements, hence the need for a robust MRP (Materials Requirement Planning) system to fulfil all the necessary requirements at each stage in the logistics process.

communicate with the SDSS on a reciprocal basis, providing the necessary feedback to enable the SDSS to control the support systems.

Using electronic systems, we are able to automate the whole decision-making process in the form of an enterprise resource planning (ERP) application. This in itself also fulfils the principle of the ANN, thus producing an ANN diagram as follows (National Distribution Centres are NDCs, while Regional Distribution Centres are RDCs) (Figure 8.7).

The ANN combined with the DSS enables the electronic ERP system to determine the exact demand of each RDC depending upon the regional demands for the products concerned, and thus allocate product resources to the areas that require these the most, on a constant basis. However, the essential factor that drives this process is feedback from each of the RDCs to the central electronic control function. Where the feedback is positive, no remedial action is required, and the process continues on a constant basis. Where the feedback is negative, i.e. the RDC is suffering a shortfall in inventory, the process is adjusted to account for the shortfall, and more materials are transported to the RDC concerned.

It should also be noted that this is a purely hypothetical situation in itself, but it does represent typical scenarios based on topical situations that some might recognise with relation to their own experiences and observations. In reality, this scenario can apply just as well to the health-care sector, in order to address the pandemic where it matters and to supply the necessary healthcare products to ensure that all necessary steps are taken to cater for all national health needs. It could be observed that in several national cases, this policy was not adopted from the outset of the present/recent COVID pandemic, and the result was a severe shortage of certain products in places where they were needed as a matter of urgency, owing to deficient planning. This is not to say that cybernetic synergy would have fully worked in every case, based on the collective ability organisations to coordinate their activities at short notice, but it could have more quickly alleviated the critical situation as it emerged. The original Cybersyn project was designed to provide immediate solutions based on the information provided through feedback from the relevant sources, hence its ability to provide short-term immediate solutions. In this respect, accurate feedback is essential to the provision of the right and expedient solution, especially in terms of organisation and planning at each stage in the process. It should also be recognised that Cybersyn was based largely on physical management decisions taken by human individuals, i.e. top management based in the capital Santiago, using a central control room with limited technological resources. This was the early 1970s, and Chile had few computer systems available at the time. However, today, such solutions are automated and are carried out electronically as part of the computer system. To a degree, this not only removes the human element but also speeds up the decision-making process based on the electronic information provided.

9

Cybernetics and Quality Control

Chapter 8 covered the use of cybernetics in project management and addressed the issues of planning and control. This chapter addresses the issues of quality control and Statistical Process Control (SPC) in the cybernetic perspective, as all these elements overlap in terms of process and quality control in a variety of areas. However, before analysing the relationship between cybernetics, quality control, and lean management, it is necessary to determine the background to these areas in the form of SPC.

SPC is a method of quality control which employs statistical methods to monitor and control a process. This helps to ensure that the process operates efficiently, producing more specification-conforming products with less waste (rework or scrap). SPC can be applied to any process where the "conforming product" (product meeting specifications) output can be measured. Key tools used in SPC include run charts, control charts, a focus on continuous improvement such as Six Sigma, where a maximum of 3.4 defects is allowed per 1 million opportunities or events (i.e. data measurements), and the design of experiments. An example of a process where SPC is applied is manufacturing lines.

SPC must be practiced in two phases: The first phase is the initial establishment of the process, and the second phase is the regular production use of the process. In the second phase, a decision of the period to be examined must be made, depending upon the change in 5M&E conditions (Man, Machine, Material, Method, Movement, Environment) and wear rate of parts used in the manufacturing process (machine parts, jigs, and fixtures).

An advantage of SPC over other methods of quality control, such as "inspection", is that it emphasizes early detection and prevention of problems, rather than the correction of problems after they have occurred. This reduces costs as well as time wasted on inspections at a later stage.

In addition to reducing waste, SPC can lead to a reduction in the time required to produce the product. SPC makes it less likely the finished product will need to be reworked or scrapped.

SPC was pioneered by Walter A. Shewhart at Bell Laboratories in the early 1920s. Shewhart, who was a physicist, engineer and statistician, developed the control chart in 1924 and the concept of a state of statistical control. Statistical control is equivalent to the concept of exchangeability developed by the logician William Ernest Johnson also in 1924 in his book *Logic, Part III: The Logical Foundations of Science*. Along with a team at AT&T that included Harold Dodge and Harry Romig, he worked to put sampling inspection on a rational statistical basis as well. Shewhart consulted with Colonel Leslie E. Simon in the application of control charts to munitions manufacture at the US Army's Picatinny Arsenal in 1934. That successful application helped convince Army Ordnance to engage AT&T's George Edwards to consult on the use of statistical quality control among its divisions and contractors at the outbreak of World War II.

W. Edwards Deming, the creator of the Plan-Do-Check-Act (PDCA) cycle, invited Shewhart to speak at the Graduate School of the US Department of Agriculture and served as the editor of Shewhart's book *Statistical Method from the Viewpoint of Quality Control* (1939) which was the result of that lecture. Deming was an important architect of the quality control short courses that trained American industry in the new techniques during WWII. The graduates of these wartime courses formed a new professional society in 1945, the American Society for Quality Control, which elected Edwards as its first president. Deming travelled to Japan during the Allied Occupation and met with the Union of Japanese Scientists and Engineers (JUSE) in an effort to introduce SPC methods to Japanese industry. Some 10 years later, Japanese statistical quality methods were further developed into the concept of Quality by Design by the Japanese engineer Genichi Taguchi, the author of the famous statistical Taguchi methods, i.e. the quality of a product is based on the principle of the eradication of the potential problem or fault in the production system at its design or development stage. These concepts were used successfully by the Japanese automotive company Nissan to improve its quality methods and create the successful range of cars that exist today.

Shewhart read the new statistical theories coming out of Britain, especially the work of William Sealy Gosset, Karl Pearson, and Ronald Fisher. However, he understood that data from physical processes seldom produced a normal distribution curve (that is, a Gaussian distribution or "bell curve"). He discovered that data from measurements of variation in manufacturing did not always behave the way as data from measurements of natural phenomena. Shewhart concluded that while every process displays variation, some processes display variation that is natural to the process (*common* sources of variation); these processes he described as being *in (statistical) control*. Other processes additionally display variation that is not present in the causal system of the process at all times (*special* sources of variation), which Shewhart described as *not in control*.

In manufacturing, quality is defined as conformance to specification. However, no two products or characteristics are ever exactly the same, because any process contains many sources of variability. In mass manufacturing, traditionally, the quality of a finished article is ensured by post-manufacturing inspection of the product. Each article (or a sample of articles from a production lot) may be accepted or rejected according to how well it meets its design specifications. In contrast, SPC uses statistical tools such as the normal distribution and standard deviations to observe the performance of the production process in order to detect significant variations before they result in the production of a sub-standard article. Any source of variation at any point of time in a process will fall into one of two classes.

1. *Common* causes

    "Common" causes are sometimes referred to as "non-assignable", or "normal" sources of variation. It refers to any source of variation that consistently acts on process, of which there are typically many. This type of causes collectively produce a statistically stable and repeatable distribution over time.

2. *Special* causes

    "Special" causes are sometimes referred to as "assignable" sources of variation. The term refers to any factor causing variation that affects only some of the process output. They are often intermittent and unpredictable.

Most processes have many sources of variation; most of them are minor and may be ignored. If the dominant assignable sources of variation are detected, potentially they can be identified and removed. When they are removed, the process is said to be "stable". When a process is stable, its variation should remain within a known set of limits. That is, at least, until another assignable source of variation occurs.

For example, a breakfast cereal packaging line may be designed to fill each cereal box with 500 g of cereal. Some boxes will have slightly more than 500 g, and some will have slightly less. When the package weights are measured, the data will demonstrate a distribution of net weights.

If the production process, its inputs, or its environment (for example, the machine on the line) change, the distribution of the data will change. For example, as the cams and pulleys of the machinery wear, the cereal filling machine may put more than the specified amount of cereal into each box. Although this might benefit the customer, from the manufacturer's point of view, it is wasteful and increases the cost of production. If the manufacturer finds the change and its source in a timely manner, the change can be corrected (for example, the cams and pulleys replaced).

The data from measurements of variations at points on the process map is monitored using control charts. Control charts were originally devised by Walter Shewhart (that is why they are often known as Shewhart charts) and attempt to differentiate "assignable" ("special") sources of variation from "common" sources. "Common" sources, because they are an expected part of the process, are of much less concern to the manufacturer than "assignable" sources. Using control charts is a continuous activity, ongoing over time. The control chart is based on a mathematical mean, i.e. the statistical average, being set as a horizontal line across the chart, otherwise called the Centre Line, with two sets of upper and lower limits imposed above and below it. These limits are divided into two sets of parameters, i.e. the Upper and Lower Warning Limits (UWL/LWL), and outside them, the Upper and Lower Action Limits (UAL/LAL) or Upper and Lower Control Limits (UCL/LCL). The Warning Limits are calculated by ±2 Standard Deviations away from the mean, and the Action Limits are calculated by ±3 Standard Deviations away from the mean. The range between these limits is determined by the calculation of the standard deviation for the data sets involved for an established production process. The greater the standard deviation, the wider the spread of data in relation to the mean. In general, the data being analysed is not acted upon as long as it lies between the mean and the warning limits, despite the fact that there may be a wide range of data allowance as dictated by the upper and lower limits. However, should the observed data exceed the warning limits, more attention is paid to the process. If any of the data sets should exceed the action limits, the process is shut down automatically and the whole process reviewed. This whole process should thus be made part of the cybernetic process, as it has significant implications for the Viable Systems Model (VSM) of Stafford Beer. A typical example of a control chart is shown in Figure 9.1.

When the process does not trigger any of the control chart "detection rules" for the control chart, i.e. the tendency of the data towards the lower/upper warning or action limits, it is said to be "stable". A process capability analysis may be performed on a stable process to predict the ability of the process to produce "conforming product" in the future. However, in the following diagram, one data set exceeds the Upper Control Limit (UCL). This would suggest that a problem has occurred with this particular data set and that the process needs to be shut down in order to investigate the problem, and completely review the process before it can be allowed to continue, as the process is deemed to be unstable (Figure 9.2).

A stable process can be demonstrated by a process signature that is free of variances outside of the capability index. A process signature is the plotted points compared with the capability index.

When the process triggers any of the control chart "detection rules", (or alternatively, the process capability is low), other activities may be performed to identify the source of the excessive variation. The tools used in these extra activities include Ishikawa diagrams, designed experiments,

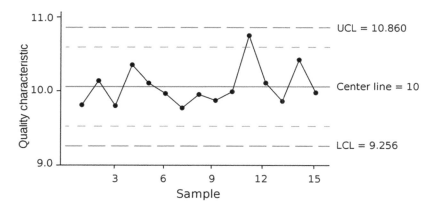

FIGURE 9.1
Statistical Process Control (SPC) chart.

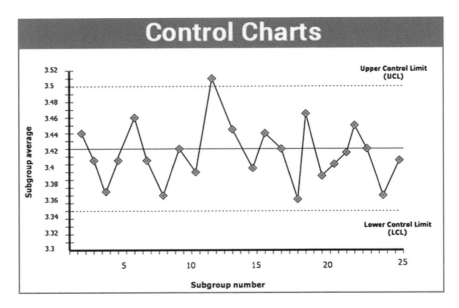

FIGURE 9.2
Control charts.

and Pareto charts. Designed experiments are a means of objectively quantifying the relative importance (strength) of sources of variation. Once the sources of (special cause) variation are identified, they can be minimised or eliminated. Steps to eliminating a source of variation might include development of standards, staff training, error proofing, and changes to the process itself or its inputs.

It is the SPC system, coupled with control charts, that can be incorporated in an overall cybernetic approach to quality control and ultimately, overall corporate efficiency, especially where a production facility is involved. To this extent, the value of the cybernetic approach to quality control reveals much in the way of detailed analysis that is still in its infancy and needs to be developed much further.

In general terms, cybernetics is about having a goal and a self-correcting system that adjusts to the perturbations in the environment so that the system can keep moving towards the goal. This is referred to as the "First Order Cybernetics". An example (remaining true to the Greek origin of the word) we can use is a ship sailing towards a destination. When there are perturbations in the form of wind, the steersman adjusts the path accordingly and maintains the course. Another common example is a thermostat. The thermostat is able to maintain the required temperature inside the house by adjusting according to the external temperature. The thermostat activates when a specified temperature limit is tripped and cools or heats the house. An important concept that is used for cybernetics is the "Law of Requisite Variety" by Ross Ashby. The law of requisite variety states that only variety can absorb variety, or more simply, the controlling element must have enough degrees of variety, or systems available, to at least match, if not envelop, the varieties which it is to control. If the wind is extreme, the steersman may not be able to steer the ship properly. In other words, the steersman lacks the requisite variety to handle or absorb the external variety. However, if the steersman is of strong physique, is an experienced navigator and knows both his ship and the nautical conditions that he is steering the ship through, he will therefore be able to prevail over the elements and steer the ship through the natural adversities. The main mechanism of cybernetics is the closed feedback loop that helps the steersman adjust accordingly to maintain the course. This is also the art of a regulation loop, namely **compare**, **act**, and **sense**.

Warren McCulloch, the American cybernetician, explained cybernetics as follows:

> Narrowly defined it (cybernetics) is but the art of the helmsman, to hold a course by swinging the rudder so as to offset any deviation from that course. For this the helmsman must be so informed of the consequences of his previous acts that he corrects them – communication engineers call this 'negative feedback' – for the output of the helmsman decreases the input to the helmsman. The intrinsic governance of nervous activity, our reflexes, and our appetites exemplify this process. In all of them, as in the steering of the ship, what must return is not energy but information. Hence, in an extended sense, cybernetics may be said to include the timeliest applications of the quantitative theory of information.

Walter Shewhart's ideas of statistical control work well with the cybernetic ideas. Shewhart purposefully used the term "control" for his field. The term control or regulation is a key concept in cybernetics, as explained above. Shewhart defined control as:

> A phenomenon is said to be controlled when, through the use of past experience, we can predict at least within limits, how the phenomenon may be expected to vary in the future. Here it is understood that prediction within

limits means that we can state, at least approximately, the probability that the observed phenomenon will fall within the given limits.

Shewhart expanded further:

> The idea of control involves action for the purpose of achieving a desired end. Control in this sense involves both action and a specified end.
> ...We should keep in mind that the state of statistical control is something presumable to be desired, something to which one may hope to attain; in other words it is an ideal goal.

Shewhart's view of control aligns very well with the teleological aspects of cybernetics. From here, Shewhart develops his famous Shewhart cycle as a means to maintain statistical control. Shewhart wrote:

> Three steps in quality control. Three senses of statistical control. Broadly speaking, there are three steps in a quality control process: the specification of what is wanted, the production of things to satisfy the specification, and the inspection of things produced to see if they satisfy the specification.
> The three steps (making a hypothesis, carrying out an experiment, and testing the hypothesis) constitute a dynamic scientific process of acquiring knowledge. From this viewpoint, it is better to show them as a forming a sort of spiral gradually approach a circular path to which would represent the idealized case, where no evidence is found in the testing of hypothesis indicates a need for changing the hypothesis. Mass production viewed in this way constitutes a continuing and *self-corrective* method for making the most efficient use of raw and fabricated materials.

The Shewhart cycle as he proposed is shown in Figure 9.3.

One of the criterions Shewhart developed for his model was that the model should be as simple as possible and adaptable in a continuing and self-corrective operation of control. The idea of self-correction is a key point of cybernetics as part of maintaining the course.

The brilliance of Shewhart was in providing guidance on when we should react and when we should not react to the variations in the data. He stated that

> a necessary and sufficient condition for statistical control is to have a constant system of chance causes... It is necessary that differences in the qualities of a number of pieces of a product appear to be consistent with

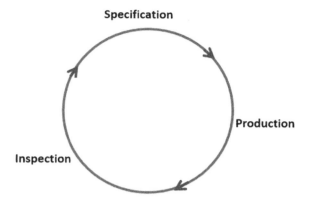

Specification

Production

Inspection

FIGURE 9.3
The Shewhart cycle.

the assumption that they arose from a constant system of chance causes…
If a cause system is not constant, we shall say that an assignable cause is
present.

Shewhart continued:

My own experience has been that in the early stages of any attempt at control of a quality characteristic, assignable causes are always present even
though the production operation has been repeated under presumably the
same essential conditions. As these assignable causes are found and eliminated, the variation in quality gradually approaches a state of statistical
control as indicated by the statistics of successive samples falling within
their control limits, except in rare instances.

We are engaging in a continuing, self-corrective operation designed for
the purpose of attaining a state of statistical control.

The successful quality control engineer, like the successful research
worker, is not a pure reason machine but instead is a biological unit reacting to and acting upon an everchanging environment.

James Wilk defined cybernetics as:

Cybernetics is the study of justified intervention.

This is an apt definition when we look at quality control, as viewed by
Shewhart. There are three options when it comes to quality control:

1. If we have an unpredictable system, then we work to eliminate the causes of signals, with the aim of creating a predictable system.
2. If we have a predictable system that is not always capable of meeting the target, then we work to improve the system in a systematic way, aiming to create a new a system whose results now fluctuate around a better average.
3. When the range of predictable performance is always better than the target, then there is less of a need for improvement. We could, however, choose to change the target and then continue improving in a systematic way.

Source: Measures of Success (Mark Graban, 2019)

Shewhart wrote "Statistical Method from the Viewpoint of Quality Control" in 1939, 9 years before Wiener's Cybernetics book. The use of statistical control allows us to have a conversation with a process. The process tells us what the limits are, and as long as the data points are plotted randomly within the two limits, we can assume that whatever we are seeing is due to chance or natural variation. The data should be random and without any order. When we see some manner of order in the likes of a trend or an outside data point, then we should look for an assignable cause. The data points are not necessarily due to chance anymore. As we keep plotting, we should improve our process and recalculate the limits.

It is good to illustrate Dr. Deming's enhancement of Shewhart's cycle, which is taken from a presentation by Clifford L. Norman. This was part of the evolution of the PDSA (Plan-Do-Study-Act) cycle which later became famous as PDCA cycle. This showed only three steps with a decision point after step 3 (Figure 9.4).

The updated cycle has significant value to it, such as experimenting on a small scale, reflecting on what we learned and have understood.

The PDCA cycle became more applicable over time, as it detailed specific processes in the cycle.

The PDCA cycle provides a simple and effective approach for solving problems and managing change. It enables businesses to develop hypotheses about what needs to change, test these hypotheses in a continuous feedback loop, and gain valuable learning and knowledge. It promotes testing improvements on a small scale before updating company-wide procedures and work methods. The PDCA cycle consists of four components:

Plan – Identify the problem, collect relevant data, and understand the problem's root cause, develop hypotheses about what the issues may be, and decide which one to test.

Do – Develop and implement a solution; decide upon a measurement to gauge its effectiveness, test the potential solution, and measure the results.

Check – Confirm the results through before-and-after data comparison. Study the result, measure effectiveness, and decide whether the hypothesis is supported or not.

Act – Document the results, inform others about process changes, and make recommendations for the future PDCA cycles. If the solution was successful, implement it. If not, tackle the next problem and repeat the PDCA cycle again (Figure 9.5).

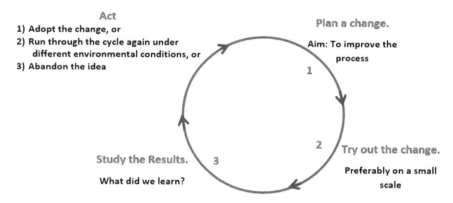

FIGURE 9.4
PDCA cycle.

FIGURE 9.5
Simplified PDCA cycle.

LEAN MANAGEMENT

The process of lean management is to strip away all unnecessary costs and activities and ensure that the systems in place are not only manageable but also totally efficient. This can be carried out using tools such as Six Sigma and KPIs, but it can also be managed through the use of the cybernetic-based VSM devised by Stafford Beer, each of whose five systems contributes to the lean management process.

System 1: Operational Control

System 1 controls an Operational Unit. The VSM is recursive, i.e. characterised by recurrence or repetition, thus supporting the essential cybernetic definition of circularity. Every recursion, i.e. recurrence, of the VSM can contain any number of Systems 1. This means that every element of System 1 is viable in itself, as it fulfils all the requirements of System 1. As observed by Beer, System 1 is the model of the human body's nervous system. When modelling a corporation as a VSM, System 1's task is to control a business division, in response to policy directives and over-riding instructions from above, in reaction to the direct demands of the external world upon it, and in awareness of the needs of other divisions.

System 2: Coordinating Function

System 1 exists permanently and inseparably in a meta-systemic coordination tool, i.e. System 2. In other words, System 2 controls and encompasses System 1. It subsumes all elements of System 1 and links them to System 3. The coordination activity, i.e. allocation of resources etc., should be carried out in a way that ensures maximum autonomy of the parts or elements "just short of threatening the integrity of the whole". This notion is also known as the Law of Cohesiveness, i.e. all elements acting separately but in a manner to contribute to the operation of the entire entity.

System 3: Managing the "Inside and Now"

System 3 is the model of the autonomic nervous system of the human body. Its purpose is to monitor the autonomic functions, implement plans within physiological limits, and report upwards. This can be translated in corporate terms to represent the feedback reported by individual elements of the departments within the corporate entity. When decisions are made by the top management, these will have an impact on the operations of each department, which in turn will report back their findings and concerns to the management. If all works, well, this is deemed to be positive feedback, and the policy is consolidated and perhaps extended. If the feedback is negative, rectification policies are implemented, and the process continues on an amended basis. System 3's purpose can also be formulated as assuring that the coordinated systems in System 1 can achieve a greater effect than the sum of the systems' individual activities. When modelling a corporation as a VSM, System 3 resembles the middle management that is responsible for all divisions.

System 3A: Auditing and Monitoring

System 3A's function is to watch for signs of strain and stress in the operational units of System 1; it does not however exert any command function whatsoever. System 3A bypasses the operational control of System 1 and thus provides an opportunity for System 3 to obtain a genuine impression of the state of affairs in the operational units. According to Beer, an example of System 3A in the context of a corporation is an Audit Channel. The system is described as a means to investigate and validate the information flowing between Systems 1, 2 and 3.

System 4: Managing the "Outside and Future"

Systems 4 and 5 represent the externalities imposed on the system and how it can adapt to these externalities or influences. Systems 1, 2, and 3 assure a stabilisation of the internal structure, but they do not take account of "progress" or change. Therefore, System 4 is dedicated to the larger environment, and hence to regulation of the system in relation to this. In terms of lean management and Six Sigma, these are deemed to be externalities, and therefore impact significantly on Systems 1, 2, and 3 in terms of operational efficiency.

System 5: Policy/The "Three-Four Balancer"

The task of System 5 is to monitor the balancing operation between Systems 3 and 4, according to Beer. The need for a balancing system between the

"Inside and Now" and the "Outside and Future" emerges from Beer's observation that in practice, Systems 3 and 4 will not achieve an equilibrium state without regulation. Viability of the organisation can only be achieved if neither one dominates over the other, i.e. the must both be properly balanced. On a corporate recursion level of the VSM, System 5 is responsible for the policy of the corporation.

To supplement these systems, an algedonic loop in management cybernetics, i.e. rewards and punishments, or approvals or alarms, regulates in a non-analytic mode. Although algedonic loops are not, per se, part of the VSM, they are nevertheless essential in its overall structure, as they have to account for the different types of feedback which will be reported. In the VSM, an algedonic control loop exists between Systems 3 and 1, which ends in System 5. Company policy, after all, has to result from internal activities and has to be able to resolve internal conflicts.

An algedonic loop can be used to override an analytic control circuit. For example, a whole plant is shut down because some critical operational variable is exceeded, as per the Control Chart example quoted earlier in the chapter. On the plant management level, nobody knows why the shutdown occurred. The signal does not contain the information why the operation must be shut down, only that it is mandatory to maintain viability.

The core idea of management cybernetics is that if Systems 1–5 are present and work as intended in a system, its viability in a complex environment is ensured and that its efficiency is maximised. However, as these systems do not naturally occur in an organisation, the VSM must be applied as a control measure and the organisational structure adapted to accommodate it.

Built-in Quality (BiQ) builds on the PDCA process, the so-called Deming cycle, with the aim of ensuring that the outcomes of a production process meet the expectations ideally without requiring ad hoc inspection or rework. The main process flow is to identify the customer expectations, upon which the operation is designed. This results in directives for the operating process, based on which the process is executed. The operating process produces the output that is checked in the quality control part of the BiQ procedure. If the output conforms to the established quality criteria, it is accepted, and if not, it is rejected. In either case, the stakeholders are informed, and, if needed, rectification measures are undertaken. For example, in the case of conformance, the stakeholders are informed that the output is going through and the operations are running well, according to plan.

However, in the case of non-conformance, expectations can be changed, inputs replaced, or new resources obtained where appropriate. If the non-conformance lies in the production system, then machines need to be recalibrated or repaired, or the whole production process needs to be reviewed. Changes to how the process is executed and carried out could be undertaken by changing or updating the operational directives. Whichever methods are required or appropriate depends on the circumstances. Either way, the purpose of the exercise to reduce non-conformance to zero or, at very least, a manageable minimum, and ensure that the whole process revolves around the maximisation of conformance, thus guaranteeing an acceptable quality level, and ultimately, complete customer satisfaction.

ISO

The **ISO 9000** family of quality management systems (QMS) is a set of standards that helps organisations ensure they meet customers and other stakeholder needs within statutory and regulatory requirements related to a product or service. ISO 9000 deals with the fundamentals of quality management systems, including the seven quality management principles that underlie the family of standards. ISO 9001 deals with the requirements that organisations wishing to meet the standard must fulfil.

Third-party certification bodies provide independent confirmation that organisations meet the requirements of ISO 9001. Over 1 million organisations worldwide are independently certified, making ISO 9001 one of the most widely used management tools in the world today. However, the ISO certification process has been criticised as being wasteful and not being useful for all organisations. In a sense, this is true, as there is a large amount of bureaucracy and process methodology to fulfil on the way to full certification, and most all enterprises are equipped for this depending upon their activities.

ISO 9000 was first published in 1987 by ISO (International Organization for Standardization). It was based on the BS 5750 series of standards from the British Standards Institution (BSI) that were proposed to ISO in 1979. However, its history can be traced back some 20 years before that, to the publication of government procurement standards, such as the US Department of Defense MIL-Q-9858 standard in 1959, and the UK's Def

Stan 05-21 and 05-24. Large organisations that supplied government procurement agencies often had to comply with a variety of quality assurance requirements for each contract awarded, which led the defence industry to adopt mutual recognition of NATO AQAP, MIL-Q, and Def Stan standards. Eventually, industries adopted ISO 9000 instead of forcing contractors to adopt multiple—and often similar—requirements.

The global adoption of ISO 9001 may be attributable to a number of factors. In the early days, the ISO 9001 (9002 and 9003) requirements were intended to be used by procuring organisations, as the basis of contractual arrangements with their suppliers. This helped reduce the need for "supplier development" by establishing basic requirements for a supplier to assure product quality. The ISO 9001 requirements could be tailored to meet specific contractual situations, depending on the complexity of product, business type (design responsibility, manufacture only, distribution, servicing, etc.), and risk to the procurer. If a chosen supplier was weak on the controls of their measurement equipment (calibration), and hence QC/inspection results, that specific requirement would be invoked in the contract. The adoption of a single quality assurance requirement also leads to cost savings throughout the supply chain by reducing the administrative burden of maintaining multiple sets of quality manuals and procedures.

A few years later, the UK Government took steps to improve national competitiveness following publication of CMD 8621, and Third Party Certification of Quality Management Systems was born, under the auspices of the National Accreditation Council of Certification Bodies (NACCB), which has become the United Kingdom Accreditation Service (UKAS).

In addition to many stakeholders' benefits, a number of studies have identified significant financial benefits for organisations certified to ISO 9001, with an ISO analysis of 42 studies showing that implementing the standard does enhance financial performance. Corbett et al. showed that certified organisations achieved superior return on assets compared to otherwise similar organisations without certification.

Heras et al. found similarly superior performance in the use of ISO 9000/1 and demonstrated that this was statistically significant and not a function of organisation size. Naveha and Marcus claimed that implementing ISO 9001 led to superior operational performance in the US automotive industry, although much of the improvement process also emanated from the use of Six Sigma as advocated and championed by Jack Welch, former chairman and CEO of the US multinational and conglomerate General Electric (GE). The US automotive industry had also benefitted from quality control techniques such as the Japanese Taguchi methods, implemented in the Japanese automotive industry in the 1960s. Sharma identified similar improvements in operating performance and linked this to superior financial performance. Chow-Chua et al. showed better overall financial performance was achieved for companies in Denmark. Rajan and Tamimi (2003) showed that ISO 9001 certification resulted in superior stock market performance and suggested that shareholders were richly rewarded for the investment in an ISO 9001 system.

While the connection between superior financial performance and ISO 9001 may be seen from the examples cited, there remains no proof of direct causation, though longitudinal studies, such as those of Corbett et al. (2005), may suggest it. Other writers, such as Heras et al. (2002), have suggested that while there is some evidence of this, the improvement is partly driven by the fact that there is a tendency for better-performing companies to seek ISO 9001 certification.

The mechanism for improving results has also been the subject of much research. Lo et al. (2007) identified operational improvements (e.g., cycle time reduction, inventory reductions) as following from certification. Internal process improvements in organisations lead to externally observable improvements. The benefit of increased international trade and domestic market share, in addition to the internal benefits such as customer satisfaction, interdepartmental communications, work processes, and customer/supplier partnerships derived, far exceeds any and all initial investment.

The ISO 9000 series are based on seven quality management principles (QMP). The seven quality management principles are as follows:

- QMP 1 – Customer focus
- QMP 2 – Leadership
- QMP 3 – Engagement of people
- QMP 4 – Process approach
- QMP 5 – Improvement
- QMP 6 – Evidence-based decision making
- QMP 7 – Relationship management

Principle 1 – Customer focus
Organisations depend on their customers and therefore should understand current and future customer needs, should meet customer requirements and strive to exceed customer expectations.

Principle 2 – Leadership
Leaders establish unity of purpose and direction of the organisation. They should create and maintain the internal environment in which people can become fully involved in achieving the organisation's objectives.

Principle 3 – Engagement of people
People at all levels are the essence of an organisation, and their full involvement enables their abilities to be used for the organisation's benefit.

Principle 4 – Process approach
A desired result is achieved more efficiently when activities and related resources are managed as a process.

Principle 5 – Improvement
Improvement of the organisation's overall performance should be a permanent objective of the organisation.

Principle 6 – Evidence-based decision-making
Effective decisions are based on the analysis of data and information.

Principle 7 – Relationship management
An organisation and its external providers (suppliers, contractors, service providers) are interdependent, and a mutually beneficial relationship enhances the ability of both to create value.

These seven principles also relate to the VSM, primarily Systems 1–3, although the ISO process itself accounts for System 4 of the VSM. Principles 1–3 are encompassed in Systems 1 and 2 (Departments and Relationships), while Principles 4–7 are encompassed in System 3 (Coordination and Monitoring).

ISO 9001:2015 Quality management systems — Requirements is a document of approximately 30 pages available from the national standards organisation in each country. Only ISO 9001 is directly audited against for third-party assessment purposes.

Contents of ISO 9001:2015 are as follows:

- Section 1: Scope
- Section 2: Normative references
- Section 3: Terms and definitions
- Section 4: Context of the organisation
- Section 5: Leadership
- Section 6: Planning
- Section 7: Support
- Section 8: Operation
- Section 9: Performance evaluation
- Section 10: Continual improvement

Essentially, the layout of the standard is similar to the previous ISO 9001:2008 standard in that it follows the PDCA cycle devised by W. Edwards Deming in a process-based approach but is now further encouraging this to have risk-based thinking (Section 0.3.3 of the introduction). The purpose of the quality objectives is to determine the conformity of the requirements (customers and organisations), facilitate effective deployment, and improve the quality management system.

Before the certification body can issue or renew a certificate, the auditor must be satisfied that the company being assessed has implemented the requirements of Sections 4–10. Sections 1–3 are not directly audited against, but because they provide context and definitions for the rest of the standard, not that of the organisation, their contents must be taken into account.

The standard no longer specifies that the organisation shall issue and maintain documented procedures (where AEO does), but ISO 9001:2015 requires the organisation to document any other procedures required for its effective operation. The standard also requires the organisation to issue and communicate a documented quality policy, a quality management system scope, and quality objectives. The standard no longer requires compliant organisations to issue a formal Quality Manual. The standard does require retention of numerous records, as specified throughout the standard. New for the 2015 release is a requirement for an organisation to assess risks and opportunities (Section 6.1) and to determine internal and external issues relevant to its purpose and strategic direction (Section 4.1). The organisation must demonstrate how the standard's requirements are being met, while the external auditor's role is to determine the quality management system's effectiveness. More detailed interpretation and implementation examples are often sought by organisations seeking more information in what can be a very technical area.

The new *ISO 9001:2015* management system standard helps ensure that consumers get reliable, desired quality goods and services. This further increases benefits for a business.

The 2015 version is also less prescriptive than its predecessors and focuses on performance. This was achieved by combining the process approach with risk-based thinking, and employing the Deming PDCA cycle at all levels in the organisation.

Some of the key changes include the following:

- High-Level Structure of ten clauses is implemented. Now all new standards released by ISO will have this high-level structure.
- Greater emphasis on building a management system suited to each organisation's particular needs.
- A requirement that those at the top of an organisation be involved and accountable, aligning quality with wider business strategy.
- Risk-based thinking throughout the standard makes the whole management system a preventive tool and encourages continuous improvement.
- Less prescriptive requirements for documentation: the organisation can now decide what documented information it needs and what format it should be in.
- Alignment with other key management system standards through the use of a common structure and core text.
- Inclusion of Knowledge Management principles.
- Quality Manual & Management representative (MR) are no longer mandatory.

However, it must be pointed out that for compliance-related activities, many authorities still require documented procedures manuals, as these are essential in ensuring that staff unacquainted with ISO-based procedures can learn the systems and structures in a straightforward and methodical manner. The other reason for such procedures manuals is that they can be audited and checked by external auditors whenever an external audit is required. This is also a pre-requisite for Sarbanes-Oxley auditing as required by the US Sarbanes-Oxley Act of 2002.

Two types of auditing are required to become registered to the standard: auditing by an external certification body (external audit) and audits by internal staff trained for this process (internal audits). The aim is a continual process of review and assessment to verify that the system is working as it is supposed to, to find out where it can improve, and to correct or prevent identified problems. It is considered healthier for internal auditors to audit outside their usual management line, so as to bring a degree of independence to their judgements.

The debate on the effectiveness of ISO 9000 commonly centres on the following questions:

1. Are the quality principles in ISO 9001 of value?
2. Does it help to implement an ISO 9001-compliant quality management system?
3. Does it help to obtain ISO 9001 certification?

The effectiveness of the ISO system being implemented depends on a number of factors, the most significant of which are:

1. Commitment of senior management to monitor, control, and improve quality. Organisations that implement an ISO system without this desire and commitment often take the cheapest road to get a certificate on the wall and ignore problem areas uncovered in the audits.
2. How well the ISO system integrates into current business practices. Many organisations that implement ISO try to make their system fit into a cookie-cutter quality manual instead of creating a manual that documents existing practices and only adds new processes to meet the ISO standard when necessary.
3. How well the ISO system focuses on improving the customer experience. The broadest definition of quality is "Whatever the customer perceives good quality to be". This means that a company does not necessarily have to make a product that never fails; some customers have a higher tolerance for product failures if they always receive shipments on-time or have a positive experience in some other dimension of customer service. An ISO system should take into account all areas of the customer experience and the industry expectations, and seek to improve them on a continual basis. This means

taking into account all processes that deal with the three stakeholders (customers, suppliers, and organisation, essentially the integrated supply chain). Only then can a company sustain improvements in the customer's experience.

4. How well the auditor finds and communicates areas of improvement. While ISO auditors may not provide consulting to the clients they audit, there is the potential for auditors to point out areas of improvement. Many auditors simply rely on submitting reports that indicate compliance or non-compliance with the appropriate section of the standard; however, to most executives, this is like speaking a foreign language. Auditors that can clearly identify and communicate areas for improvement in language and terms executive management understands facilitate action on improvement initiatives by the companies they audit. When management does not understand why they were non-compliant and the business implications associated with non-compliance, they simply ignore the reports and focus on what they do understand.

The ethic and practice of proper corporate quality management can lead to significant improvements in business performance and hence its profitability, often having a positive effect on investment, market share, sales growth, sales margins, competitive advantage, and avoidance of litigation, thus also satisfying the conditions of Porter's Five Forces model. The quality principles in ISO 9000:2000 are also sound, according to Wade and Barnes, who state that "ISO 9000 guidelines provide a comprehensive model for quality management systems that can make any company competitive". Sroufe and Curkovic (2008) found benefits ranging from registration required to remain part of a supply base, better documentation, to cost benefits, and improved involvement and communication with management. According to the ISO, the 2015 version of the standard brings the following benefits:

1. By assessing their context, organisations can define who is affected by their work and what they expect. This enables clearly stated business objectives and the identification of new business opportunities.
2. Organisations can identify and address the risks associated with their organisation.
3. By putting customers first, organisations can make sure they consistently meet customer needs and enhance customer satisfaction. This

can lead to more repeat customers, new clients, and increased business for the organisation.

4. Organisations work in a more efficient way as all their processes are aligned and understood by everyone. This increases productivity and efficiency, bringing internal costs down.
5. Organisations will meet necessary statutory and regulatory requirements.
6. Organisations can expand into new markets, as some sectors and clients require ISO 9001 before carrying out business transactions.

In the above respects, the VSM covers much, if not all, the requirements of the ISO process. The cybernetic process requires the full scope of control to be exercised over the full organisational entity, as per Ross Ashby's Law of Requisite Variety, and this is achieved by addressing and covering all the systems contained in the VSM. Given that the model covers internal relationships and synergies as much as it does management and control mechanisms, the cybernetic approach which also covers feedback and circularity, as well as recursion in the entity and its functions, provides an excellent basis for creating the control vehicles that satisfy the ISO 9000/9001 process. Indeed, the VSM model is more stringent and vigorous than the ISO process itself, as the VSM process demands far greater levels of continuous monitoring, feedback, and control and as a result can be used more effectively to manage the viability and efficiency of any organisation. The VSM is, in reality, more thorough and all-embracing than the ISO regime of standards, as the ISO system requires a series of different individual benchmarks and standards to cover all perceived aspects of the organisation. The VSM covers all these aspects as a matter of course.

10

The Relationship between Cybernetics and AEO Status

Chapters 8 and 9 have detailed the principles of cybernetics and Authorised Economic Operator (AEO) or Trusted Trader status. This chapter seeks to establish the solid relationship between the two, and how the cybernetics process can influence how successful an organisation can be in gaining AEO status.

The cybernetic principle applies a series of control mechanisms to the AEO process, and in many ways relies heavily on the viable system model (VSM), encompassing first-order and second-order cybernetics, where the second order effectively controls and observes the first order. Where the first-order controls each individual function, the second-order acts as an umbrella over the sum of all of the first-order functions. The purpose of this is to ensure that the organisation as a whole functions as a fully coordinated entity, with all elements of the entity under a strict regime of controls. The AEO process effectively slots this into an overall compliance process, where the ultimate purpose of both first- and second-order cybernetics is to achieve total compliance and control over the whole corporate process.

The first order deals with causation processes, i.e. processes that involve control, adaptation, negative feedback, and computing, i.e. operational systems. **Second-order cybernetics**, also known as the cybernetics of cybernetics, is the recursive application of cybernetics to itself, in other words, monitoring and controlling the process of first-order cybernetics, i.e. the cybernetics of the *Observed*. Heinz Von Foerster referred to it as the cybernetics of "observing systems", whereas first-order cybernetics is that of "observed systems".

In the AEO process, each section of the AEO questionnaire deals with each individual function of the organisation and can therefore be classed as "First Order". The second order concerns the overall coordination and management of the controls for each process and therefore concerns overall organisational strategy. It also concerns the principles of Input and Output. The input of information will reveal potential and actual shortcomings in the system, and this is the purpose of the AEO self-assessment questionnaire. The results obtained from this initial analysis generally provide negative feedback which can then be addressed to rectify these shortcomings. The output is the resulting change in regimes, structures, and processes which are deemed to be acceptable to HMRC when it conducts the AEO audit following submission of the application and questionnaire.

The following AEO criteria set out by HMRC illustrate the application of the VSM, and how it can be applied to the AEO application process.

Section I. Company information

This section is a listing of information necessary for the Customs authority to provide itself with a "picture" of the company and the company's activities. Some of this information may already be available if the company has already received Customs authorisations, and may contribute to a lower level of risk as a result (Tables 10.1 and 10.2).

Subsection 1.01 Organisational characteristics

TABLE 10.1

1.01.	Indicator	Risk Description	Points for Attention
1.	Date and place of registration	If registration is from a recent date Customs will not have information on the operator's history, which could lead to more controls.	a. Date and place of registration of the company. b. When the company started its business.
2.	Operator's statute	Concentrated ownership can influence the reliability of the information from the operator to customs.	a. The company's legal form. b. Has the company a concentrated ownership?

(Continued)

TABLE 10.1 (*Continued*)

1.01.	Indicator	Risk Description	Points for Attention
3.	The share capital and shareholders, owners, and legal representatives	The owner can influence the (provision of) information to the customs authorities.	a. Provide an overview of the principle owners/shareholders and legal representatives of the company, stating names and addresses and their proportional interests.[a] b. Provide an overview of the members of the board of directors of the company.
4.	Trade sector	• Shortage of transparency of the accounting system. • Omission of the connection between the flow of goods and the flow of money With manufacturing companies the reconciliation between the flow of goods and the flow of money can be difficult to equate. • A diverse range of activities could increase potential for errors or omissions.	a. Describe the company activities. b. What is the typology of the company (service company, manufacturing company, trading company)?
5.	Number of sites and subsidiaries	• Non-transparency of transactions. • Non-transparency of the flow of goods and/or the flow of money. • Multiple locations could increase the potential for errors. • Affiliated transactions.	a. Specify the location details of the various sites and/or subsidiaries of the company and briefly describe the company's activities in each site/subsidiary. b. Specify if the company and each site/subsidiary acts within the supply chain in its own name and on its own behalf, or if it acts in its own name and on behalf of another person or company or if it acts in name of and on behalf of another person or company. c. Specify whether goods are bought from and/or supplied to companies affiliated with the applicant's company.

[a] This question should be considered in relation to the described risk. Only owners/shareholders that have a direct influence on the decision making in the company are relevant.

Subsection 1.02 Internal organisation

TABLE 10.2

1.02.	Indicator	Risk Description	Points for Attention
1.	Internal organisation	• Limited control of the companies' activities. • Lack of segregation of duties between functions. • Lack of adequate cover when key personnel are absent.	a. Specify the internal structure of the organisation. b. Has the company documented the functions/competencies for each department and/or function? c. Specify how many employees there are in your company, in total and for each department. d. Give the names of the key office-holders working in your company (managing director, divisional heads, accounting manager, finance manager, head of customs routines, etc.). e. Describe the adopted routines covering the situation that the competent employee is not present, temporary, or permanent.
2.	Appropriate level of knowledge of customs procedures	• Lack of knowledge about customs regulations, customs legislation, customs procedures, and customs routines including non-fiscal aspects. • Lack of internal training could indicate a bad compliance attitude of the company.	a. Give the names and the position within the organisation of the persons that have specific customs expertise (fiscal and non-fiscal aspects). b. Asses the level of knowledge of the above-mentioned persons in regards of the use of IT technology in customs and commercial processes and general commercial matters, such as the labelling of goods.

Section II. Compliance record

Criteria: *An appropriate record of compliance with customs requirements*

The applying economic operator, the persons in charge of the company or exercising control over its management, and, if applicable, the applicant's legal representative in customs matters and the person responsible in the company for customs matters have not committed a serious infringement or repeated infringements of customs rules over the last 3 years preceding the submission of the application. If the applicant has been established for less than 3 years, his compliance shall be judged on the basis of records and information that are available.

The applicant's compliance will be judged on the basis of the records of the Customs administration, including intelligence information and results of anti-fraud investigations. If the persons exercising control over the management of the applicant are established or located in a third country, their compliance will be judged on the basis of records and information that are available in the country of application (Tables 10.3–10.5).

Note: The information of the two following subsections can mainly be gathered by the customs authority itself, on the basis of information from various sources within the customs administration including national and international enforcement agencies.

Subsection 2.01 Compliance history as regards customs authorities and other relevant governmental authorities

TABLE 10.3

2.01.	Indicator	Risk Description	Points for Attention
1.	Customs transactions	Irregularities in combination with a high volume of business can result in a high fiscal or non-fiscal risk.	• Total number of customs declarations over the last 3 years by type. • Total number of customs declarations expected over the next 2 years by type. • Customs offices involved. • Overview of the custom brokers/ agents (names, address, number) involved. • Details of Customs Duty, VAT, Value and GSP sought, licences, quotas, antidumping over the last 3 years. • Overview of the origin of the goods declared for import.

(Continued)

TABLE 10.3 (*Continued*)

2.01.	Indicator	Risk Description	Points for Attention
			• Overview of goods in which the company seeks preferential tariffs. • Procedures involved for determining value of goods imported. • Specify the authorisations for simplified procedures and/or customs procedures.
2.	Compliance check[a]	Non-compliant behaviour	Was the result of the last compliance check positive? If no, which measures has the company taken to avoid non-compliant behaviour?

[a] Compliance checks are for instance: audits, pre clearance checks, post clearance controls.

TABLE 10.4

2.01.	Indicator	Risk Description	Points for Attention
3.	(Former) Applications for authorisations	Noncompliant behaviour	Specify whether, in the last 3 years, a customs authorisation in the company's name has been revoked, suspended or whether an application for a customs authorisation did not lead to the issuing of a license, and if so what was the motivation of the customs administration.
4.	Customs compliance	Inadequate awareness of breaches against customs rules.	Has the company established procedures on disclosing irregularities to the relevant governmental agencies? For example, a contact point could be appointed who can arrange immediate access to contact with the local customs authorities when matters are identified as being of compliance and/or enforcement interest for customs. Staff should be aware of these procedures. Describe the routines for handing over information to Customs where criminal activity is suspected?

Subsection 2.02 Intelligence information

TABLE 10.5

2.02.	Indicator	Risk Description	Points for Attention
1.	Irregularities	Non-compliant behaviour	a. Specify any fiscal and non-fiscal irregularities as regards customs law and procedures as well as other relevant legislative obligations in respect of the import, export and transport of goods. b. Has the company been the subject of anti-fraud investigations? c. Is there intelligence information on the company, its owners, and or main shareholders or legal representatives from national and/or international enforcement organisations? d. Is the company handling in specific high risk goods such as weapons, dual-use goods, excise goods or CAP goods? Compare to – when available – fraud patterns available in respect of these goods?

Section III. The Company's Accounting and logistical system

Criteria: *A satisfactory system of managing commercial and where appropriate, transport records, which allow appropriate customs controls*

The applying company should maintain an accounting system which is consistent with the generally accepted accounting principles applied in the Member State where the accounts are held and which will facilitate audit-based customs control.

To enable the customs authorities to apply the necessary controls, the company has to allow the customs authority physical or electronic access to the customs and, where appropriate, transport records. Electronic access is not a pre-requisite to comply with this requirement.

The applying company should have a logistical system which distinguishes between Community and non-Community goods, the fulfilment of this criterion is not needed in the case of an AEO Certificate – Security and Safety;

Subsection 3.01 Audit trail

In accounting, an audit trail is a process or an instance of cross-referring each bookkeeping entry to its source in order to facilitate checking its accuracy. A complete audit trail will enable to track the lifecycle of operational activities, in this respect related to the flow of goods and products coming in, being processed and leaving the company. Many businesses and organizations require an audit trail in their automated systems for security reasons. The audit trail maintains a historical record of the data that enables you to trace a piece of data from the moment it enters the data file to the time it leaves (Tables 10.6–10.8).

TABLE 10.6

3.01.	Indicator	Risk Description	Points for Attention
1.	Trade sector	• Shortage of transparency of the accounting system. • A diverse range of activities could increase potential for errors or omissions.	a. Describe the company activities. b. What is the typology of the company (service company, manufacturing company, trading company)?
2.	Level of access for competent administrations	• Inability to readily undertake an audit due to the way in which the company's accounting system is structured. • Lack of the control over the system's security and access.	a. Customs authorities shall have access to the company's records for control purposes including pre-arrival and pre-departure information, as required. b. Is an audit trail for fiscal and/or customs purposes available?

Subsection 3.02 Accounting system

TABLE 10.7

3.02.	Indicator	Risk Description	Points for Attention
1.	Computerised environment	Complex management system offers possibilities to cover-up illegal transactions. Omission of the connection between the flow of goods and the flow of money.	Organisation of the company's computerised environment. The following elements should be included: • The extent of the computerisation on the basis of the following scale: mainframe /mini/PC network or stand-alone PC. • The hardware platform available and the operating system running on it. • The separation of functions (between development, testing and operations) within the computer department (functions) organised.

(Continued)

TABLE 10.7 (*Continued*)

3.02. Indicator	Risk Description	Points for Attention
		• The separation of functions between users and computerisation organised. • The separation of functions among users organised in the system. • How is access to the various parts of the system controlled? • Which applications have been accommodated elsewhere? • To which software house have these been assigned?

TABLE 10.8

3.02. Indicator	Risk Description	Points for Attention
2. Integrated accounting system	Incorrect and/or incomplete recording of transactions in the accounting system. Lack of segregation of duties between functions. Lack of reconciliation between stock and accounting records.	Are the financial accounts and the logistical accounts part of one integrated accounting system? **Financial administration** Give an outline description of the financial system. Incorporate the following elements in your description or in the answer to the following questions: a. Specify which software package your company uses. b. Is this a bespoke or a standard package? c. Who is the manufacturer/supplier of the package? d. Have any adaptations been made to the standard package. If so, what adaptations have been made and for what reason? e. Where and by who is the financial administration carried out? f. Give a list of the ledger accounts that are used. g. Who checks whether the entries in the sub-administration match those in the ledger? h. Does the system make use of verification interim accounts? Who is responsible for the coordination of these verification interim accounts? If so, give an overview of the ledger accounts with descriptions of where this registration takes place.

(Continued)

TABLE 10.8 (*Continued*)

3.02. Indicator	Risk Description	Points for Attention
		i. Are the liabilities to import duty/excise recorded in the ledger in an intra-accountable manner? If so, give an overview of the ledger accounts with descriptions of where this record takes place.
		j. Can non-community goods suppliers be distinguished from community goods suppliers?
		Logistical administration
		a. Which software package the company is using?
		b. Is this an in-house or a standard package?
		c. Who is the manufacturer/supplier of the package?
		d. Have any adaptations been made to the standard package. If so, what adaptations have been made and for what reason?
		e. Where and by whom is the logistical administration carried out?
		f. Is there a separation between the office stock and the warehouse stock administration?
		g. Is there a batch administration?
		h. What are the units in which the logistical administration is carried out?
		i. Is the stock administration linked up with the financial administration in an automated fashion? If not, what is the interface between the stock administration and the financial administration?
		j. How can the non-community goods or goods subject to customs control in the logistical administration be distinguished from the community goods?

Criteria: *A satisfactory system of managing commercial and, where appropriate, transport records, which allow appropriate customs controls*

The applicant shall have an administrative organisation which corresponds to the type and size of business and which is suitable to the management of the flow of goods, and have internal controls capable of detecting illegal or irregular transactions.

The applicant shall have, where applicable satisfactory procedures in place for the handling of licenses and authorisations connected to commercial policy measures or to the trade in agricultural products (Tables 10.9–10.12).

Subsection 3.03 Internal control system

TABLE 10.9

3.03.	Indicator	Risk Description	Risk Description
1.	Internal control procedures	• Incorrect and/or incomplete recording of transactions in the accounting system. • The use of incorrect or outdated standing data, such as article numbers and tariff codes.	a. Have guidelines been issued within the company by the board of directors, which employees within the purchase, storage, production, and sale processes must abide by? If so, have these guidelines been registered? b. Give an overview of the guidelines laid down. c. Does the company use ISO standards? d. Are guidelines regularly updated and reviewed? **Internal assessment** a. Describe in outline the internal procedures which are aimed at assessing the existence and operation of the administrative organisation and internal controls (henceforth: AO/IC) in relation to the flow of goods. If findings have been reported in the framework of this assessment in the last three financial years, provide an overview of those findings and of the measures that have been taken to improve matters. **Standing data** a. Describe the procedures concerning the change of standing data (master files) which are relevant for customs (for instance, standing files of creditors, article numbers, commodity codes and statistical numbers).

(Continued)

TABLE 10.9 (Continued)

3.03. Indicator	Risk Description	Risk Description
		b. Who/which department(s) is (are) responsible for these?
		c. In what way are adjustments archived?
		d. In what way are permanent (standing) data stored in digital form?
		e. Is a record being kept of permanent (standing) data?

TABLE 10.10

3.03. Indicator	Risk Description	Points for Attention
2. Internal control procedures specifically for production	• Inadequate control within the company over the business processes. • No or weak internal control procedures offer possibilities for fraud, unauthorized or illegal activities.	a. Is the production function separate from the purchase function, the sale function, and the administration? b. Does it involve a direct or indirect determination of use? c. Who/which department performs the recalculation and on the basis of what data? d. Is there calculation drawn up for each period or for each production run? e. Describe the discrepancy settlement procedure regarding the pre- and re-calculation. By whom is this carried out? f. Who enters what data in the supply and financial administration in relation to the supplies, which have been deployed in the production process? On what basis are these carried out? g. In what way are production results processed in the financial administration? h. What kind of journal entries does the production process give rise to?

Subsection 3.04 Flow of goods

TABLE 10.11

3.04.	Indicator	Risk Description	Points for Attention
1.	General	• Lack of control over stock movements offers possibilities to add dangerous and/or terrorist related goods to the stock and to take goods out of stock without appropriate registration.	a. Are internal goods movements recorded and are the connections between the different steps in these internal goods movements established? If so, with what frequency and by whom? b. Is this done in quantities and/or in money? c. Who analyses these goods movements and how often? d. Who authorizes the processing of the deviations established? e. Which standards are being applied in this connection?
2.	Incoming flow of goods	• Lack of reconciliation between goods ordered, goods received and entries to accounting records. • Lack of control over stock movements offers possibilities to add dangerous and/or terrorist related goods to the stock and to take goods out of stock without appropriate registration.	a. Purchase and receipt procedures for goods imported from non-Community Countries. b. How (on the basis of which documents), when and by whom are imported goods entered in the stock administration system? c. At which point in time is the entry booked in the stock? d. Accounting systems associated with purchasing, receipt, and payment of goods. e. Arrangements for returning goods. f. Arrangements for intake deviations. g. Arrangements for incorrect entries in the stock administration. h. Details of inventory procedures.

TABLE 10.12

3.04.	Indicator	Risk Description	Points for Attention
3.	Storage	• Lack of control over stock movements. • Lack of control over stock movements offers possibilities to add dangerous and/or terrorist related goods to the stock and to take goods out of stock without appropriate registration.	a. Does the company have appropriate procedures in place to control the goods in stock? Such procedures can – among others – be comprised of the following measures: • a clear assignment of a location for storage of the goods; • existence of a stock-taking procedure; • procedures in case a temporary location is chosen to store the goods; • arrangements for controlling breakage, decay or destruction of goods.
4.	Production	• Lack of control over stock used in the manufacturing process. • Lack of control over stock movements offers possibilities to add dangerous and/or terrorist related goods to the stock and to take goods out of stock without appropriate registration.	Identify if the company has appropriate procedures in place to control the manufacturing processes. a. Describe the procedure as regards the request for raw materials and the delivery from the warehouse. b. Describe the procedure as regards logging the use of the raw materials in the production process. c. Describe the procedure as regards the registering of the finished manufactured product. d. Describe the procedure as regards losses in the production process. e. Describe the procedure as regards the release of the finished product to the warehouse. Such procedures can – amongst others - be comprised of the following measures: • A department which is responsible for the assignment for production. • The people responsible for the assignment for production register this in the administration.

(Continued)

TABLE 10.12 (*Continued*)

3.04.	Indicator	Risk Description	Points for Attention
			• Use of standard manufacturing methods in the production.
			• Appropriate documentation of the manufacturing methods.
			• Regular control of the manufacturing methods.
			• End products should be subjected to a quality inspection.
			• Inspection results should be registered.
5.	Outgoing flow of goods Delivery from warehouse and shipment and transfer of goods	• Lack of control over stock movements offers possibilities to add dangerous and/or terrorist related goods to the stock and to take goods out of stock without appropriate registration. • Lack of reconciliation between stock records and entries to the accounting records. • Failure to make appropriate voluntary disclosures	Identify if the company has appropriate procedures in place to control the release of goods from the warehouse and the shipment of goods. Such procedures can – among others – be comprised of the following measures: • Sales department informs – on the basis of standardized procedures – the warehouse of the sale order/release of the goods. • Persons are appointed as authorized to decide if the goods are ready for sale/release. • Release of the goods is appropriately registered. • A standardized information procedure between the warehouse keeper and the company's unit/department responsible for customs matters, to enable internal synchronization of the delivery of goods and starting of the export procedure. • A final check before release to compare the order of release against the goods which are loaded. • Standard operating procedures for returned goods – inspection, counting, and registering.

Subsection 3.05 Customs routines

3.05.	Indicator	Risk Description	Points for Attention
1.	General	Ineligible use of the routines	Describe the details of handling routines of Customs declarations/accompanying documents. There should be Internal procedures to verify customs transactions conducted by direct and or indirect representatives (e.g. customs agents or forwarders).
2.	Economic licenses for import and/or export	Ineligible use of goods	Identify if the company does trade with goods that are subject to import licences; export restrictions and/or goods that are subject to an embargo. If that is the case there should be appropriate routines and procedures in place for administering the licences related to the import and/or export of goods. Such procedures can – among others – be comprised of the following measures: • Registration of the licenses by on the basis of standard procedures. • Regular control of the licenses on validity and registration. • Registration of the licenses is done be a separate person or a group of persons than the control of the licenses. • Standards for reporting irregularities with the licenses.

Criteria: *A satisfactory system of managing commercial and, where appropriate, transport records, which allow appropriate customs controls*

The applicant shall have satisfactory procedures in place for the archiving of the company's records and information and for protection against the loss of information.

The applicant shall maintain anti-smuggling measures and raise awareness among the staff in particular upon employment and during training.

The applicant shall have appropriate information technology security measures – for example firewalls and anti-virus protection – to protect the applicant's computer system from unauthorised intrusion and to secure the applicant's documentation.

Subsection 3.06 Procedures as regards back-up, recovery, and fall-back and archival options

3.06.	Indicator	Risk description	Points for attention
1.	Requirements for record retention/ archiving	• Inability to readily undertake an audit due to the way in which the company's accounting system is structured. • Deliberate destruction or loss of relevant information	Give a description of procedures regarding backup, recovery, and fall-back option, taking account of the following questions – where applicable. • How long do data remain available online, in its original form? • How long does data remain accessible online, and how long does it remain available for an archive/history or statistical summary? • How long is data kept on record off-line? • On what kind of media is data stored? • In which (software) format is data stored? • Does data get compressed and at what stage? • What are the guarantees as regards the long-term availability (technical quality of the recording media, availability of the hardware and program code, descriptions of the data and the program code)?

Sub-Section 3.07 Information security – protection of computer systems

3.07.	Indicator	Risk Description	Points for Attention
1.	Certification standards for securing computerised environment	Unauthorized access and/or intrusion to the economic operator's computer systems.	Are any existing certification standards applied for securing computer systems?

(Continued)

3.07.	Indicator	Risk Description	Points for Attention
2.	Internal control procedures	• Unauthorized access and/or intrusion to the economic operator's computer systems. • Deliberate destruction or loss of relevant information.	a. What measures are in place to protect the economic operators' computer systems against unauthorized intrusion? b. Has any penetration test been made with positive results? If no, the company should do these tests to show the security of their system. Such procedures can – amongst others – be comprised of the following measures: • An updated, documented policy on protection of the company's computer systems; registered access for authorized persons; regular change of passwords; monitoring systems etc. • An updated safety plan describing the measures in place protecting computer systems from unauthorised access as well as deliberate destruction or loss of information.
3.	Computerised environment	• Unauthorized access and/or intrusion to the economic operator's computer systems. • Deliberate destruction or loss of relevant information.	a. What policy/procedures exist for issuing authorizations for access and the level of access to the computer systems? Access to sensitive information should be limited to the staff members who are authorized to apply changes and additions to the information. b. Who is responsible for the protection and running of the company's computer system? Responsibility should not be limited to one person only but to several persons who are able to monitor each other's actions.

3.07.	Indicator	Risk Description	Points for Attention
4.	Contingency plan	• Unauthorized access and/or intrusion to the economic operator's computer systems. • Deliberate destruction or loss of relevant information.	The company should have an action plan with procedures in case of incidents.
5.	Routines in case of computer failure	• Unauthorized access and/or intrusion to the economic operator's computer systems. • Deliberate destruction or loss of relevant information.	The company should have backup routines when computer systems don't work. There should also be procedures on bringing the information in the computer systems when they operate again.

Subsection 3.08 Information security – documentation security

3.08.	Indicator	Risk Description	Points for Attention
1.	Internal control procedures	• Misuse of the economic operator's information system to endanger the supply chain. • Deliberate destruction or loss of relevant information.	a. What measures are in place to protect the economic operators' documentation against unauthorized intrusion? b. Has any penetration test been made with positive results? If no, the company should do these tests to show the security of their system. Such procedures can – amongst others – be comprised of the following measures: • An updated, documented policy on documentation security: registration methods of document, access authorisations, backup of documents, etc. • An updated safety plan describing the measures in place protecting documents from unauthorised access as well as deliberate destruction or loss of documents. • Procedures on filing and storage of documents.

(Continued)

3.08.	Indicator	Risk Description	Points for Attention
2.	Contingency plan	• Misuse of the economic operator's information system to endanger the supply chain. • Deliberate destruction or loss of relevant information.	Identify if during the last year incidents have occurred and what type of measures have been taken as a result thereof to improve the information/documentation security.
3.	Authorisation level for staff categories	• Misuse of the economic operator's information system to endanger the supply chain. • Deliberate destruction or loss of relevant information.	Which staff categories have access to particulars concerning goods and information flows? Which staff categories are authorised to change these particulars?
4.	Safety and security requirements imposed on others	• Misuse of the economic operator's information system to endanger the supply chain. • Deliberate destruction or loss of relevant information.	What security requirements have you placed on your trade partners and other contacts handling sensitive information provided by you?

Section IV. Financial solvency

Criteria: *Proven financial solvency*

The condition relating to the financial solvency of the applicant referred to in Article 5a(2), third indent, of Regulation (EC) No. 648/2005 is considered met, if his solvency can be proven for the past 3 years. Solvency, for the purposes of this Article, shall mean a good financial standing which is sufficient to fulfil the commitments of the applicant, with due regard to the characteristics of the type of the business activity.

If the applicant has been established for less than 3 years, his financial solvency shall be judged on the basis of records and information that are available.

One of the techniques and tests used by HMRC in this section is the examination of Current Assets and Liabilities for each accounting year, hence the requirement for 3 years' worth of company accounts. The tests used are the Quick (Acid Test) Ratio, which is: Current Assets LESS Inventory/Current Liabilities, and the Liquidity Ratio, which is: Current Assets/Current Liabilities. The lower the ratio, the higher the financial risk to the company. This, like the other sections detailed above, would fail under System 1 of the VSM.

Subsection 4.01 Insolvency

4.01.	Indicator	Risk Description	Points for Attention
1.	Insolvency	Noncompliant behaviour	Check and analyse the balance and financial movements of the company to analyse the company's ability to pay their legal debts. In most time the banking relation of the company will be able to report on the financial solvency of the company. In case the operator is subject to any insolvency or recovery proceedings, information should be gathered on the circumstances, which have led to the initiation of the recovery proceedings, as well as on the amounts due. It has to be analysed if the insolvency can effect in a negative way the compliance of the company and its business processes.

Section V. Practical Standards of Competence and Qualification
Criteria: *Practical Standards of Competence*

The operator should demonstrate a high-level of staff competence in Customs matters, and how it deals with day-to-day Customs issues, including import and export procedures. In preparation of the pre-audit of customs authorities the operator can conduct a self-assessment to enable himself to analyse if the company is able to meet the competence and qualification requirements.

The assessment is an attempt to identify the risks and threats which might occur in that part of the company's function where overall staff knowledge of and competence in Customs matters is essential, and consequentially look into the measures in place to minimise these risks.

5.	Indicator	Risk Description	Assessment Questions
1.1	Practical Experience of 3 years or more in Customs matters	Inadequate levels of competence	Do you or the person in charge of your Customs matters have practical experience of a minimum of 3 years in Customs matters?
1.2	Customs quality standards	Inadequate levels of standards. In the United Kingdom, this does not necessarily apply	Do you or the person in charge of your Customs matters comply with a quality standard concerning Customs matters adopted by a European Standardisation body, when available?
2.1	Professional Qualifications	No Professional Training or Qualification	Have you or the person in charge of your Customs matters successfully completed training covering Customs legislation consistent with, and relevant to, the extent of your involvement in Customs-related activities, provided by any of the following: a. A Customs Authority of a member State b. An educational establishment recognised, for the purposes of providing such qualification, by the Customs Authorities or a body of a Member State responsible for professional training c. A professional or trade association recognised by the Customs Authorities of a Member State or accredited in the Union, for the purposes of providing such qualification?

It must be noted that in all the above, there is a column which deals with risk assessment. This tells HMRC the level of risk assigned to each sections, and to what degree this risk impinges upon the eligibility of the company for AEO approval.

The VSM applies in the following way:

System 1: Operational Control

System 1 controls an Operational Unit, each of which is detailed in the AEO Questionnaire. The VSM is recursive, i.e. characterised by recurrence or repetition, thus supporting the essential cybernetic definition of circularity, and therefore refers to the operations of each department, and how they are coordinated as far as the AEO criteria are concerned. Every element of System 1 is viable in itself, as it fulfils all the requirements of System 1 and therefore can be audited and controlled in a cohesive manner as far as AEO is concerned. When modelling a corporation for AEO purposes as applying to the VSM, System 1's task is to control a business division, in response to policy directives and over-riding instructions from above, in reaction to the direct demands of the external world upon it, and in awareness of the needs of other divisions.

System 2: Coordinating Function

System 1 exists permanently and inseparably in a metasystemic coordination tool, i.e. System 2. In other words, System 2 controls and encompasses System 1, and therefore fulfils the requirements of the criteria of AEO. It subsumes all elements of System 1 and links them to System 3. The coordination activity, i.e. allocation of resources etc., should be carried out in a way that ensures maximum autonomy of the parts or elements without threatening the integrity of the whole entity.

System 3: Managing the "Inside and Now"

The purpose of System 3 in this instance is to monitor the autonomic functions, implement plans within physiological limits and report upwards, and therefore satisfy the requirements of AEO status for full compliance. This can be translated in corporate terms to represent the feedback reported by individual elements of the departments within the corporate entity concerning the systems in place for full coordination of the various divisions within the company, and therefore full control of the whole process with regard to compliance and control from an AEO perspective.

When decisions are made by the top management, these will have an impact on the operations of each department, which in turn will report back their findings and concerns to the management. If all works, well, this is deemed to be positive feedback and the policy is consolidated and perhaps extended. If the feedback is negative, rectification policies are implemented and the process continues on an amended basis. System 3's purpose can also be formulated as assuring that the coordinated systems in System 1 can achieve a greater effect than the sum of the Systems' individual activities. When modelling a corporation as a VSM, System 3 resembles the middle management that is responsible for all divisions.

System 3A: Auditing and Monitoring

System 3A's function is to watch for signs of strain and stress in the operational units of System 1 without exerting any command function whatsoever. System 3A bypasses the operational control of System 1 and thus provides an opportunity for System 3 to obtain a genuine impression of the state of affairs in the operational units, which amounts to the audit channel and therefore satisfies the AEO criteria of audit trails and accountability. System 3A therefore satisfies the need to investigate and validate the information flowing between Systems 1, 2, and 3, and render the whole system transparent and accountable, as well as being totally compliant. It provides the checks and balances capable of ensuring compliance, as well as complete control over Systems 1–3.

System 4: Managing the "Outside and Future"

As described in Chapter 9, Systems 4 and 5 represent the externalities imposed on the system and how it can adapt to these externalities or influences. These include the criteria imposed by the AEO process. Systems 1, 2, and 3 assure a stabilisation of the internal structure, but they do not take account of "progress" or change. Therefore, System 4 is dedicated to the larger environment, especially in a global context, and hence to regulation of the system in relation to this. In terms of AEO, these are deemed to be externalities imposed by government and quality standards authorities such as ISO, and therefore impact significantly on Systems 1, 2, and 3 in terms of operational efficiency.

System 5: Policy/he "Three-Four Balancer"

The task of System 5 is to monitor the balancing operation between Systems 3 and 4, and thus control the whole corporate structure and systems. The need for a balancing system between the "Inside and Now" and the "Outside and Future" emerges from the observation that in practice, Systems 3 and 4 will not achieve an equilibrium state without regulation, hence the checks and balances required as part of the AEO process based on quality management. On a corporate recursion level of the VSM, System 5 is therefore responsible for the policy of the corporation and acts as an umbrella for the entire structure.

All the sections detailed above fall under Systems 1–4 of the VSM. Section 5 deals primarily with policy, which is also an important element of the AEO process, as it defines the modus operandi of the company and therefore covers and is related to all the other sections of the VSM.

In essence, the VSM would need to determine the following, according to its five structural levels:

1. The synergy within departments
2. The synergy between departments
3. The transparent structure and system defining these synergies
4. The effects of Externalities on the corporate systems and synergies
5. The overall control system and structure encompassing the whole company

The VSM would automatically highlight the areas of deficiency in terms of cybernetic management and would therefore determine the extent to which the model is satisfied in the company's case. Where the risk for each section is high, deficiencies occur, and these must be rectified before the company can progress any further with its AEO application. Once these issues have been rectified, a further application of the VSM can be conducted, and the AEO application can be progressed further. Overall, the application for AEO approval relies heavily on these criteria, as these systems demonstrate that the organisation is in full control of its business activities and can therefore prove compliance in all activities that it conducts.

11

Conclusions

We live in a world of economic and financial uncertainty. There is an increasing need for accountability, transparency, efficiency, and competitiveness in the commercial world, borne out to be a series of tools and guidance to this end, from Porter's Five Forces model through the processes of Lean Management, Continuous Improvement and Six Sigma. However, it has become clear that not much attention is paid to the principles of Management Cybernetics. Cybernetics as a whole appears to have been relegated to a backroom status in the face of the concepts of Continuous Improvement and Six Sigma. While these concepts are important and indeed very powerful, they do not represent the whole story concerning business efficiency and cost-effectiveness.

Although cybernetics as a stand-alone subject was first consolidated and proposed in 1948 by Norbert Wiener, its origins date back much further, and its subsequent applications have become increasingly diverse and complex. Wiener proposed the concept as a reference to the human body and the machine, both of which have a central control function, which, in the case of the human body, is the brain. For machines, the control function lies in the factory, in the form of an electronic control mechanism supervised by a division of the company usually concerned with a combination of the manufacturing and information technology processes. The main issue is that, as a result, cybernetic applications and processes have also become increasingly scientific and mathematical, with a vast array of complex mathematical formulae created to cover a variety of functions, along with an equally vast array of technical jargon, even to the point of renaming the concept "Control Theory", which, in reality, is only part of the concept. For the layman and business practitioner, this presents a nightmare in terms of basic understanding of the subject, especially when much of what is analysed and disseminated does not refer to basic business disciplines, which is an area of major importance in terms of the study and practice of cybernetics. Cybernetics, in its relationship with Operations Research (OR), is a major tool in the improvement and enhancement of business practices and processes. It has been sued in the past to enable governments and top-level businesses to achieve far greater levels of efficiency and indeed has been developed for the present-day world of influence by the major multinational companies. However, for reasons best known to the business world, the extent to which it could be used has never been fully recognised or exploited, hence the need to revive the concept for a world of change and uncertainty.

Cybernetics applies to all aspects of business, from the Small-to-Medium-sized Enterprise (SME) right up to the large multinational corporation. Indeed, the whole nature of corporate management in itself provides an ideal target for the study and application of cybernetics as a major business discipline. The works of the English cybernetician Stafford Beer go a long way in defining the need for the use and application of cybernetics in business processes, but the existing material available is very technical, and in many ways, goes far further in terms of technical descriptions and explanations than is necessary, especially for the business practitioner whose knowledge of mathematical concepts and formulae may be somewhat limited. Consequently, this book has been written to remove some of the mystique from the subject and make it far more understandable and accessible to everyday practitioners involved in business management and control.

It is understood that present-day business are occupied with short-term management, especially where profitability and liquidity are concerned. However, there is also the need for a long-term strategy, as it is vital to know where the company is progressing in terms of its future plans. Long-term investment is at stake, especially in terms of new technology and the need to keep apace with an ever-changing world. The Five Forces of Michael Porter concentrate on business competitiveness, and this revolves increasingly around efficiency and cost-effectiveness rather than purely concentrating on an increase in sales activity. The keywords in this are therefore productivity and viability, i.e. determining if the company in reality is a viable proposition. Many companies may generate a degree of revenue, but this does not make them viable institutions. Indeed, their present modus operandi and structure flies in the face of viability, as in many cases, the sheer costs of running the company, as well as reflecting in the balance sheet, mask any generation of revenue. The business turnover may look reasonable, but the ratios concerning the relationship between assets and liabilities suggest otherwise. Liabilities can reflect the relative inefficiency of an organisation, and much of this is due to an inherent lack of internal control, as well as an inherent lack of basic intra-company synergy. If organisations cannot properly communicate within themselves, then how can they be expected to communicate with other entities? Certainly, internal problems cannot be resolved if there is no proper line of communication. Indeed, what may start out as a small and potentially solvable problem rapidly becomes a nightmare, as there is no proper means of addressing the issue based on team thinking or the creation of a solution based on consensus ad idem, and the organisation suffers as a result. In many cases, there is no contingency planning, nor is there any form of backup plan in case the original strategy fails. A cybernetic approach would solve this by the application of several models, depending upon the issues to be addressed. In particular, the application of the Viable Systems Model (VSM) is a major step towards the analysis of many internal issues within any organisation, as it determines the extent to which a proper level of internal communication and synergy exists within the organisation.

Cybernetics has been applied to government and its control over national issues, particularly in the case of the Chilean national economy, which, under the Marxist presidency of Salvador Allende was a command economy, and indeed studies of economic cybernetics have, in general, emanated from specialists in socialist economics. However, in the free market world, the discipline has never been taken seriously, as it has been assumed that cybernetics was only for socialist economies owing to its control structure. However, in a world of competitiveness, the cybernetic approach as a business tool can be used very effectively for the purpose of corporate control in order to maximise the efficiency of a corporate entity, in that it encourages discipline within the corporate environment as well as an appetite for control and maximisation of efficiency and cost-effectiveness. Some 40–50 years ago, cybernetics was used by several of the management consultants, especially in the United States, to encourage the big corporate entities, including the multinational corporations, to become more cost-effective and efficient in their development. However, in more recent years, this approach has waned in the face of concepts such as Continuous Improvement, Six Sigma, and Lean Management, and, to a degree, the diluted form of cybernetics, namely Control Theory, particularly in manufacturing and production environments.

To an extent, the ISO system of benchmarks has also been seen as a major quality control achievement, but all of these are somewhat more limited in that they address specific areas of development and control, rather than addressing issues of the overall corporate entity. Indeed, manufacturing productivity may be an admirable goal, but if the supply chain is still riddled with inefficiencies that compromise the overall productivity of the company, then one specific initiative of efficiency is not going to achieve the overall corporate goals. In this respect, cybernetics covers not only the whole corporate entity but also covers the relationships between the individual entity and other entities around it, i.e. an entire network. If one element of the network fails, so too does the whole network. Cybernetics addresses all these elements and seeks to ensure that all parts of the network function as a unified body, in ways similar to the human body. Indeed, much of the original work on cybernetics concentrated on the function of the human body as an example of a totally integrated function. If one part of the human body malfunctions, the whole body suffers as a result. Rectifying the problem benefits the whole body as a result.

There is still a significant amount of room for business cybernetics to develop. The original studies undertaken by Stafford Beer can be seen as a foundation, but not necessarily the ultimate resolution to the concept. Much more can yet be achieved in terms of addressing corporate needs, especially in a world of uncertainty, and because of the need for increasing levels of efficiency and competitiveness, there is a need for far closer and integrated coordination of any corporate entity. This book goes some of the way in providing a direction in how to achieve this, in the same way that a helmsman guides a ship through troubled waters. The song by Rod Stewart *Sailing* perhaps sums it up:

> We are sailing stormy waters, to be near you, to be free.

As in one of the principles of cybernetics, the navigator is the means by which the Input information is processed, and emerges as the Output, i.e. the navigation of the vessel through the waters in perfect safety. The navigation itself serves as the process and rectification of the challenge to cross the stormy waters. The outcome of the challenge is to convert the input into a successful output. The cybernetic approach addresses this challenge and converts it into a successful reality, as well as successfully surmounting and challenges or adversities as they arise.

Lessons from the past tell us that, like any boy scouts, we must always be prepared. That means that there must be some form of control strategy in place to avoid chaos in the event of national crisis or emergency. Indeed, this strategy must also prevail at corporate level for the same reasons. Experience tells us that in good times, most issues take care of themselves, but when times are more challenging, there needs to be a contingency policy that steers the nation or the corporate entity through the crisis. In business terms, this may be a Business Continuity Plan (BCP). However, such a plan may only account for a basic means of continuing business activities. It does not provide an overall solution. The cybernetic approach, however, goes far deeper and provides a long-term if not permanent solution based on a solid control mechanism. The same premise holds for a national solution based on a cybernetic approach, i.e. cohesion of the whole structure based on a neural system where all elements of the system function alongside each other under an overall control system that is planned and operated in an orderly manner, and where that control system accounts for and surmounts all challenges as they arise.

This neural system, as shown in the Chilean Cybersyn project, can actually work for any country. It enables any government to adopt a strategy of command and control and use it in times of emergency, while relaxing it when the crisis has abated. Even under a normal situation, a cybernetic synergy allows the government to take control over all its functions in an efficient way, ensuring that each government department is allowed to practise its own functions in an efficient manner, while remaining responsible and accountable to central government. Given that each government department has its own responsibilities and portfolios, it is responsible for running national functions such as Finance, Defence, Health, Education, Transport, Internal Security and so forth in an effective manner. However, this still has to be coordinated and managed by central government, i.e. the elected body that constitutes Parliament or Congress, depending upon the national structure. However, such a system still requires feedback in the form of reporting mechanisms, where each department reports to the top, and indeed where lower levels report to the department itself. This is effectively top-down management based on bottom-up feedback. After all, management is only as good as its ability to control and manage, and that, as analysed in the chapter on the cybernetics of economics, cannot be achieved by coercion. It must be achieved by consensus ad idem, where all parts of the system function in complete harmony with all the others, just as with the human body.

Government in itself is a complex affair. Government comprises politicians belonging to different political parties elected to represent their constituents, with the party with the majority of representatives becoming the duly-elected government. In a parliamentary system, the leader of the party with the majority becomes the Prime Minister, or Premier, and forms a government from those elected as representatives. The government is answerable to the people as well as to the head of state, be they a monarch or an elected president, but to this extent, the government makes legislation which is ratified by the head of state and becomes law. In this respect, the government acts as the "brain" of the national entity. In a presidential system, the President is elected by the nation and is the ultimate leader; the Congress, namely the legislature which is separately elected, debates policy, including that submitted by the President, and approves it. In this respect, the President is the "brain" of the system. In both cases, government makes legislation, but a separate body, namely the national administration, executes policy and makes it happen. The national administration is composed of professional civil servants, who formulate government policy according to the national legislation and convert it into the means by which the country operates.

The net effect is as shown in in Figure 11.1.

As can be seen from the diagram, government makes policy and passes it down, eventually directing and managing industry, commerce, and

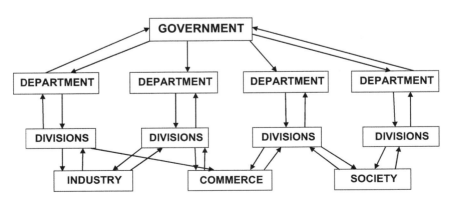

FIGURE 11.1
Government hierarchy.

society, and all the other elements that make up a national social and business network. In turn, society gives feedback to the government departments or their divisions, which in turn report to the departments, which in turn report to government itself.

An example of this is the national transport infrastructure, whether private or state-run. If the railways do not function properly, the passengers complain to the transport authority. The transport authority in turn complains to the government transport department, which in turn reports to the Transport Minister, who is part of top government. Decisions are made by the government, which then transfer down to the transport authority, which makes appropriate changes to the way in which the network operates. This can only work properly if there is a coordinated control system in place, which not only receives the feedback from below but also acts upon it and rectifies the problems identified. As shown in Chapter 6, there has to be a full structure of planning, coordination, command, and control for the system to work, very much along the lines of the VSM.

The corporate structure must operate in the same way, except that Government is replaced by Top Management, albeit in a governing role. Departments and Divisions remain much the same, depending upon the function of each department. The bottom level is the workforce, which ensures that the tasks delegated to it are completed in a timely, efficient, and cost-effective manner. If a problem occurs at the lower levels, the workforce reports this to the departments, which in turn report to top management. The difference is that with the corporate sector, externalities such as customers, suppliers, and stakeholders, i.e. the supply chain, or those entities involved in having a role or influence in the running of the entity, can bear a significant influence on the company as a whole, especially where problems occur as a result of breakdowns in the supply chain for whatever reason. In the governmental structure, external problems resulting from externalities, such as international conflicts or pandemics, are rarely conveyed fully to society unless the issue threatens national security or the national well-being, in which case government must have contingency plans in place to deal with the crisis as it arises and develops. A typical diagram of the corporate structure can be illustrated as in Figure 11.2.

In this respect, cybernetics works at both government and corporate level. Indeed, a cybernetic approach must be deployed, as it is the only way in which there can be a full measure of command and control, as well as a

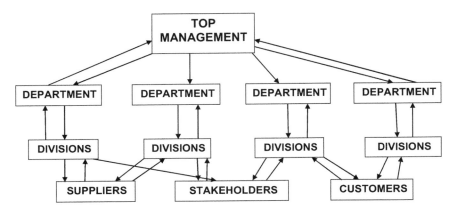

FIGURE 11.2
Management hierarchy.

means of rectification of prevalent issues through effective reporting and feedback. Without effective feedback, the system cannot operate effectively and adapt to any changes necessary. As seen in previous chapters, not all change is good, but some of it may be necessary, even in the interim on a temporary basis, if only to bring a semblance of order to a critical situation. The coronavirus pandemic has shown that radical measures have been necessary to bring a degree of order and security to the crisis, but the inherent failing on the part of many governments is that there had been little or no contingency planning implemented prior to the crisis in anticipation of it. Coordinated planning and control could have ensured that adequate levels of proper preventive solutions could have been implemented in order to address a medical crisis and hopefully alleviate it in time. In some cases, changes that were implemented on a temporary basis may have to become permanent, such as mandatory forms of basic hygiene or even better management of retail strategy, particularly in terms of ensuring that essential supplies of food and other items were always available at all stores and supermarkets, in order to counteract the adverse effects of panic buying. A central control mechanism would have ensured that all problems could have been anticipated in advance and measures taken to avoid such problems before they actually happened. Corporate policy already encompasses this, with alternative suppliers being available to act should there be a deficiency with existing suppliers. This is where cybernetic synergy applies at its best and helps to address and resolve problems as soon as they arise, even to avoid those problems arising in the first place.

In brief, the main elements of an ideal cybernetic structure are as follows:

- the VSM;
- Command and Control;
- Synergy (*consensus ad idem*);
- Communication and connectivity;
- Feedback; and
- Rectification.

As long as all these functions work in harmony, the system maintains robustness and efficiency. However, it also requires will and commitment to make it work.

An ideal checklist could thus include the following:

- Does the VSM apply to the organisation?
- Do the 5 Systems apply and are they in place?
- Is there an existing control system in place?
- Does it fulfil the criteria of the Law of Requisite Variety?
- Is the analysis of positive/negative feedback part of the control system?

This concept is not, as could be put, rocket science. Unfortunately, it has been made somewhat difficult to understand by the application of a large number of formulae and mathematical concepts, especially in terms of manufacturing, production, and scientific operations, as well as its use with Artificial Intelligence (AI) and indeed various aspects of Operations Research (OR). It is, however, the application of some basic principles in order to provide a coordinated and well-run structure, where communication, feedback, and effective management operate in total cohesion and harmony to ensure the smooth and efficient operation of any organisation, be it commercial, administrative, or governmental. In this respect, it uses the human body, with its brain, various organs and limbs, neural and nervous systems, as its primary model. It can apply to organisations of all sizes and types and is a tangible and methodical solution. It can be complex, but that depends largely on how complex the organisation is that the approach and concept is targeted at. Cybernetics is not some vague concept, ideal or dream. It is a concept, but it is based on reality and real-time issues which need resolving in a practical way, hence the application of cybernetic synergy to both business and government, regardless of politics and personal interest. The result is well-being for government, business, commerce, and society. Everybody gains, which in itself is the overall benefit to the national entity as a whole. This gain is based on an orderly form of management, where business becomes more competitive through closely controlled management and thus becomes more robust and in a better position to compete in the market place. Although the economic principles of the economist Adam Smith advocated a *laissez-faire* approach, i.e. they allow companies to govern themselves and thus find a natural equilibrium in the market, this can only be achieved where the company itself engages in a policy of management control and coordination, in order to become more efficient and hence more competitive.

Various crises over the past few decades have shown that business is keen to embrace economic growth, but is reluctant to anticipate recession. The present crisis has shown that few companies have been prepared for social lockdown imposed as a result of the coronavirus pandemic, owing to the assumption that times would always be good. However, this reveals a lack of planning and contingency. Cybernetic strategy takes into account the need for contingencies and the influence of externalities on corporate systems. Indeed, the coronavirus pandemic, if viewed as an externality, plays a significant role in defining System 4 of the VSM, i.e. the externalities which influence the overall structure of an entity and indeed drive its overall policy, especially concerning the need for adaptation to significant or radical change. On this basis, more needs to be done to anticipate such issues and prepare for them when analysing corporate systems and how they need to adapt to changing global trends. Successive global crises have demonstrated a need to break away from traditional ethics and concepts, and effectively to think "outside the box", i.e. adopting far-reaching practices that are designed to implement significant means of efficiency but are also designed to create a paradigm shift in terms of management principles and techniques based on systems which encompass greater levels of control, synergy, and feedback.

Overall, this kind of cybernetics is not designed as a political tool, but as a management and business tool. It is designed to address economic needs, and hence business needs, but can also be used successfully as a management tool for government itself, regardless of the political direction of the government concerned. It can be argued that cybernetics was exploited more by left-leaning administrations and was thus a socialist tool, but it does not follow that this was the only raison d'être for the concept. Other than Stafford Beer, who did somewhat sympathise with socialist regimes, most of those who developed the field of cybernetics had no interest in its political implications; they were more interested in its scientific ramifications. Other practitioners of cybernetics, especially those practitioners located in Central and Eastern Europe, did manifest distinctly left-leaning politics, as they saw economic cybernetics as applicable to the functioning and maintenance of the Socialist State. However, cybernetics in itself knows no political limitations; it surpasses these and encompasses all disciplines and all elements of today's society. It has more relation to the human form, and the nature of control and coordination of everything to which it is supposed to apply.

In some ways, cybernetics has evolved into the term "Control Theory". However, it is not just a theory but also a practical concept, given the diversity and variety of its applications. Cybernetics takes on board not just the principle of control, but also the various means by which that control can be applied and exercised. The principle of "Control" does not do total justice to the concept of cybernetics, as the whole principle of cybernetics also includes guidance and direction. Furthermore, cybernetic synergy implies the role of communication and feedback in the cybernetic process, as these two principles are vital in ensuring that control is exercised over a given structure.

"Feedback" and "regulation" have been successfully analysed and developed in detail for thermostats and autopilots, or "black boxes" whose relationship to traditional cybernetics (or control theory) is fairly straightforward. Clearly, it is a relatively simple matter to design and build a box to guide vehicles from point A to point B in space, which was initially demonstrated in the late 1950s with the Soviet Sputnik programme, whereas it has been far more difficult, and not yet entirely solved, to produce one that will guide a vehicle between two locations on the ground, other than driverless mass transit urban rail systems. One of the more perplexing aspects of this distinction between the two types of devices is the notion of "system": how it is derived and how it is designed and implemented.

From the very beginning, there has been a misconception that cybernetics implies that the concept of control in the animal and the machine are the same. In reality, they are not. As a fundamental premise, this relationship is questionable, and there are good arguments that show that it cannot be true, as an animal is a natural being, whereas a machine is an artificial being, without a brain to enable it to function. A machine needs to be pre-programmed by man, whereas an animal is naturally pre-programmed as a living being. A second reason why the concept of control across animal and machine has become blurred is the persistence, especially by general systems theorists about a single notion of "system", which in reality can mean and apply to anything which has some form of network and structure. Suffice to say that systems can be classified as of two varieties, namely natural (e.g. the solar system) versus man-made or artificial (e.g. a satellite communication system).

Political, cultural, and even professional issues also have tended to make cybernetic concepts obscure and unclear and even unintelligible, often with scientific and general systems overtones. After Wiener's cybernetics book was published, its ideas spread quickly around the world. They were obviously well-received in the Soviet Union where Wiener made several trips, the most important of which was in 1960. After that, cybernetics began to play, at least from the perspective of their planned societies and economies, an extremely important role in political, economic, and cultural evolutions and counter-evolutions, i.e. East versus West. The books about economic cybernetics all originated in the eastern bloc, and the Cybersyn project was initiated as part of the ultra-Left-Wing economic policy of the Allende administration in Chile in the early 1970s.

In retrospect, there have been some very interesting, albeit diametrically opposite, effects of the concept of cybernetics. In the East, cybernetics became a salient feature in communist pedagogy, as institutes were established with cybernetics as both the core academic discipline and the institutional political dogma. Meanwhile, in the West, there has been a corresponding decline in cybernetics witnessed by fewer university course offerings and an ever-decreasing number of publications and forums. This was partly because of the emergence of control theory, which deals with the control of continuously operating dynamical systems in and engineering context, but can also be applied to areas such as linguistics, psychology, and sociology. In other respects, the principle of cybernetics has been mistakenly associated with the term "cyber" in terms of the digital age, with the term "cyber" referring to cyberspace and cyberattacks, which have far more to do with computer technology, which relates more to pure Artificial Intelligence than it does to pure cybernetics.

However, the concept of control theory has not been applied to business, and this is where the application of cybernetics to business is perhaps as important as ever, if not increasingly important, in a world of economic and productive efficiency, especially concerning both economic and business policy. Cybernetics allows for increased corporate cost-effectiveness and efficiency in general, especially within the context of a free market, where competition rules. In this respect, cybernetics has moved from being a political tool to being a business tool, and thus from being state policy to becoming corporate policy. In short, cybernetics is not dead as a concept, nor has it completely metamorphosed into control theory. It has become more specific, and equally far more diverse in its applications, especially in a business concept. It must therefore remain a key area of research in terms of business and management practice.

In addition to these measures, other considerations also prevail. We live in a world of ever-developing technology, where electronic management has replaced manual systems. Much of any control mechanism is carried out by electronic means, using databases and Enterprise Resource Planning (ERP) systems. Much of the field of cybernetics, therefore, can be carried out using such electronic methodology such as Artificial Neural Networks (ANNs) and Decision Support Systems (DSS) supporting Strategic Decision Support Systems (SDSS). The technology and architecture behind these systems is not rocket science by any means but is based on the control systems described earlier in this book. The requirement is still the issue of accurate and efficient information based on algedonic feedback, and this is still a crucial element of any cybernetic process. To a degree, this also revolves around the use of Artificial Intelligence (AI), but the whole process is still a specific cybernetic process based on original concepts which have not changed radically since they were first developed in the middle of the 20th century. The cybernetic principles remain the same; the means by which they are implemented and operated has changed. The main concern is that they have not been taken as seriously by business as they should, and this is where more work needs to be carried out to apply such principles to much of business practices and procedures.

ANNs can be viewed as supporting at least two types of DSS: data-driven and model-driven. First, neural networks can be employed as data analysis tools for forecasting and prediction based on historical data in a data-driven DSS. Second, neural networks also can be viewed as a class of quantitative models to be used in a model-driven DSS. However, models are theoretical and require much manipulation to apply them to actual practices and procedures.

ANNs apply to dynamic networks. A number of important engineering applications require the processing of time-varying information, such as speech recognition, adaptive control, time series prediction, financial forecasting, radar/sonar signature recognition, especially for use in maritime defence and security applications, and non-linear dynamic modelling. To cope with time-varying signals, neural network topologies have to be enhanced with short-term memory mechanisms, especially those embodied in electronic applications. This is probably the area where neural networks will provide an undisputed advantage, since other technologies are far from satisfactory. However, it should be pointed out that this area is still in a research stage. It should also be noted that many real-world problems fall in these categories, ranging from classification of irregular patterns, forecasting, noise reduction, and control applications. Humans solve problems in a very similar way. They observe events to extract patterns and then make generalisations based on their observations.

In recent years, the increasing complexity and uncertainty involved in managerial decision situations has necessitated more sophisticated DSS equipped with models that go well beyond capturing only the simple linear relationships. This need was the main thrust and motivation behind the vast amounts of research that aimed to leverage the power of ANNs in DSS. According to recent research literature, one of the areas that attracted the most attention out of this non-linear modelling paradigm is finance.

In the field of finance, most attention of ANN-enabled DSS is dedicated to predicting stock markets for investment and banking purposes, as well as international currency exchange for commerce purposes. Since such a prediction may lead to a rather quick and easy way to make money, many research efforts are reported in this area with variable levels of success. There have been several studies and reports made on successful applications of neural network modelling in predicting the stock market movements, while others concentrated on the exchange rate predictions. In addition to the prediction of movements in stock markets exchange rates, some other researchers applied the same techniques on bankruptcy prediction, portfolio management. More detailed reviews of application of ANNs in decision support in finance and banking can be found in various places, although the studies referred to are largely academic and do not specifically refer to actual financial practice. Other problem areas where ANNs are used in conjunction with DSS include environmental issues, the service industry (including customer relationship management and e-commerce), engineering design, manufacturing, tourism, and hospitality, among others.

Several hardware and software vendors now offer off-the-shelf products that enable end users to develop and test neural networks with minimal programming. It is possible that these programs will eventually become popular business tools such as statistical packages and spreadsheet programs. The issue appears to go far beyond user interface and performance considerations, as it is related to deeper issues regarding the appropriateness of neural computing to the specialist nature of business applications, in general, and DSS, in particular. On this basis, one can take the position that neural networks offer a great deal of promise and potential, on the one hand, and a great degree of uncertainty, on the other, given the lack of research into the issues concerned.

Lessons from the past tell us that there is always a need for a control mechanism, as well as for monitoring and auditing processes to reinforce that control mechanism. A system cannot be controlled unless it has been checked and monitored. Control can be exercised at any level, be it government, the public sector, corporate, divisional, or individual. It can also be exercised at any stage during the process, i.e. at design, production investment, actual production, and testing of the product. Indeed, the principle of the Japanese Taguchi Methodology ensures that all flaws and weaknesses are removed from a manufacturing project at design stage. In some ways, therefore, cybernetic strategy links with the quality and continuous improvement methodologies of Six Sigma and other forms of quality control, hence the Control Theory derivative of cybernetics. However, as has been demonstrated, cybernetics goes much further than either Control Theory or Time and Motion studies; it encompasses the whole of management theory and practice, which in turns governs the whole structure of the organisation and ensures absolute control over all aspects of the organisation. In some ways, Time and Motion, or Work Measurement studies can observe working practices and their relative efficiencies. However, such studies observe working practices and do not necessarily examine the corporate or organisational systems themselves. Data can be derived from such studies to engender statistical analysis, but such analysis is of no effect if it does not also relate to the organisational or corporate structure encompassing such work activities. If the structure is not disciplined or does not encourage a state of internal discipline, then neither will the working practices within the organisation. A lack of control in any organisational entity leads to disorganisation and ultimately chaos and possibly destruction. As Wiener showed, even in the animal kingdom, there is a form of organisation and control, with packs of animals controlled by a form of leadership. This is a necessity, since if there were no form of control, mayhem would break out within the pack, leading to the wilder instincts of animals taking over and the pack being destroyed owing to internal conflict. In a man-made organisation, if work measurement studies are conducted properly, they will identify weaknesses, anomalies, and inefficiencies in the system and will consequently encourage management to amend its own policies accordingly by way of feedback. Failure to do so can ultimately lead to systemic failure and possible disaster. The responsibility for viability and efficiency ultimately therefore rests at the top of the tree, at senior management level, with policy thus trickling down to the lower levels of the organisation, encouraged by an approach of leading by example, not by directive.

The synergy element of this perspective tells us that communication, both internal and external, is a necessary part of this coordination and control. There has to be a consensus ad idem, i.e. a meeting of minds and thoughts. If everybody worked independently without consulting with others, there would be no synergy, i.e. organised coordination, and hence, there would be no common policy or means of decision-making. Cybernetic synergy, as this book has set out to prove, is essential in maintaining order and control. This synergy brings together groups of people, either as individuals, or as organisational divisions, with the common purpose of creating a common policy or objective within the organisation, through discussion, debate, or simply verbal communication leading to written policy in the form of documentation that is agreed by all concerned, i.e. consensus ad idem, including the management, along with the collective will of all concerned to abide by and execute that policy. Ultimately, management cannot rule by decree, but by consultation. Once this has happened and mutual agreement is reached by all concerned, that process becomes policy and ultimately the set of directives that governs and facilitates the smooth and efficient operation of the organisational entity.

As the biblical verse states: *The body has many parts, and each has a function to play.*

Glossary of Terms

AAT: Autonomous Agency Theory

AEO: Authorised Economic Operator

AI: Artificial Intelligence

Algedonic Feedback: Positive or Negative Feedback, i.e. the feedback loop that generates reward or punishment, and thus indicates the environment's response to the organism's behaviour

ANN: Artificial Neural Network

BiQ: Built-in Quality

BOAC: British Overseas Airways Corporation

CIA: US Central Intelligence Agency

COVID: Coronavirus Disease 19

CRI: Composite Risk Index

CPSU: Communist Party of the Soviet Union

Cybersyn: The Cybernetic Synergy model used in Chile 1971–1973

DMAIC: Define, Measure, Analyse, Implement, Control (Part of the Six Sigma Process)

DRP: Distribution Requirement Planning

DSS: Decision Support System

EPA: (US) Environmental Protection Agency

ERP: Enterprise Resource Planning

EU: European Union

First Order Cybernetics: Observing the System

GATT: General Agreement on Tariffs and Trade

GVC: Global Value Chain

ISO: International Organization for Standardization

MCAS: Manoeuvring Characteristic Augmentation Software

MRP: Material Requirement Planning

OC: Organisational Cybernetics

OR: Operations Research

PDCA: Plan Do Check Act

PESTEL: Political, Economic, Social, Technological, Environmental, Legal (Market Access)

PLC: Product Life Cycle

QMP: Quality Management Principles
R&D: Research and Development
RAF: Royal Air Force
SCM: Supply Chain Management
SCRM: Supply Chain Risk Management
Second-Order Cybernetics: Observing the Observer
SOP: Standard Operating Procedures
SPC: Statistical Process Control
TNC: Transnational Corporation
UNCTAD: United Nations Conference on Trade and Development
USSR: Union of Soviet Socialist Republics
VSM: Viable Systems Model
WCO: World Customs Organization
WTO: World Trade Organization

Literary References

BOOKS

Beer, S; *Beyond Dispute* (1994) (Wiley).
Beer, S; *Brain of the Firm* (1995) (Wiley).
Beer, S; *Decision and Control* (2000) (Wiley).
Beer, S; *Designing Freedom* (1974) (Anansi).
Beer, S; *The Heart of Enterprise* (1995) (Wiley).
Lange, O; *Introduction to Economic Cybernetics* (1970) (Pergamon Press).
Wiener, N; *Cybernetics: Or Control and Communication in the Animal and the Machine* (1948) (MIT Press).

ARTICLES

Badillo, I; Tejeira, R; Morales, O; Briones, A; A Systems Science/Cybernetics Perspective on Contemporary Management in Supply Chains (Chapter 7, Intech) (2015).
Dubberly, H; Pangaro, P; Introduction to Cybernetics and the Design of Systems (2004).
Gill, A; Management Cybernetics (1988).
Haber, J.; Modeling Distributed Cybernetic Management for Resource-based Economics (June 2015).
Kamran, Q; Cybernetics and Strategy: A Necessary Synergy for Strategic Models (2014).
Nittbaur, G; Stafford Beer's Syntegration as a Renascence of the Ancient Greek Agora in Present-day Organizations (2005).
Rowbotham, J.M; Cybernetic Synergy (Austrian Economics Center & Hayek Institute, 2020).
Steinhaeusser, T; Elezi, F; Tommelein, I.D; Lindemann, U; Management Cybernetics as a Theoretical Basis for Lean Construction Thinking (2014).
Umpleby, S; Management Cybernetics presentation (July 2007).

Index

Note: *Italic* page numbers refer to figures.